WATERWALK

A PASSAGE OF GHOSTS

STEVEN FAULKNER

RDR BOOKS
MUSKEGON, MICHIGAN

Waterwalk: A Passage of Ghosts

RDR Books
1487 Glen Avenue
Muskegon, MI 49441
phone: 510-595-0595
fax: 510-228-0300
www.rdrbooks.com
email: roger@rdrbooks.com

Portions of this book have appeared in *DoubleTake,*
Wisconsin Trails magazine, *North American Review,*
Southern Humanities Review, and *The Dos Passos Review.*

ISBN: 978-1-57143-170-7
Library of Congress Control Number: 2007930522

Cover design and production: Seth Faulkner
Text design and production: Richard Harris
Maps: David Faulkner

Distributed in the United Kingdom and Europe by
Roundhouse Publishing Ltd., Millstone, Limers Lane,
Northam, North Devon EX39 2RG, United Kingdom

Distributed in Canada by
Scholarly Book Services, 127 Portland Street, 3rd Floor,
Toronto, Ontario, Canada M5V 2N4

Printed in the United States of America

Contents

For Joy—and all the years

. . . walk out as a man, which is to say sovereign
wanderer, lordly exile, worker and waiter and watcher.
—Walker Percy, *Love in the Ruins*

PART ONE
CHAOS

... ruin upon ruin, rout on rout,
Confusion worse confounded ...
—*Paradise Lost*

After

Justin is alone. The black night is loud with wind and rain. He is rushing down Interstate 70 at 80 miles-an-hour in his little red convertible, wind tearing at his canvas top, heavy rains flooding his windshield. He eases off to 70. The highway before him is hardly visible, a dark running pool of rain-needled headlights. Sudden lightnings hammer the heavy clouds into shapes metallic, colors steel, bright brass, and arsenic grey. The approaching taillights of an eighteen-wheeler blur red as its tires slash spray onto his windshield. He maneuvers and pushes the little car past the trailer and truck, hurrying home. Another semi-truck appears directly ahead of the last one; all three vehicles are rushing up a hill in a chaos of driving rain, flung spray, and incessant lightning. Justin slips past the surging trucks, skims over the crest of the hill, and plunges down the other side on a thin slick of black running water. The glare of the semis gradually diminishes behind him as he picks up speed. His tires rip through standing water——he's sliding—hydroplaning—slip-

ping—sideways—going—the boy pulls the wheel left to correct the slide—his turned tires hit pavement, and the little car whips around and slams head-on into the concrete partition that divides the highway. He is not wearing a seatbelt.

Night Life

I had lost touch with my son Justin. His sixteen years of growing from baby to young man in this supposedly quiet Midwestern city had been sixteen years of runaround mayhem in my life. He was a vague figure, an occasional apparition flitting in and out. And what was I to him? Busy beyond belief. Running newspapers after midnight, rushing off to college classes by day, racing on to evening meetings for another job, studying, teaching, writing research papers: a father phantom disappearing by day, slipping away by night, always evading him.

It's two in the morning. My aging truck, weighed down to the axles with 1421 copies of the *Topeka Capital Journal*, sways around a corner, its suspension emitting almost human groans. I swerve from one newspaper rack to the next, hurrying from red box to red box like some huge mechanical insect pollinating large metallic flowers.

Counting out sixteen papers, I shove open the truck door, walk to the paper rack, yank open the steel door, pull out yesterday's worthless news and drop in today's. Hurrying back to the truck, I glance about, wary of anyone approaching along the shadowed sidewalks.

A storm is moving in. I keep an eye on the frenetic lightning jumping and glaring from between the highrise office buildings of downtown Topeka, Kansas. Hot air, humid, motionlesss, smothers the streets and alleys. I am sweating in a T-shirt. Thousands of tiny green bugs swirl around the street lamps, some darting toward my eyes and ears and mouth. They crawl in chaotic carpets up the sides of lighted storefronts, attracted always to the lights that kill them. But few stores downtown are lighted anymore; businesses have fled to the garish suburban malls where traffic slows to a crawl and thousands of shoppers move along the brightly lit shops while these old buildings, some a century old, stand gaunt and vacant along the deserted streets.

The prostitutes still find customers. Some in miniskirts, some in sweats, some in long overcoats in the summer heat; one on this street, a couple more two streets down, they pace the brick walks watching the coming cars. But they know my old truck. There's no money here. I nod as I go by, and they look the other way.

Thunderheads are building in the northwest. A faint percussion of thunder reaches me as I pull into the Amoco station. The air waits, full of that oppressive heat that has made the asphalt, the brick, the concrete its own through the long summer day.

I think of my friend who left M.I.T. where he was working on a Ph.D and moved to a Kentucky farm with no electricity. He tells me he learns about who was elected president or if we've gone to war again about a week or two after the event. Word of mouth, he says, is a kind of filter that eliminates most of the trivia. He and his family live a quiet life, chopping their wood, baking their bread, collecting rainwater in a barrel for showers, plowing a couple acres with a horse and plow. He knocked on my door one day and said some land was available; we could move there. But I wanted to finish my long-delayed university degree. I let it go and kept on running papers seven nights a week, 365 days a year, no time off for good behavior.

Jumping out of my truck, a gust of wind snatches a paper from my hands and chases it like a wounded goose down the sidewalk. Thundersqualls can be vicious. A few weeks ago I saw oak trees a foot-and-a-half in diameter snapped in two, crabapple trees ripped up like radishes, power lines mangled by flying debris.

There's Burt with his long, twisted walking staff. He waves from an alley as I drive by. He pushes a garbage-can-grocery-cart-contraption he uses to collect aluminum cans. One night he found a teenager in a dumpster shot through the head.

At the Kwik Shop old Kelly Joe is getting coffee. He lives in a nearby halfway house for the mentally impaired. He's a congenial old man who has trouble with his consonants. When he's drunk they disappear altogether. He looks around as I drop off 35 papers. "Orna ain," he says.

"Better get back home before it breaks loose," I say.

"Na. O ine a ain."

"Take it easy, Kelly."

"Ee ya ayer, Eve."

In a highrise for the elderly and handicapped, I hurry down the concrete-block hallways, slapping down papers for paying customers. Old Helen, who is addicted to games of chance, meets me at three-thirty in the morning with her strange concoction of herbal tea. She used to grow the stuff, whatever it is, in her farm garden. Little pieces of green swim in a dark brown liquid. It tastes bad, but I sip at it to thank her for her kindness. She shows me the latest letter from the contest she's sure she's won.

"Read the fine print, Helen. They're just trying to get you to buy stuff. You didn't buy it did you?"

"It was just pencils," she says. "You want some pencils?"

"Don't buy their stuff, Helen. They're leading you on."

She shrugs. Her farm is gone. Her people are absent. She can't sleep. I hand her the teacup and the newspaper, then hurry on.

Alone. The elevator hums up to the top floor of another gov-

ernment-subsidized highrise. In a ninth-floor apartment, old
Jack Music is going mad. He's convinced that "Old Greasy" is
out to get him; she's the woman down the hall who eats fried
hamburger smeared with strawberry jam for breakfast every
morning. Her leathery face is patchy and creased by years of
smoking, the varicose veins on her lower legs bleed through
gauze wrappings. Jack tries to point out the powdered chemicals Old Greasy is using to poison him. I run my finger along the
floor and smell it; it's nothing but dust. His apartment is empty:
no bed, no chairs, just a few cushions scattered across the vi-
nyl tiles. Some nights I hear him, alone in there, pouring out a
stream of hideous invective against the bare walls.

Four a.m. I swerve into another gas station. One night I smelled
gasoline fumes here. Someone had just stepped from behind the
building and emptied his pistol into an occupied car. He missed
everyone, but a bullet punctured a gasoline hose.

Across the street, the high dome of the state capitol building
stands serenely before the nervous flashes of the approaching
storm. I swerve across the street, counting out fifteen papers,
pull to the curb, and jump out. Thunder crashes simultaneously
with the agitated lightning. The storm has lost all patience with
this city. Great sheets of cold wind plunge down the highrise office buildings and rush up the streets and alleys scattering leaves
and papers. The trees that grace the capitol grounds thrash this
way and that as the mad winds riot. I run for the newsstand as
the rains rush me from across the street.

Justin is ten years old. He lies on the bed beside me watching
my face. It's 10 p.m. Three hours before paper route time. I'm
reading him a bedtime story about a boy and a raccoon named
Rascal. The boy's father is often away from home for days, even

weeks. The boy finds a wild raccoon to keep him company. . . but I can't keep my eyes open. I keep dozing off. Justin gives up on the story and falls asleep. My eyes jerk open and I look at his quiet face.

On a dark summer night, for no apparent reason, a twelve-year-old boy fires a pistol at another newspaper carrier. The carrier jerks out his own pistol and empties eight shots at the twelve-year-old. They both miss.

One night a gang of young men throw a carrier against a picket fence and beat him with bats. He survives with crushing bruises on his back and puncture wounds in his chest from the pointed fence. He never finds out why.

Classes are over for the summer. Justin is twelve. He begs to go on the paper route with me. In spite of the risks, I take him along. All night long he bumps and bounces through the city streets with me, helping me count out papers for the next stop. We buy Tic Tacs and Cokes at the Kwik Shop to keep us both going.

At dawn his small hands follow me up a dark ladder in an enclosed stair well. I unlatch and push open the heavy, overhead door that opens onto the roof of a highrise. The paper route is finally over and I want to show him something. We climb onto the flat, gravel roof. The air is clear. A few wisps of cloud have caught gold from the coming sun. The city and its dark streets lie far beneath us, a maze of gabled roofs, a tangle of grey foliage, a glare of street lights. I point out the dome of the capitol building silhouetted against the brightening east, the gothic spires of Topeka High School to the north. We turn and try to locate our own neighborhood to the west and spot the white dome of the Washburn University telescope. We walk across cinder blocks to another ladder and climb up to the topmost platform. We breathe in the cool, bright air; the sun just now flashes above the eastern horizon. A moment of lucid stillness.

Another nameless night. A man lies spraddled over a curb, his head in the street. I step out of the truck, glancing this way and that, stoop down, and feel for a pulse. His stubbly neck is still warm, but he is quite dead.

A heavy man falls across the threshold of his third-story apartment. His wife is hysterical; she has already dialed 911. She begs me to do something. I press the flesh of his thick throat for a pulse. I can't find it. I lay my newspapers down and try his wrist. I don't know what to do. The medics are thumping up the stairway calling, "Code Blue!" Heart attack.

A prostitute ducks behind my truck and snarls, "That man's horrible! Horrible! Get me out of here. Just get me out of here! A few blocks. Don't let him find me." I spot a man lunging along the sidewalk across the street. I open the truck door and quick as a cat she slips in. I drop her off a few blocks away.

Justin is fifteen years old. He walks in with a black eye and a bruised head. A hallway fracas in the high school. A boy started kicking his locker for no apparent reason. Justin told him to stop. He kicked it again. Justin shoved him and turned away. The guy blindsided him up the side of his head. Justin turned and caught the boy with his fist. Teachers pulled them apart. A teacher had Justin's arms pinned to his sides when the boy jerked free and landed one in Justin's eye.

A British reporter is on the radio in the predawn darkness. He characterizes the American Midwest as "the placid, dowdy, unexcited heart" of the country. He is giving news of the Oklahoma City bombing.

It goes on like this, month after month, year by year. Justin brushes into the house after track practice. I say, "Hi. How's it going?"
   "Okay, Dad."
   "See you Friday at the track meet."
   "Okay Dad."

Not long ago I remembered a book I had read to his older brothers. Rummaging around in closets, I found it: *The Explorations of Pére Marquette*. It's a child's version of history. I turned to the Foreword:

The boys and girls who read this story will be transported in imagination to the time when the Mississippi River flowed in mysterious grandeur through unexplored prairies and forests that stretched for countless miles on either side. They will camp where only unknown fish and game and Indians lived.

But Justin was too old for a children's book. I reached for Homer's *Odyssey*. Maybe this. But when would we find time to read together? We hadn't read together now for years. I picked up the Marquette book again and paged through the account of his epic exploration to discover the Mississippi. My mind was far away, full of pioneer adventures and warm, sunlit afternoons, of leisurely rivers winding slowly, of time to spare, time aplenty, free time, time unhurried . . .
   Maybe we could read a book together again. Maybe we could find the track of those old discoverers Joliet and Marquette, find the vanishing wake of their birchbark canoes.

Before

So Justin and I bought a canoe. Canoes are quiet. John Graves, who knows about these things says, "Chances for being quiet nowadays are limited. Those for being unquiet seem to abound." "Canoes," he says, "are unobtrusive; they don't storm the natural world or ride over it, but drift in upon it as a part of its own silence."

Canoes are slow. But speed is a species of winged demon, promising quick excitement, less time in transit, more time with our families; but having paid great sums for the fiend's wings, we find ourselves living farther from our places of work, farther from friends, farther from family—speeding every which way to make up the distances.

Justin and I spent two weeks of my off hours shingling a house to buy that canoe. We needed one made not of fiberglass, canvas, or aluminum, but a canoe made of the new tough stuff that can take the abuse of slamming into rocks, scraping over tree trunks, and grinding onto gravel beaches. Shingling was hot work. The day we cut and hammered down the last line of ridge caps on that infernal roof, temperatures rose into the high nineties. We were hot-footing it over sun-roasted shingles in our socks to avoid scarring the asphalt shingles. We sweated. We panted. Sitting sideways on a hip, shingle heat seared through my jeans making me shift from side to side in order to pound in that last sweaty handful of nails. We earned that canoe.

In the basement of the University of Kansas library, I found a nineteenth-century translation of Marquette's journal of his journey with Joliet. Scrounging minutes here and there in my busy schedule, I read it and plotted our course. I ordered rain jackets and pants. Lightweight cooking pans. Backpacks. I gathered the goods: hatchet, fold-up saw, tarp, books, resolve. I or-

dered a spray skirt that would snap down over the canoe to
protect us from swamping in rough water and called in Justin
to help me drill and rivet thirty-six snaps along both lengths of
the canoe. I installed an oak thwart to keep our backpacks in
place, and rigged up loops along the gunwales to tie stuff down.
Preparations took time and a lot of work, and Justin was content to let me take care of them. I kept suggesting he read Cliff
Jacobson's book on camping and canoeing, but he couldn't be
bothered; it sounded too much like homework.

We christened our new canoe the Natty Bumpo, after James
Fenimore Cooper's hero in *The Last of the Mohicans* (I had read
the book; Justin had watched the movie). Cooper added a "p"
to his hero's name, making it Natty Bumppo. I suppose that
made it appear on the page, if not to the ear, more Indian and
less like a clumsy Yankee. I thought clumsy was about right for
us. Make it Bumpo. And nattily dressed he was when we were
through, with a yellow spray skirt I splotched a mottled green
and black for camouflage. Most boats are female, so goes the
tradition. And it's true Natty sported a skirt. But in these days
of the gender wars when half the hurricanes have undergone a
sex change, I decided boats can be male. Besides, it wouldn't be
right to spend that much time away from my wife in the arms of
another woman. Call the skirt a kilt.

Occasionally, I would stop and ask Justin if he really wanted
to do this. He would shrug and say, "I guess so." Not a lot of
enthusiasm.

I knew this was a fool's odyssey: a middle-aged, sedentary,
city-living, flabby-muscled man launching a nine-week canoe
trip with his now sixteen-year-old son. I found it impossible
to imagine weeks and weeks of canoeing, of staking out a tent
wherever we could find a patch of sand or a few feet of grass,
harder still to comprehend that passing of lingering, leisurely
time that would add slow mile to slow mile until decades of

miles passed into centuries and centuries into a millennium. How would we stand up to a two-month journey: three hundred miles along Lake Michigan's stormy northern shore, some three hundred miles upcurrent and down, crossing the entire state of Wisconsin on two rivers, and finally, over four hundred miles down the wide Mississippi? This was the route Joliet and Marquette took 300 years before, the maiden voyage of Europeans into the heart of what is now America's Midwest.

Justin and I had virtually no experience canoeing. How would we survive the Great Lakes? I didn't know, but I was determined to take a long walk, call it a waterwalk. We would walk away from the sound of the shutting of doors with the comfortable click of the lock that tells us we have food in the refrigerator, beds to ease our bones, television to unravel our minds, isolation from our neighbors, and insulation from storms. For a good stretch of time, I hoped to lose the dependable dependencies.

Part Two

A NEWER WORLD

Come, my friends.
'T is not too late to seek a newer world.
Push off, and sitting well in order smite
The sounding furrows; for my purpose holds
To sail beyond the sunset . . .
         —*"Ulysses," Alfred Lord Tennyson*

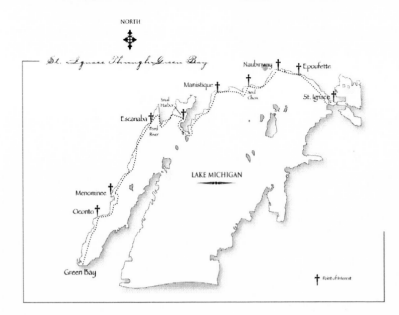

NORTH

St. Ignace Through Green Bay

Naubinway † † Epoufette

Manistique †

Seul Choix †

St. Ignace †

Escanaba †
Ford River

LAKE MICHIGAN

Menominee †

Oconto †

Green Bay

† Point of Interest

Away

Spring had arrived late on Michigan's Upper Peninsula. Some-one in a cafe had said there was still ice on Lake Superior. The news made me nervous. This was Lake Michigan, the top tip of it, and the water was frigid. A person who capsizes in 40-degree water has only ten minutes to get out before the body and mind grow sluggish and lose coordination. Knee-deep in frigid water, our legs ached with the cold. Back and forth we sloshed, lug-ging supplies from the truck backed onto a gravel beach near St. Ignace, Michigan, the place Joliet and Marquette began their epic voyage. The canoe floated fifty feet from shore in shallow water. A bright sun shone through clear water, a beautiful, ex-hilarating day. A brave little breeze from the east rocked Natty Bumpo against the tow rope as we stuffed the canoe with duf-fel bags of clothes, ¾-inch sleeping pads, sleeping bags, a two-man dome tent many years the worse for wear. No ice-filled cooler, just a canteen and canvas bucket. The food pack was filled with canned foods, bananas, coffee, peanut butter, cheese,

eggs, bacon, pancake mix: weighty stuff, but we weren't planning portages in the first weeks. The early voyageurs traveled
great distances on a daily ration of cornmeal boiled up with
whatever they could shoot or pull from the waters, but such a
diet often worked havoc on their French stomachs. I didn't have
that much of the pioneering spirit.

My lovely eighteen-year-old daughter Johanna, holding the
tow rope, made some crack about having every confidence we
would capsize in the first mile. My wife Joy stood silent on the
shore, her long blonde hair blowing in the breeze, with nothing left to do but worry. Julia the ten-year-old and Andrea the
thirteener: Snoof and Sqump as I had always called them, stood
still now, watching. Four-year-old Alexander ran back and forth
along the gravel beach picking up pebbles and throwing them,
oblivious to time and long absences.

Justin leaned over and attached the rifle to the loops near his
seat in the prow. I tried strapping my fishing rod in place, but
the tip caught on a pack and snapped off. I stood up, holding
the broken rod. There was no repairing it now.

I looked down at the chaos of our packinge—every space
jammed tight: book bag, jackets, camera, maps. Beginnings are
always chaotic. We pulled the bungi cords over the packs and
slipped them into loops along the gunwales. We jerked the skirt
over the front half of the canoe and snapped it down as best we
could and straightened up. I saw Justin glance away toward the
horizon: water as far as you could see, as open-ended as the sky
itself.

The boat rocked heavily, tugging at the long, braided rope.
We stepped in, holding onto the gunwales for balance, and sat
down. The canoe settled into the water. A man is a fool, said
one expert, to take a canoe onto rivers or lakes without at least
nine inches of freeboard between water and gunwale. It looked
close to nine inches to me.

Johanna let slip the rope. I began wrapping the long wet coil firmly under my elbow and up between thumb and forefinger, over and over; the rope slid away from shore and we floated away with the wind.

Within minutes they were small colorful figures on a distant shore. We lifted our paddles over our heads and held them. We saw their hands come up.

Our plan was to follow the original voyage of the French trader Joliet and the Jesuit missionary Marquette. Besides Joliet and Marquette, there were five other French-Canadians who accompanied them in the canoes. These were the first Europeans to discover the upper Mississippi River. Their journey began near here in a shallow bay on Michigan's Upper Peninsula, in the town that still bears the name of the old Jesuit mission, St. Ignace. It's a tourist town now, but three long centuries ago, there was nothing there but a rough, log chapel and a collection of bark lodges surrounded by a palisade of sharpened poles. Three-hundred-and-eighty Huron Indians had fled to this bay in 1671. They found a wide, sandy beach that sloped gently into a broad meadow protected from bitter winter winds by a range of low, forested hills. They were fleeing the mighty Sioux nation in the west who had sworn vengeance on them after some young Hurons had killed several Sioux men. But the Hurons were afraid to venture farther east because the great Iroquois confederation had for years raided the shores and islands of Lake Huron, slaughtering or enslaving a good portion of the Huron tribe. Caught between Sioux, Iroquois, and arctic winds, they lived a hard life.

Jacques Marquette was their priest. He had journeyed with them in their long flight eastward from Lake Superior's western shore and would suffer with them through that first winter after their corn crop failed to mature. But this thirty-four-year-old Jesuit from the prosperous town of Laon, France, had long hoped to venture farther west. A gifted linguist, he had heard from members of various tribes about a great river far to the west that ran from north to south. Some said the great river ran into a sea, but no one knew whether that sea was the Gulf of California, the Gulf of Mexico, or perhaps the coastal swamps of Georgia.

The Indians warned against searching out that river's end. Travelers told of roaring river monsters that swallowed canoes whole, of demons that skipped across the waters and killed, of tribesmen who tomahawked visitors without a word of warning, of heat so intolerable that humans could not survive. But Marquette dismissed the dangers, telling his Indian friends he was not afraid to die.

On December 8, 1672, Louis Joliet and a few companions paddled their birchbark canoe into the little bay of St. Ignace Mission. He had been commissioned to pick up Marquette and journey westward in search of the rumored river that ran down to an unknown sea. Joliet was a trader, hoping to find routes for the fur trade, sources of copper, iron, perhaps even gold. A whole world of economic opportunity lay before him.

I wanted to know this man Joliet and his companion Marquette, not only through their writings, but I hoped to so repeat their experiences that for us they would become more than ghostly abstractions, figures painted on a page. I wanted to discover the kind of knowledge that comes from real participation in a journey, to feel the beat of the sun, and the pull of the waves, and the fearful anticipation of discovery. More than this, these two seemed to me to represent two continuous streams of American experience and American values, the religious and the commercial. It seemed an unlikely partnership. One thinks of commerce flowing one way, setting its own ethical (or unethical) standards, religion coursing another. Yet, these two men would try to join the two streams, or, more accurately, join together in a single stream. In their unusual collaboration lay a secret of one of America's early, great successes.

Marquette was the missionary, intent on communicating faith and culture to the people of the new world. He came from a country that considered itself the height of civilization, and had good reasons to think so. The French town of Laon, where he grew up, boasted sixty-three churches, including a cathedral with massive square towers that rose 130 feet from the pavement. Some consider its great rose window second only to that of the cathedral at Notre-Dame in Paris. He was educated in some of the best schools of that civilization. In the city of Rheims, he once participated in a theatrical production complete with orchestra, ballet, and drama for the sixteen-year-old King Louis XIV and his entourage.

But he chose to leave France. He joined the Jesuits who were then extending missions as far as Japan, China, and Argentina. For twelve years he went through the rigorous Jesuit course of studies to prepare for a mission, and was finally sent, in 1666, not to the Far East, which he had originally hoped for, but to New France in North America.

If the missionaries hoped to elevate the minds and spirits of those they taught, the French trading monopolies were set up to secure financial profits for their shareholders. Historian Joseph Donnelly writes, "From the outset, traders and other company officials in New France learned that debauching the Indian was the most effective means of compelling the native to gather a rich fur harvest. Because the missionaries could not in good conscience tolerate that policy, they were soon at loggerheads with the company's representatives in Canada as well as its officials in France." Letters and emissaries crossed and recrossed the Atlantic carrying complaints, explanations, and demands. As early as 1666, there was already conflict between these two sets of values: the entrepreneurs' and the missionaries'.

Late in 1672, it was the inspiration of the administrator of New France, Jean Talon, to dispatch both a trader and a missionary to make one of the great exploratory journeys of North America. Thus, on the same expedition, came these two Frenchmen, hoping to consummate a union between forces seemingly irreconcilable. At one level the purpose of their journey seemed the same as ours, to join two unlikely men in a common endeavor and to heal their divisions. Justin was a stubborn boy, sometimes moody, sometimes angry, impulsive as the wind. I was a father sometimes moody and angry, preoccupied with his own affairs. I was hoping the work of our own exploration and a length of time spent together would form a lasting bond.

We were drifting far from shore. I paddled awkwardly, first on one side, then on the other, calling out to Justin to switch sides when I did. Natty Bumpo swerved left and right, but a following breeze was playing along, nudging us forward on a gentle swell, the day was cool and bright, and the spirit of adventure was upon us.

Far off to our left an island like a brush stroke in watercolor floated up from a blue-grey sea. To our right low hills grey and sooty with firs and pines, scratched here and there with the white lines of leafless birches held a rocky shore. Though spring had arrived two months ago in Kansas, here the day's sun and wind were just beginning to shake open the budding leaves.

I stared down at my first topographical map but had trouble translating the head-on view of shore and island into the overhead view of the map. A small bay receded into the land, leaving us a half mile of cold waves from shore. What was that rise of hill and forest ahead? Gros Cap, said the map: Fat Cap? Cape Fat? I didn't know my French.

Every time I looked down at the map, Natty Bumpo veered one way or the other and Justin would glance back to see what his intrepid guide was doing. But the weather was fine and we were full of the energy and optimism of all things new. Our paddles pulled us through clear water, little vortexes of bubbles swirling past with each stroke, the lines of our wake spooling away into the little waves.

Alone on the sea. A perfect Saturday afternoon and not another soul in sight. A vast seascape, and the joy of this deep solitude was washing beneath me in the gently rocking waves and in the silence breathing all around us in the easy wind. Ducks rose from the surface and winged away and far away we heard, for the first time, the strange, tremulous call of a loon. We were a long way from Kansas.

It was not difficult, as we paddled along, to imagine those seven Frenchmen in their two birchbark canoes just ahead of us, stroking smoothly and swiftly through clear waters, bound for regions unknown. But we crawled along like some awkward, two-footed amphibian just learning to swim. On we paddled, trying to find a rhythm, stutter-stepping through the waves like bootcamp recruits. The water moved beneath us, transparent green, shot through with sunlight, fathoms of Chablis changing as the sun declined to a golden Chardonnay. We were voyaging over a wine-light sea.

As we passed a point of land, rocks twenty feet below us rippled into view and then rose rapidly to meet us. Pale shelves of boulders and broken rock neared the surface and we maneuvered away to stay in deeper water. Dark shadows darted away among the rocks and Justin cried out that he had seen the first fish. We laughed and pointed and shouted like children.

The sun burned down through cool air ahead of us and we began to search for our first campsite. Ahead of us sand dunes sloped away through dried grasses into wooded hills: Pointe aux Chenes, read the map. It was almost six-thirty and we had paddled about eight miles in four hours (a distance that would take less than eight minutes in an automobile).

It was enough for a first day. We slid into a sandy shore and climbed out, feeling a stiff ache in our legs and backs. It was enough.

Toehold In Time

The wind had died. A small fire flickered and spurted and glowed between us. A cold evening had settled in and a strange melancholy had hold of me. We had set the grey dome tent behind the first line of sand dunes with oak trees climbing the hill behind us and several birches forming a ragged semi-circle. We'd had problems with our old tent. Someone must have stored it away wet; two of the four long nylon channels that held the flexible rods that formed the tent's frame had rotted with mildew. The bowed rods had ripped through the channels in several places. The frame was holding its shape for the time being, but something had to be done. A half moon had drifted out from behind the hills, shining through a thin lace of cloud. We had already eaten, but neither of us felt like sleep. I looked across the fire at Justin and was glad to have him there, stretched full length in the sand.

I wanted one day to be able to hold these memories like quiet flames in the dark of forgotten things. Against the gathering night of things lost, I would re-collect these visions of our time together and burn them against the power of time. I would hold his young face of sixteen years there beside that fire, cheeks flushed by the cool of the night and the heat of the fire, hold him in that limbo of time that memory preserves, for memory and hope are our only defenses against the ceaseless rush of time.

What is this gift-giving thief we call time? I have never been able to understand it. As great a mind as St. Augustine said, "What then is time? If no one asks me, I know: if I wish to explain it to one who asks, I know not." And neither do I. How do you define this restless, silent, invisible thing that whirls us along, both granting and erasing our memories? For most of my life I have been spinning too fast to catch the memories, gyrating out and away from myself and from those I love. I have long needed to slow down and drop into a lower rotation, a place nearer the still center of the turning wheel. And now, having taken the time, I vowed not to lose these transient moments, these days of constant motion over wave and current, but find each moment its local habitation, locate each day, root each selected memory in its place, so that fickle, reeling time might be held and arrested. "There is a time," says Eliot, "for the evening under starlight."

Earlier, as the red sun melted into the western sea, I had sent Justin to find rocks to surround the fire while I searched for firewood. I had dragged in broken limbs of oak and birch, unfolded our camp saw, and cut up ten-inch lengths while Justin carried in several large rocks and dropped them in a tight circle. After finding some branches of short flat hemlock needles, dried to a brittle orange, for kindling, I struck a match. A small flame crackled and spat through the hemlock and into carefully laid twigs. If I couldn't steer a canoe, at least I could lay a fire. Then a thought struck me. "Where'd you find the rocks?"

"Along the beach."

"That's not really a good idea."

"Why not?"

"They collect water in crevices and pores. When the fire heats them, they might explode."

"So what are we going to do?"

I stared at the brightly burning sticks now licking up through thicker logs and decided, at this point, we would just take our chances; I had seen a rock actually explode only once as a boy, camping in the Kansas hills. It was a long time ago and it had done no damage. I decided to leave not-well-enough alone.

Justin lay down next to the fire and began feeding it sticks. I warned him to move back a little in case I'd been right about the rocks. He scooted back six inches. I was pulling out our little cloth sack of cooking pots when a rock went off like a rifle shot. Justin leaped back from the fire as sharp pieces of hot stone pattered down across the campsite. We looked around for damage and found ten or eleven holes melted through the weather tarp that covered our packs, but somehow the tent was still intact. A few minutes later, as we ranged around the perimeter of the camp like hungry wolves, another rock exploded and we scampered into the dunes howling and laughing. We kept our distance for about half an hour until we were sure the artillery was over, then, cautiously, we moved back in and took possession of our camp.

I set down the square bars of the grill on what was left of the stones and cooked up a can of beef soup mixed with a can of corn. We ate the stuff with bagels and then put on our first pot of coffee, French roast beans boiled over an open fire.

Ernest Hemingway used to camp in these parts. In a story that takes place in this area, Nick Adams spoons sugar into an empty apricot can. He brings the coffee to a boil. There's a good smell. The coffee bubbles, pouring coffee and grounds down the side of the pot into the hissing fire. He uses his hat to take hold of the hot coffeepot and pours it into the apricot can. He takes a sip and says it's a triumph.

It was a triumph for us too. I screwed off the lid of our sugar container and shook some into my cup, then handed the sugar to Justin. I picked up the coffeepot using my bandana to protect my hand and poured Justin a cup, then me. We looked over our steel mugs at each other as we sipped a little off the top; it was too hot to take it faster. The coffee was rich and good, really good. Justin sucked in air to cool his lips and said it tasted better than coffee at home, and I said it was better than coffee in any coffee shop, and we were both right.

I was sipping my second cup now, thinking of things lost and things gained. It was Saturday night. For twenty-two years my wife and I have laid down a tradition of always going out together on Saturday nights. When we were dirt poor, living on $1.75 an hour I earned by driving dump trucks, we looked forward to Saturday nights. We would dress up a bit and walk down the wooden steps of our upstairs apartment, out onto a brick street, past the old Carnegie library where I had learned to love books, past the county courthouse, and on around a corner to a little Persian restaurant where we ate beef-tongue sandwiches for two bucks apiece. Even when the children came, we found ways to leave them with friends for a few hours every Saturday night. Saturday nights were more than useful; they were stolen hours of unhurried pleasure, a stillness in the mad rush of things: taking our food slowly, sharing a lingering pleasure in each other while time loosened its grip, as it did when we were first in love and could talk the night away. For brief hours the Now would transcend tomorrow's insistent needs or the past's lame conclusions.

I was missing her already. Nine weeks cut out of our long-held routine seemed like a lot just then. After looking forward to this journey for so long, I was surprised by this sudden sadness.

I pulled my paperback version of Homer's *Odyssey* from my book bag and began to read aloud, turning my body so the orange flamelight wavered across words maybe 3000 years old. Justin was lying on his back looking up at old stars, his camouflaged hat still on his head, his jacket buttoned against the cold, a silent figure near me but far. The fire flared up as a breeze moved over the dunes, nosing around our tent and tarp, and wandered away along miles of dark sand.

Somewhere in the dark woods a whippoorwill startled us with its loud, unmistakable cry. As a boy, I used to read of the whippoorwill's call in my storybooks. I remember looking closely at the word and trying to imagine the three-note whistle that repeats its own name. I'd never heard one myself until this night. The words once read as a child were suddenly given in the original tongue: that sharp, lilting, insistent flame of sound from the forest floor. It seemed so near. In the intervals. . . far away. . .we could hear another whippoorwill calling . . . calling.

After a chapter, I closed the book and looked across the fire at Justin. How do you find a teen-age son who lives only in the Now? How do you enter his present world and somehow draw him into my world of things past, literature, history, poetry, and then on into the larger world?

I don't know.

The tent was a quiet shadow beyond our little, flickering circle of flames. It was late. I put the book away and pushed myself stiffly to my feet. We unzipped the tent door and crawled into the dark. The sleeping bags were already laid out. If I had read Hemingway's advice on camping up here before I took the trip, I would have chosen a heavier sleeping bag. Justin's was a fine, thick bag with a hood to keep the head warm, but I had had a choice of several bags back home. It was hot in Kansas when I made that decision, so hot it was hard to imagine that temperatures up here could still drop into the thirties at night. Hemingway had said, "In a succession of one-night camps on a canoe trip . . . take twice as much cover as you think that you will need." You pay dearly for small mistakes in the wild. I pulled my hat down over my head and slept badly.

Next morning I ripped up a red nylon tote bag and sewed it over the worst of the holes that the bent tent poles had torn in their channels. The blackflies found me at work, zooming in at my eyes and ears. I spat and slapped and sewed. Justin found the head net I had bought for him and pulled it over his hat and around his face to keep the little demons at bay.

When we reset the tent, the channels held.

Just then, two white swans came winging along about fifty yards out to sea. They were flying close together in perfect unison, each wingtip scarcely missing the waves, each downbeat accompanied by a coarse honk so that they kept up a perfectly synchronous duet of rough sound and graceful motion as they flew past. It seemed a hopeful omen.

Slow Fast

We had been paddling for three hours over a calm, jade-green sea. The sand beach and wooded hills on our right had steadily dropped away; we were a mile out to sea, too far for inexperienced canoers. The distant point of land that curved out into the lake ahead of us seemed to recede at the same rate we paddled. Time slowed down. The shore stood still. We were not used to this discipline of will and muscle that required such labor to move so slowly.

Around noon, my lower back began to protest the journey and I called for a break. Justin flopped back on the backpacks, tent, clothes duffels, and mattress rolls that overfilled the center of the canoe, and I eased back onto the bookpack, jackets, camera pack, fishing gear, metal coffee thermos and other odds and ends that we had stuffed in the stern.

"When do we eat?" Justin asked.

I sat up and took stock of our position. The prow of our canoe had drifted around. I told him we'd eat when we reached the sea wall I'd seen on our map.

"How far's that?" he asked.

I looked down at my map. "Somewhere near that head-land."

He pushed himself up and looked. "How far is that?" He didn't like the look of the distance.

"Maybe another half hour or so," I said, but I had no idea of distances yet. I looked at the map again and shrugged, "Maybe a little longer." Maps are a comfort if you know how to read them. Marquette drew a rough map as he paddled into the fu-ture, paddled into the unknown. The drawing of a map was for him, and for those who sent him, a necessary step in gaining control of space and of the future. Of course maps have one severe limitation; they never tell us why we are there.

We took up our paddles and turned west. We were under a spell. The sea was lethargic, rippling away on our left to a grey horizon; the sun shone faintly through the haze; the only sound was the dip of our paddles, the light gurgle of our wake, and occasionally, far out on the water, the quavering warning of a loon. The low line of grey hills, the black trees, the pale sand were fixed to the horizon.

Far ahead we saw a long low line on the water.

"That might be the sea wall I saw on the map," I told Justin. "We'll eat lunch when we get there."

A half-hour later lazy ripples stirred by the merest breath of a breeze had erased that hoped-for line.

"So much for the sea wall," said Justin. "When do we eat?"

"When we get there," I said and paddled on.

Black flies resting on the surface would rise to meet us, swerv-ing around our heads and diving for our necks and faces. Their bite is sharp and irritating. They were easy to kill, but always there were more.

An hour later, we rested again, pulling off our jackets and ly-ing in the soft sunlight. My back was feeling the strain. Justin's empty stomach was straining his patience. He pulled his camouflaged hat from his tousled hair and groaned, "Come on Dad, let's just eat."

I pushed myself upright and poured coffee from our thermos, then passed the thermos up to Justin. My lower back ached, my buttocks ached, my legs were stiff. We sipped our coffee and swatted flies.

But Justin wasn't complaining. Pretty good for a TV-bred kid used to seeing a two-month trip condensed into 50 minutes of highlights. And we were getting better at steering, using the J-stroke I'd read about in Jacobson's book. Given the hazards ahead, it was a most fortunate thing we had these first two days of calm weather to learn how to steer our craft.

Five minutes later Justin handed back the thermos and we were paddling again, our impatience channeled into the steady stroking of our paddles. But why impatient? Isn't it our aversion to manual labor that cuts us off from nature itself? We spend long hours seated in air-conditioned indolence only to long for such hours on the lake, for hours of real work under an open sky. But once on the lake, here we were, losing patience with slow time, which is the only time the sea and the seasons know.

About three in the afternoon we thought we had spotted a line of rocks in the water near the shore. We paced on through the water, hungry for a late lunch. Justin was very hungry, and fed up with the whole idea of canoeing The Great Lakes. This was no lake, he said, it was an ocean.

Time is a tyrant. Always on the run. Moving through us whether we are moving or not. Driving us forward into what now seems inevitable, but was not . . .

A little red convertible is sliding sideways, slipping at 70 miles-an-hour—yawing through a stiff spray of thrown water—the wheel jerks and the little car whips left and explodes into concrete. The impact slams his body into the passenger door, the car flips onto that passenger door and shoots down the pavement in a hail of glass . . .

> Time present and time past
> Are both perhaps present in time future,
> And time future contained in time past.

About four in the afternoon, we finally reached a rough limestone bulwark against the sea; the rocks were as big as pickup trucks. We coasted along the jumble of stone that rose twelve or fifteen feet out of the water until we found a place to disembark. Justin climbed out and looped the yellow prow rope around a boulder. I forced myself out of the canoe and onto a flat rock where I unbent my body. I climbed painfully from rock to rock to where Justin was trying to secure the rope and showed him how to tie it off with two half hitches, then crippled my way back down to the canoe and unraveled the stern rope, tying it off to another boulder. We unsnapped Natty's spray kilt, unstrapped the cover of the food pack, and took out a can of Spam, some cinnamon-raisin bagels, and two bananas. Cinnamon-raisin was not my choice to go with Spam, but we were starved. Hunger is a dictator.

We climbed over the rocks to the other side. Inside the wall, a bay of tiffany greens, browns and blue glass stretched flat away to the conveyor belts and metal buildings of what seemed to be some kind of loading facility. It was Memorial Day; no one was working. As we finished our Spam and bagels, we noticed a school of fish nosing over submerged rocks near the wall. Justin hurried back over the boulders for the fishing gear, and I showed him how to tie on a leader and snap on a spinner.

After several casts and retrievals, we could see that the fish were not paying attention. I climbed down toward them to get a better look. They were only carp and suckers, cruising the shore and smacking their round lips on dark moss.

I told Justin to try Spam. He baited a hook with a little square of the pink stuff and cast out again. No luck. Again and again he sent weight, bobber, and bait flopping over the school and reeled it all past the noses of the preoccupied fish. Once, the hooked square of meat slid right over the back of a big carp; it turned and darted away. They were on low-fat diets.

We were disappointed, but then, carp are something of a disappointment anyway. Lake trout, northern pike, white fish, walleye, maybe we'd settle for a crappie—that's what we were hoping for on The Great Lakes. We have plenty of carp in Kansas.

Just then we heard a sound of crashing waves.

We looked at each other puzzled. All was calm in the bay. Not a stir of a breeze. But behind us, over the seawall, we heard the unmistakable sound of waves pounding the rocks. We leapt up and mountain-goated from rock to rock over the seawall. White caps covered the open sea and Natty Bumpo was being systematically slammed against a boulder. Where did these waves come from? There was no wind.

We snatched up the fishing gear, slipped on our life preservers, and scrambled down to the canoe. Standing on a large slab of stone whose surface was just inches above the crash and spray of the waves, I squatted down to quickly hog tie the top of the open food pack while Justin was steer-wrestling Natty Bumpo's head, trying to steady him against surging waves. Every wave slammed our canoe against rough limestone, leaving long grooves in his hull. I jerked the spray kilt down over the packs and snapped it to the hull. Justin climbed into the skirt's front passenger opening and pulled the cord to tighten it around his waist. I wrapped up the stern rope and stepped into the swinging boat, shoving off with my paddle at the same time.

We angled away from the rocks into open water, paddling hard, rocking up and down on three-foot waves. After we cleared the seawall we were able to ride with the waves, each rising swell heaving us along the way we were going. There was very little breeze, but the waves were rolling along as if a storm had scared them witless.

At first I wasn't sure how we would handle a running sea, but soon we found it was great fun to ride with the waves. The hard work of the morning and early afternoon, slogging endlessly through a lazy sea, was no more. We were moving swiftly now with white caps flipping the crests of the waves all around us.

For an hour we rose and fell with the waves, making sure we never yawed into a trough, for I had read that in high seas you must always angle into the waves, that getting caught parallel to the run of the waves will capsize a canoe.

Rounding a point, we spotted white water breaking over barely submerged boulders. I yelled to Justin to keep a sharp eye out for rocks—a phrase I had learned in books. We maneuvered around jagged boulders that raked the surface of the oncoming waves. Other rocks would raise their heads for a moment like rough-skinned walruses, then duck beneath the heaving swell; it was anxious but exhilarating work. We shouted back and forth, pointing out boulders, whooping when a wave gave us a good shove. It was risky and great fun.

Hours later, we made a turn into Epoufette Bay. The jumble of boulders and pine trees we were passing came between us and the wash of the waves, and the sea immediately calmed and cleared. Gravel and multicolored rocks were gliding by several feet below us: "paven pools as clear as air," to quote Robert Louis Stevenson. And then, having dodged countless boulders in a running sea, in the placid bay I guided our heavily loaded canoe onto a rock.

"Dad! You've stuck us on a rock! I can't move."

It took a deal of pushing and pulling, knee-deep in cold water, to refloat and left a deep scar on Natty Bumpo's bottom.

Twenty minutes later, we had set up our tent near a thick

stand of brush and were unloading our duffles, our food pack, and the pack of pots, pans, toilet paper, and other essentials I always called the Rude Mechanicals pack after Shakespeare's working fools. I stood up and looked about. We stood alone in a small campground.

I looked at my sixteen-year-old. "Well," I said, "we survived our first heavy sea."

He shrugged and grinned. "And got stuck on a rock in calm water."

"Hey," I responded, "you're supposed to announce coming rocks, boy."

"I did!"

"Not soon enough."

"Yes I did."

Epoufette

Our tent was set in a little oval of grass surrounded by tall dark firs and thick brush that was giving birth to thousands and thousands of small green buds. Three Canadian geese waddled away through the yard of an adjacent house, but there were no humans in sight. It was like wandering into a Gulliver's world of intelligent geese. They would look at each other, offer a comment or two, glance back at us, then mutter a few cutting remarks as they sauntered away into the next yard.

Rooting around in the Rude Mechanicals, I could not find my toothbrush. This was not a problem Marquette or Joliet would have worried about, but one grows used to little conveniences. When I was a child in Africa, my native friends used to chew the end of a twig and then brush their teeth with that. So the absence of a toothbrush was not a problem, but it did provide a good excuse to take the little side road marked on the map and walk up to Highway 2. Perhaps there would be a small grocery there, or maybe a cafe.

And so we took our leisurely way up the gravel road that rose steeply from the little collection of houses that is Epoufette. In the ditches, foot-high stands of green-leafed trillium lifted white three-petalled flowers to the eye, and spice to the passing bees. They were the first ground flowers of spring we had seen. After hours and hours of sitting cramped in Natty Bumpo's bowels, it felt fine to walk again, to move by the strength of our legs the way humans were intended to move: homo erectus, if not always homo sapien.

When we reached the roaring semi trucks and whizzing cars of the highway, we found the Cut River Inn. Inside a few men and women were gossiping around the wood-panelled bar or keeping an eye on televised hockey. We needed to keep expenses down, so we just ordered dessert: apple dumplings in a special rum sauce, with a cup of coffee. I had brief thoughts of Joliet and Marquette: cornmeal mush for them, apple dumplings in rum sauce for us. And did I feel guilty that those intrepid explorers should eat so ill while we latter-day imitators should eat so well? I certainly did, and ordered ice cream to smooth my conscience.

Our repast past, we wished for more, but the discipline of meager finances forced us away from the table. Next door, at a little place that sold smoked fish, smoked turkey, smoked buffalo, smoked venison, and other authentic foods of the past we could not afford, we bought two toothbrushes and headed back down to camp.

The gold sun declined toward the sea. A forested peninsula beyond the bay now shadowed the shallow waters below us and all the wooded hills were darkening. The smell of pine was in the air: warm air, bee-winging weather, honey-light air.

Let us go then, you and I,
When the evening is spread out against the sky:
A woman mesmerized. . . a-rest on hair of sable.
Let us go, along certain half-deserted ways,
The whispering byways
Of silent nights and solitary campers,
And wainscot restaurants with rum-sauce cobblers,
Gravelled roads that lead to simple enchantments
Of good, in tents.

And indeed there is time,
There is time
To wonder, if you dare and if I dare
To disturb the universe.

I have heard the mermaids singing, each to each,
And I believe that they have sung to me.
I have seen them riding seaward on the waves
Combing the white hair of the waves blown back
When the wind blows the water white and black.
(with apologies to Mr. Eliot)

Later that evening, I heard Justin hacking at a dead tree trunk. Our journey could have ended there with a single stroke. His hatchet sliced down through soft wood and slammed against his shin. Fortunately the sharpened edge turned just enough to miss breaking open the bone. It left a nasty bruise. He limped in with his log and told me of the near miss.

Justin isn't much for following directions, especially when it is fatherly or motherly advice concerning safety. Once, on a rare vacation, we were camping in a birch forest in the Rocky Mountains. Justin, about twelve at the time, picked up a camp saw. I told him to keep both hands on the saw and "whatever you do never put your other hand on the log." Saws have a tendency to jump toward living flesh. Three minutes later he quietly walked back holding a bloody finger with a severed tendon.

"Did you put your hand on the log?"

Yes he had.

My wife hustled him into our truck and ran him down the mountain to a hospital an hour away to sew him up.

We heated our soup and corn in the already blackened pan, poured it out into our plates, and ate it with bread. As darkness settled in, Time eased down beside our fire and slept. The cold came down with the stars, and I could hear in the whisper and crackle of the flames the old stories of adventure I had loved as a child, and could see in the flickering shadows around me those past explorers laughing and storytelling of more ancient adventurers still.

We sipped hot coffee and listened to the constant running water from a nearby artesian well. Justin rubbed his shin.

"Do you like it so far?" I asked.

He looked up. "That was *really* boring until lunch."

I shrugged. "It's going to be a long trip. I guess we'll get used to it."

Justin wasn't sure you could get used to boring. I was hoping he'd stay the course. So far no serious arguments, just a debate that first morning over who would do the dishes. I had insisted he do them, and after a time he had relented, though he secured an agreement from me to trade off with him; dishwashing being the bane of all teenagers. I really didn't mind washing our few dishes in water drawn from the lake on a beautiful morning, using sand to scour the skillet, rinsing them with clean water, but there had to be some division of labor and we hadn't as yet fallen into a routine.

Out there in the darkness the artesian spring ran steadily. No radio. No television. Just the sound of the running water, and behind us the slow washing of waves. A whippoorwill called from the other side of the bay. We watched the little flames subside and flicker up again, smolder and then slumber into embers. I let the lingering hours soak slowly into my speed-hardened soul.

Next morning Justin dropped four eggs into popping bacon grease while I stirred an egg and water into pancake batter. The sky was bright and cold. We ate the eggs and bacon while the batter began that lethargic bubbling that makes for light pancakes. But Justin was impatient to flip the flapjacks and we ended with scrambled pancakes. He shoveled it all into our metal plates, we poured on the syrup, and it tasted better than those perfect discs in restaurants.

We then tried washing our hair in the water that ran from a bent and rusty pipe that tapped the artesian well. That water was cold, so cold it hurt. I backed away from it and lathered my hair and upper body, then cupped my hands in the liquid ice and slapped it over my chest, back, and stomach. Brutally cold. Maliciously cold. This is why our ancestors avoided baths in winter. (For that matter, they took few in summer either.) And right they were to avoid them.

I plunged my head under the running water and tried to slap the soap from my hair; within seconds my whole scalp ached as if someone were crushing my head with rocks. But there was no help for it; we couldn't go all day with soap-slimed heads. So I kneeled beneath the pipe doing penance for my rash lust for cleanliness and let the winter water do its worst. By the time the head was clean, the scalp felt no pain, completely anesthetized. But the upper body was still very much alive to the pain. I leapt up, grabbed a towel, and bounded about like a jackrabbit, vigorously rubbing life back into scalp and shoulders.

Justin was much amused. But there was no escape for his

soaped head either, though he wisely refused to wash his upper body.

We threw on t-shirts and sweaters and began packing our equipment with unusual energy. While we were taking down the tent, a man drove a pickup truck into the camping ground and unloaded a riding mower. We saw him climb on and begin mowing the far side of the field. I was a little nervous, not knowing if we were legally camped or not. On our way out of camp the previous afternoon, we had noticed a wooden sign that set five dollars as a camping fee. But there had been no one to pay but the geese and I had had little intention of finding the rightful recipient.

The mower droned away on the far side of the acre of grass as we carted our packs down to the canoe. Then we saw him stop, climb down, unscrew the lid of his coffee thermos, pour himself a cup, and walk on over. But he was a good man; he asked for no money. He was middle-aged with a stubble of beard and wore a flannel shirt, a nylon-quilt vest, a baseball hat, and black-rimmed glasses. He took a sip of coffee and asked, "Cold last night?"

"Cold enough," I said.

"Don't see too many people camping this early."

I nodded and briefly filled him in on the general scope of our journey.

He pointed across the bay toward the peninsula of rocks and trees on the far side. "They say some father camped right over there. You see that white house through the trees? Right over there somewheres. Might have been Father Marquette, I don't know." He sipped his coffee.

"This is Epoufette," he added. "Means Halfway in French. It's halfway between St. Ignace and Manistique. The fur traders used to stop off here. Some people say Epoufette means peaceful. I don't know which it is, Peaceful or Halfway."

"Either way," I said. "It's halfway peaceful."

"Yeah, except for these damned black flies. It's been real dry this spring. The mosquitoes ain't been botherin' me much. But them damned black flies come at ya, they come at ya and they get behind yer glasses on that mower. I don't mind the bites so much, they just worry me, worry me to death."

Justin and I smiled. He was a mower of public fields like my grandfather, one of those who carry on the continual labor of this land for little pay and less gratitude, but without whom all the rest of us would have no houses to live in, no working furnaces or running pipes, no automobiles to drive, and very tall grass in our public parks.

Some people have heard of Joliet and Marquette, but there were five others whose expertise and sweat and courage made the great exploration possible: Jacques Largillier, called the Beaver, Pierre Moreau, called the Mole, Jean Tiberge, Jean Plattier, and a fifth whose name and life were lost—these were the relative unknowns who suffered as much, endured as much, whose courage was tested as much as the leaders.

A little small talk and the man was off to his mowing again. I expect I will never see him again. He spoke only of the usual things: the place, the weather, the insects, the perennial subjects of chance meetings. But those few words made the necessary connection. It seems that Justin and I, strangers and interlopers, were worthy of a little politeness, a little respect, a little camaraderie. I used to disparage small talk. Not anymore. It's the language of civility, one of the ceremonies of innocence. And here in this bay, where Joliet and his men may well have camped, I had found my way to a place where sky and sea, speed and slowness, impatience and peace, and father and son were meeting at least halfway.

High Adventure

As we launched Natty Bumpo into the blue waters of the bay, several hundred geese came winging low over the stand of firs and pines, filling the air with yelps and honks and the thrumming of their wings. It sounded as if we'd been caught in a city traffic jam. But they were soon out of sight, out of sound, and on their way. We were all on our way again, and glad to be going. The sky was clear, the rocks beneath us shone copper and bronze through the shallow waters; out ahead of us the little waves rippled, intensely blue under a cold sky.

Epoufette Island, rocky and forested like the shore, stood some fifty yards off the peninsula. A connecting ledge of rocks ran just inches beneath the surface. After some maneuvering along that ledge of submerged rock and breaking waves, we found a narrow passage where the waves surged through a fissure in the rock. We paddled hard and shot through the gap, aided by a wave that lifted us through the fissure and over the ledge. We were getting better at this.

A half-hour of paddling through deep blue-green waters brought us to a little gravel island peppered black with hundreds of long-necked cormorants. As we approached, all of them took flight, leaving only a salting of white seagulls perched on rocks or pecking away at the eggs the cormorants had left in their nests—for the cormorants had covered the whole rocky island, about a hundred yards long, with their rude stick nests.

We stepped out of the canoe in shallow water and pulled Natty Bumpo ashore. In each nest lay two or three eggs, about the size of chicken eggs, pale blue, covered by a kind of skummy-looking white. Here and there we found a similar nest of brown seagull eggs; the white gulls and the black cormorants seeming to reside in mutual toleration, though the gulls took advantage of the cormorants' flight to breakfast on their neighbors' eggs.

The place stank. White guano had killed what brush there was; only a few skeletal limbs reached up from the whitened rocks. Greenish-black guano floated in the shallows. The captain of a lake steamer told us later that in his youth there had been few cormorants here, but that in recent years they had flown in from the ocean by the thousands and were killing off the trees and brush on islands all over the lakes. I have since learned that catfish farms in the south have given the cormorants food-rich wintering grounds, multiplying their numbers.

As we walked about examining the eggs and nests, the cormorants kept circling the island, all of them flying in the same direction. Round and round the island they flew in squadrons of hundreds. They are orderly and quiet birds: a swift, silent procession of rapacious hunters.

We took one cormorant egg with us, hoping to fry it up that evening and have a taste. An Indian elder we met later that day told us he hated the cormorants. "They eat the fish. They are like living nets," he said. "They all dive down together into the water and the fish can't get away." He said it did no good to go to the islands and steal the eggs because the birds would lay another three in their place. The thing to do, he said, was to shake the eggs up and leave them on the nests. But we, in the interests of culinary research, took but one.

A couple of hours later, we stopped for lunch on Little Hog Island. We ate sardines and peanuts, resting in the gin-strong sunlight, feeling the heat on our faces, watching large seagulls floating on their reflections in the calm water on the leeward side of the island.

After eating, we pushed through a tangle of brush and fir trees to see what the other side of the island held. As we ducked under the last branches, hundreds of seagulls rose screaming from their nests. They turned and wheeled above us, a fierce white squall. Unlike the cormorants that flew in formation, it was every seagull for itself, pivoting and dipping, snapping at the others and rising again in raucous disarray. They are intense competitors: entrepreneurial birds. We picked our way between nests along the south, sunward side of the island; it was all a seagull suburb. Between the trees and the rocky shore, the grass was greening and in places went pink and blue with carpets of tiny flowers. Large herons flapped heavily from high stick nests in the fir trees. The island was fat with spring.

Late that afternoon, we rounded Biddle Point and saw, some three miles across the bay, the white houses and greening lawns of the little town of Naubinway. I estimated we'd be there in an hour; Justin thought it would be two hours. We always disagreed about this; I would optimistically underestimate; he was usually dead on. This time we were both wrong.

The light breeze had stilled and we glided on through small, rolling waves, taking off our life jackets and shirts in the warm sun. The sea lapped and rocked, and we with it in a kind of easy-going cadence. Every wave near and far sparkled; the sea was a deep, blue, rumpled garment, spangled everywhere with floating diamonds, a king's robe laid down for our passage. Justin was commenting on this effect when, looking to land, I noticed white caps all across the water.

"Justin," I said. "Why are there whitecaps near shore and none out here?"

Just then, a strong, warm wind off the land struck us. Natty Bumpo immediately began to rise and fall with the waves. I knew we were in trouble. It was one thing to have a wind driving us toward shore, but quite another to fight against a force driving us out to sea. Behind us lay 50 or 60 miles of open water.

The sea rose all around us; white water curled and hissed

along the summits of running waves, and the wind blew warm and strong in our faces. Ahead of me, Justin would plunge into a trough while I rose up on a passing crest.

"Justin! Put on your life jacket!"

He did, but I could not stop paddling even for a moment to put on mine for fear of turning sideways to the waves and capsizing. By this time, our third day of paddling, we had gained some measure of coordination. I could generally keep us on course with my J-stroke, but we had not yet fought the wind. Ahead of me Justin would plunge into a trough while I rose up on the passing crest.

The wind grew stronger, a constant pressure against face and chest and canoe. That soft, diamond-sparkled robe of blue we had been skimming over during the long afternoon hours was now a grey beggar's robe ripped by the winds. We leaned into the wind and pulled hard on our paddles.

Wave after wave rose against us. The canoe pitched and crashed into breaking waves. The curling crests slapped over the gunwales, shocking us with icy water. Fortunately, most of the water sloshed off the spray skirt and back into the sea. But we had been unable to snap the spray skirt down over the protruding food pack in front of my legs, so the back fourth of the canoe lay open to the waves. Cold water began sloshing around my ankles, but we could not stop to bail.

It seemed impossible to be just a half mile from land and yet so incapable of reaching it. Every ten minutes or so, I would cry out, "Switch!" and we would deftly change sides with our paddles to give overworked muscles a chance to rest. But I found that paddling on the windward side made steering almost impossible.

"Switch back!"

Justin obeyed, but soon yelled for us to switch back again to give his muscles a rest.

"I can't steer it on that side!" I shouted.

He obeyed without argument and kept stroking.

I searched the shore for evidence that we were making some creeping progress toward land and safety. A low red house rested beneath sun-soaked pine trees ahead of us. Another half hour of constant wave-digging, thirty minutes of ceaseless plowing a vanishing furrow through rough terrain moved house and trees a slow acre to the right. I yelled encouragement to Justin, who kept on digging.

After another anxious hour of paddling, I feared our strength would give way, but there was no rest possible, each oncoming wave seemed to shoulder us back as far as we had paddled forward. The wind had grown stronger. The waves bucked and kicked all around us. No way out. "Being in a ship," said Samuel Johnson, "is being in a jail, with the chance of being drowned."

I kept angling into the oncoming waves, rising and falling, rising and crashing. When a particularly large wave staggered us sideways, I feared capsizing and swung the prow head on into the waves. But then Justin would lift above the wave and slam down into a trough spraying his face and chest in an icy shower.

A growing weariness began to tell on me; we had been fighting wind and wave for two hours without rest. The pleasant little houses, so secure on their rise of land, so serene in the bright afternoon sunlight, moved slow-step by slow-step along to our left; the green grass of a golf course and its thin beach of gravel and sand seeped slowly toward us through the wild waves. We were forcing some progress through this tumult, but I knew that a sudden mistake would kill us.

What had I gotten my son into? Taking time with your son is one thing, but smashing him into freezing waters through a gale wind may be a solution without repair. Beware the love of fathers. I remembered reading of a Boy Scout troop in canoes capsized by a strong wind. All the good intentions of those fathers drowned in that wind; boys and fathers lost.

But then again, what is life without high adventure? I glanced at the houses; would anyone on shore see us if we flipped in these waves? We were certainly too far from shore to swim; the cold water would take us under. And yet I was strangely unafraid. Muscling through the waves and steering for shore were all-consuming and so preoccupied me that fear blew in and away at the same time.

Two-and-a-half hours of jarring waves and charging winds and freezing spray, of strength-sapping armwork finally moved us into easier waters beneath the land. We were much relieved, but we still had a long way to go. We had angled a quarter of the compass away from Naubinway in order to maintain our course against the run of the waves and now had to turn left and follow the shore back past the golf course, past a commercial fishing dock, and on past the town, looking for a place to get off the water. Off to our left the big waves were still running hard for open water with the wind in pursuit.

A quarter mile across a small inlet, we saw a few picnic tables under some pine trees and decided it might be a suitable park. Pacing across the inlet, we noticed two white swans rising and falling on the sheltered blue waves of a little inlet. A good omen? I guided Natty Bumpo beside a wooden dock and ran him up a concrete boat ramp that someone had softened with a thick layer of sawdust. We tied up to the wooden posts and climbed out—stiff, exhausted, happy.

I looked at Justin. "How'd you do?"

He shook his head and smiled, "I was a little worried."

Naubinway

On our left a low building with showers and restrooms squatted on the point of the headland. On our right, an expanse of
mowed grass ran down to the lake, and a paved road sheltered
by a few old knotty pines circled away from the shower house
and on toward the little town of white houses. Just above the
dock where we had begun pulling out our wet canvas packs, we
noticed a black Chevy Blazer, and a man inside it watching us.
We walked up to introduce ourselves, assuming we might need
permission to camp.

He rolled down the window, and we saw a short, stocky man
with black eyes and a butch haircut. He said he was a sixty-six-
year-old elder of the Ojibwa people.

"I don't have any problem with you camping here," he said.
" I sure wouldn't send anybody back out in that wind." He said
he had seen us coming and had driven over to see if we'd make
it. His name was Wachter (his father had German blood). He
said the name meant watcher. Many years ago, he said, several
men in birchbark canoes had arrived at this point; he had gone
over to meet them too. They had been taking the trip to com-
memorate the third centenary of the Joliet-Marquette journey.
One of them had written a book about their trip and had mentioned Wachter in its pages. "I'm in the Library of Congress,"
he said. "He called me an affable man."

And an affable and talkative man he was. He talked nonstop for some forty-five minutes as we stood drying out in the
constant wind. His people, he said, used to live hereabouts in
domed houses constructed of willow poles covered with bark.
At night the old ones would sit around the fires and talk, or
drink hallucinogens.

"Hallucinogens?"

He pointed across the road at a little stand of brushwood.

"See those bushes over there? The ones with the red bark. That's dogwood ozier. You peel back the bark, scrape off the soft inner bark and mix it with bayberry or sage. It's a real hallucinogen. We had that centuries before LSD and all that stuff the hippies had. We don't give it to the white man, though," he grinned. "They're crazy already."

He told us that Naubinway used to be a sawmill boomtown. Back when they were rebuilding Chicago after the great Chicago fire of 1871, the sawmills worked twenty-four hours a day. There was an open-air dance hall with a roof, five taverns, and a cat house. "Most of that's gone now."

But Wachter's main pride was the accomplishments of his Ojibwa tribe. "The white man called us Chippewa. You see, they screwed it all up, couldn't pronounce the name right. They heard 'Ojibwa' and pronounced it 'Chippewa.' They screw everything up." He grinned.

He went on to tell us how, not many years ago, the tribe had been reduced to a half acre of tribal holdings with sixteen dollars in the bank. But then they had hired a lawyer to get the fishing and hunting rights they had been promised by treaty. The court ruled in their favor and now it's Indians who run the commercial fisheries here. "Making good money too," he said. "Then the tribal elders started building gambling casinos. We've got five now. Making millions. And they provide 2500 jobs, 500 to whites. So they're good for everybody. They bring in the tourists too." He said the tribal elders use the money to finance the businesses of tribal members, build homes for the elderly, and generally try to diversify the financial base of the tribe.

After some time he asked us where we were headed and we told him. He said we would pass the Millecoquins River around the peninsula. "That's where LaSalle [The French explorer] came with his whole fleet of canoes," he said. "The Indians around here welcomed them, real friendly, you know. But that night the Indians stole everything they could lay their hands on: axes, pots and pans, food, everything they could carry away. When LaSalle woke up next morning, he was mad as hell and called the river Millecoquins. I always heard that it meant River of a Thousand Demons. But a French student moved here one year and told me it meant River of a Thousand Rascals." He smiled, "Either way."

As we talked, a car full of teenage girls drove slowly by, turned around at the shower stalls and drove away.

"That French student couldn't paddle a canoe," he went on. "He'd sit in the back of the canoe and try to paddle it with the nose of the canoe sticking up in the air; it would just go around in circles. I told him I'd help him out. I said, See that rock? It must have weighed seventy or eighty pounds. Put it in the front of your canoe. He couldn't figure out what I was doing, but he tried it. When he got in, the canoe balanced out and he paddled away."

Another man had driven up. We pulled away from Wachter. The newcomer was a soft-spoken, grey-haired man named Larry Wyse; he was the harbormaster. We asked if we could camp overnight. He looked down and said, "Well, we don't encourage camping on this spot," then he glanced up and smiled, "but we don't stick too close to the rules here." He pointed to the showers and said he had just filled the tanks five days before and we could take showers. "I haven't turned on the heat yet, but the water might be warmer than the lake."

Another car with teenage girls idled by, turned, and headed back to town.

After Wyse and Wachter had driven away, Justin ventured into the shower house while I set up the tent. Someone had jimmied the bathroom door open that winter and pissed in the sinks and on the floor, so he picked his way carefully across the cold concrete and turned on a shower. It was Epoufette all over again; the water was ice cold. But Larry Wyse had told us about a pizza place on the highway, so we felt the need to clean up before we walked into town. Justin stripped and stepped in, and out. He soaped up and stepped back in, and out again quickly. In and out he stepped, doing the wild, body-slapping wicked-water two step; it was impossible to stand under that spray for more than a few seconds.

He returned, dressed in jeans and a wool sweater, and with a wide smile handed me a towel. "Your turn," he said. I accepted my fate and walked off to endure another cleansing. Another car of teenage girls cruised by, honked at Justin, and sped away laughing.

We were famished. After the showers, we hurriedly pulled the rest of our gear from the canoe and laid out our canvas packs in the wind to dry. The first car with teenage girls came by again, honked, and then roared away. We unpacked our sleeping gear, which was still dry, and unrolled the sleeping bags inside the tent. Another car, this one with a couple teenage boys, drove slowly by. We shoved our equipment into the tent and walked away up the paved road, hoping these drive-by teenagers were not a reincarnation of LaSalle's millecoquins.

Though we were walking on solid pavement, we could still feel the sway and rise and drop of waves beneath us, and off to our right the blue waves were still lunging and falling and running away.

The roadway passed through a reedy swamp and tall pines for a hundred yards before it entered the little town. As we walked along, two more cars cruised past, the last one carried an older couple. We were evidently something of a local attraction. We walked by small white houses resting in wide yards of greening grass, Larry & Sons Small Engine Repair, and Carl & Don Frazier Wholesale and Retail Fish. They say this little town is the largest commercial fishing port on The Great Lakes.

If that's a fact, there must be little commercial fishing on the
Lakes; maybe we missed something, but I thought we saw only
one fishing dock along the shore on our way in. The mower we
had talked to in Epoufette had told us the fishing was nothing
any more. He said when he was a boy the bays around here
were full of fish. He blamed this tremendous loss of fish in fifty
years on lamprey eels and Indian gill nets, but scientists blame
chemical runoff from farms and factories. Sometime during the
last generation, Joliet's descendants had begun to undermine
their own efforts; by joining commerce and technology with
profit as an end in itself, they had managed to kill off their own
source of income.

We found Pizza Pronto on the other side of Highway 2. The pizza we ordered was huge, slathered with yellow cheddar cheese
and extra sauce, sausage, ham, pepperoni, and who knows what
else. We devoured the pizza as evening moved into town and
settled in. I stared out the window as passing cars on Highway 2
switched on their headlights; the red light down the road blinked on and off, on and off, brighter and brighter as the steepled
church across the street slowly lost its color.

   I looked at Justin who was sitting back, eyeing the last wedge
of pizza. "So you were a little worried?" I asked.

   "Weren't you?" He looked at me and glanced back at the last
piece, trying to calculate if there was any way he could force it
down. I had already given up eating.

   "Sure I was worried. Especially with the back quarter of the
canoe open like that."

   He nodded and said something about getting continually
splashed by the waves. "It was freezing! You didn't get that in
back, did you?"

   I smiled. "Not much."

   "Maybe I should sit in back."

"Maybe later," I said. "Let me get the hang of it first. Besides, you're young; you can take a little cold water."

"A little cold water! Every time we hit a wave the spray hit me in the face; it was freezing! My hands were numb. Then the water would trickle down my neck. And now, look at my lips, they're chapped and the skin on my face burns."

He was right. His face was sun-and-wind burned and his lips beginning to crack. Even the backs of his hands were red. I told him to put on more of the sun cream we carried. He said he'd been doing that, but it didn't seem to help.

"We'll buy some chapstick for your lips," I offered. " But look, we survived our first real adventure. A couple hours ago we were fighting for our lives, now here we sit, stuffed and secure."

He smiled and sipped at his Coke.

"Stuffed and secure," I added. "That seems to be one definition of the American dream."

He shrugged and nodded. "I'm glad we made it."

"Me too. You going to eat that last piece? He looked at it with serious intent, but then pushed it away and sighed. "Too much."

We walked back through streets and houses sinking deep into a northern night. We came upon a little memorial for fishermen lost at sea. A few artificial seagulls on posts stood silent vigil around a sign under a street light listing the names of those drowned. The men from one fishing trawler had gone below deck to clean fish when their autopilot navigation device homed in on a passing Great Lakes tanker. Their trawler smashed into the steel hull of the huge tanker and the little fishing boat went right to the bottom with all hands. How often do our time-saving devices rob us of all the time we have? Of course the manual method has its risks too. We had come close enough to joining those mariners on the bottom. But the battle had been exhilarating. It wasn't a machine that had driven us through that wind; our own hands carried us through. There's a real satisfaction in handmade success.

Justin wanted to sleep outside in the warm wind. I wondered if he'd be comfortable outside; I thought the wind would worsen his chapped skin, but he said the wind felt good on his face. It wasn't worth an argument; I let him go. We were living and working together as we had never done before, but there was still a distance between us, something hard to define: a separation not to be bridged by three days of travel.

All night the wind blew, a warm steady blowing that carried scents of earth and vegetation. The tent shook and fluttered as I lay inside listening. The wind that had almost killed us was now the breath that we breathed. Some Indian tribes used to worship the wind, and this night in a frail tent I could see their point: killer and life-giver, blasting down the bitter winds of winter, carrying up the sunny breezes of spring. Even those Biblical tribes, the Hebrews and the Greeks, each used one word for both wind and spirit: "and the Spirit (or Wind) of God was moving over the face of the waters."

Marquette's first mission had been at Sault Sainte-Marie, at the confluence of Lake Superior and Lake Huron. He had gone there with several others and had built a mission headquarters of rough logs. It was a strategic location because every year twenty or thirty tribes from near and far would gather to trade with the Ojibwa who had settled there. It was the Ojibwa, Wachter's ancestors, who had learned to keep their balance while standing upright in their birchbark canoes in the surging whitewater and whirlpools of the heavy rapids of the Saint Mary's River.

According to the Jesuit account, the men would "thrust deep

into the water a rod, at the end of which is fastened a net made in the form of a pouch, into which the fish are made to enter. This is repeated over and over again, six or seven fish being taken each time, until a load of them is obtained." The Ojibwa would then sell these whitefish to the gathering tribes.

After the French arrived, the Ojibwa began buying goods from the French to resell to the other tribes. It seems the Ojibwa have a long tradition of being businessmen. After all these centuries, they are still working the tourist trade, still fishing with nets, still seeming to keep their balance in an uncertain world. Naubinway is an Indian word for 'Place of Echoes.'

First Hunt

Next morning, we pulled for deeper water and settled into a rhythm, picking our way between boulders that cut the surface or waited just inches below. The water was clear, slopes of jumbled rocks below us would rise up to glance in a hundred colors at the dazzling sun, then sink away into blue-green depths.
The waters clean, the skies blue, our spirits were riding the steady winds. We were forty miles from St. Ignace, still making our way westward along Michigan's Upper Peninsula.

By late afternoon, we were exhausted; wind and waves had turned against us. A dark, rough line of wild forest curved away through great distances until its thin line of sooty green curled over the lip of the horizon and disappeared. It was hard to pack up will enough to paddle over that receding horizon, but we kept going, taking our way over what the ancients called the swan's road, the fish-path, the realm of the woven waves.

A seagull winged along above us, cocking its head at us, then dropped like a white rock toward the surface, spreading its wings just above the waves and floating up in a quick curve, suddenly weightless as a piece of paper. It flapped its wings a time or two, then settled onto the water, paddled around for a few seconds, then flapped away again.

We had noticed that seagulls usually drop down like this, pulling up at the last second and settling down to paddle around after their prey while the V-tailed terns plunge smack into the water from forty or fifty feet up. Both species seem to miss their fish much more often than they catch.

Several miles on, we saw tiny flakes of white rising and falling along the blue horizon like wind-blown confetti. As we approached, we could see hundreds of seagulls and terns crying and diving into the shallow waves beyond a shoal of sand and gravel. Suddenly a great, dark bird plummeted from the sky and hit the surface. Then, with a great beating of wings, it dragged a fish along the waves to the beach. It was a golden eagle, and the fish was either too heavy to lift from the waves, or the southwest breeze behind the eagle prevented it from lifting off.

On shore, a deer spotted us and bounded away, raising an enormous white tail. A bald eagle rose from the branch of a dead tree and floated away over the forest. We seemed at last to have journeyed beyond houses and civilization into America's past.

As the sun glared down toward the trees ahead of us, we made our way toward a point of land lined with spruce and pine trees. From a distance it looked like a fox's tail lying on the water.

We beached the canoe and carried our heavy packs over sand dunes to a little sandy depression between pine trees. We staked our tent in the sand, found a dead pine tree from which to cut limbs for firewood, and pulled out our sack of pots and pans. Another golden eagle, resting its wings on the open air, circled above us, then drifted away.

While I was breaking up sticks for the fire, Justin went exploring. He returned with a long, grey feather and asked me what it came from. It was an eagle's feather, over a foot long. Two inches above the point of the quill, soft white down changed into light grey barbs that gradually darkened toward the squarish tip. It was in perfect shape.

I followed him back into the sand dunes. We trudged up through soft sand till we found a beaten path, then walked it as it skirted the evergreen forest and wound down through scrub juniper, dried grasses, and the grey limbs of wind-broken pines. We entered the forest and stopped. Some thirty yards away a rabbit sat, its long ears straight up, its bright eye gleaming in the waning light. We stood still and watched, waiting for it to move, but it remained fastened there, outwaiting us.

Justin whispered for me to get the rifle. I muttered back that the rabbit would never wait for me to return. "Come on Dad!" he whispered. I walked away toward the camp, fully expecting Justin to soon join me. When he did not return, I began wondering if the rabbit was that patient. I began hurrying through the sand. Perhaps there was some chance for roast rabbit tonight. I scrambled into our tent and grabbed the rifle. I looked back the way I'd come. Justin wasn't in sight. Back through the dunes I ran, huffing along the path until I saw my son still standing where I'd left him five minutes before. And there was the rabbit, outwaiting its life.

I was out of breath and asked Justin if he wanted to take the shot. He shook his head. No, he wanted me to shoot it; he had never shot an animal before and was afraid he'd miss. I took a deep breath, aimed for the shoulder . . . and pulled the trigger. The rabbit collapsed. We walked over and kneeled down beside it. Grey ticks in many sizes infested its muzzle and several fat ones had attached to the long ears; the rabbit had scratched the light fur off its own ears trying to rid itself of the pests.

Along those long, diaphanous ears, we could trace the thin dark veins.

Justin was enthusiastic. He wanted to take the rifle and hunt for more. I gave him the rifle and walked back to camp carrying the rabbit. Not long afterwards I heard a shot, then another. I had the fire going when Justin walked in, head down. He'd missed. I told him I would unroll the sleeping bags and cut some more wood if he wanted to try again. I had already told him how to hunt rabbits with a .22. You walk slowly, carefully, stopping every seven or eight paces, then, after a pause, you move on another few paces. If you keep walking without pausing, the rabbits will freeze where they are and you'll walk right by them. But if you stop, their instincts tell them the predator has scented them. As soon as you take another step, the rabbit bolts from cover. That's your moment to freeze. If you're lucky, the rabbit will bound off a few paces, ears back, listening for pursuit, then stop to find out what's taking you so long. That's the moment to draw a quick bead and fire. Three of us once shot 23 rabbits in a single afternoon.

The shadows were long and the woods dark when I heard another snap of the rifle. A minute later I heard a second shot.

Justin returned triumphant. He strode into camp holding his long-eared trophy high. His first rabbit.

We took the two tick-riddled rabbits some distance from camp to gut and skin them, wanting to keep bears from joining us in camp for a late-night snack. I dropped them on some low-lying evergreens to keep them out of the sand and showed Justin how to tear the soft fur from those long, leggy bodies. He wanted to keep the feet of his first rabbit, so I sliced through tendons and joints telling him we'd salt them and put them in a waterproof container.

Night was upon us when we laid those long muscled legs down on the hot grill to roast. Justin told me how he had stalked it, then hit it on the first shot, but when he approached the shot rabbit, he had noticed its eye still watching him. He hadn't been able to crush its head with his boot as I had done, so he had shot it a second time. And now he was full of the ages-old pleasure of the hunt.

After turning the sizzling legs several times, we scattered salt over them and ate. "Like strong chicken," said Justin. I smiled and kept on chewing. They take considerable chewing.

The night was cool, the stars bright and near, the sea wind filled the pines. Over the dunes we could hear the systematic sweep and crash of the waves on sand. I read *Odysseus* aloud for a time: Odysseus was sailing for home and his son Telemachus was sailing to find him; the ancient gods of voyage and adventure seemed near.

I closed the book and listened again to the singing of the wind. Our little fire flared and snapped and glowed. Justin lay on one elbow near the fire, fingering his eagle feather.

The Pit And The Long Ship

We traveled far. Stopping for lunch on another sandy beach, we walked away from the sounding shore into the silence of a sunlit forest of balsam fir, black spruce, and leafing aspen. We climbed over grey tangles of fallen limbs to a stream running clear over stones amber and black. Thick patches of yellow marsh marigolds gathered in forest clearings and trailed into clear rippling water, reminding me of two lines from my youngest daughter's favorite poem: "Brave marsh merry buds rich in yellow,/ Give me your money to hold." Moneyed men we were.

We drank of the cold water, ate sandwiches, and returned to our canoe, following bear tracks through the sand, then shoved off again. Again the day was fair—cloudless skies, soft winds, gentle waves, sunlight soaking our shoulders. Men of good fortune.

As another long day waned, the sun declined toward the sea straight before us, glaring full in our faces, glittering and flaring painfully off brassy sheets of water. For two more hours, we sliced through hammered sheets of brass and copper and tin, pulling our hats low and squinting into the intolerable sun.

"I'm getting sick of this, Dad."

"Me too, but we've got to find a place to camp."

An hour later, Justin complained of a headache. We rested for a few minutes while I fished through the Rude Mechanicals for aspirin. Justin swallowed them and we continued.

In the end, we gave up and drifted for shore, waterstepping carefully through a shallow, pebbly glaze of water to a flat sand beach with scattered bushes and dried weeds.

While cutting wood and setting up the tent, we kept hearing a distant rumbling, grating sound. We hung up wet pants and damp sweaters to dry, then walked through a line of fir trees. There, about a mile and a half away in a deep cove, we could see some kind of noisy, clanking industrial facility. The sounds carried across the water, a constant murmuring and grumbling, punctuated by the sharp keening of electronic bells. The whole place seemed terribly out of place in this quiet forest, but it was my oldest daughter's nineteenth birthday, and this looked like an opportunity to call home and wish her a happy day. Besides, I knew my wife would be a bit anxious by this time, not having heard from her novice voyageurs for several days. Taking advantage of the last hour's sunlight, we left camp without eating and walked the long beach toward a conglomeration of metal buildings, tall towers of steel lattice girders, conveyor belts, machinery.

Black coal had washed up peppering the pale sand here and

there. Justin watched the shore for shells. He found a hand-sized piece of weathered driftwood that looked remarkably like a sperm whale; even a tiny knot represented the eye. He slid it in his coat pocket saying he'd add it to his collection: salty rabbit feet, and now a water-carved whale.

Then he found the body of a loon. He called me over. We knelt down and examined it. The strong webbed feet it once used to dive far down into dark waters were folded against soft white underfeathers, the pick-ax bill and round black head lay half-covered by sand, the white neck band had vertical black stripes that seemed to run beneath a lower collar of black then reappeared, sweeping beautifully into white-starred wing feathers that grew into a black-and-white checker pattern across its back.

We heard a distant beeping and looked up to see one of the Great Lakes tankers backing slowly along the far shore toward the industrial facility. Even at this distance the ship was massive. A white pilot's house stood high on one end, cranes and aerials protruded all along its rusty hull. The ship slid slowly through the waves toward what we could now see were hills of grey gravel criss-crossed by walkways and conveyor belts clanking along this way and that. The complex looked like some alien colony set down in this wilderness, but it was only a rock quarry.

As we walked on, empty footprints in the sand came out to meet us, turned around an empty whiskey bottle, then accompanied us like a walking phantom toward the plant.

The ship backed with a painful slowness toward the dock beeping insistently. We made our way through a thick stand of weeds, around a pile of broken concrete, and on across a flat surface of packed gravel, looking for a phone. A front-end loader howled toward us, its black tires as tall as we were, then turned and slammed into a pile of gravel, growling, belching black smoke, lifting its great maw, lowering it again and grinding into the gravel hill, then lifting it high as a stream of gravel dribbled from the corners of its mouth. It turned and howled over to a moving conveyor belt where it slowly disgorged the gravel. The long trail of broken rock rattled up the conveyor belt, turned, and trundled along another belt toward the dock.

The great rust-hulled ship had docked. We read the sign painted on its side: Inland Steel Corporation: the *Wilfrid Sykes*. Not a name to bestir the romantic soul. We stepped through a fence and made our way toward the ship. A pickup truck dashed away to our right. Somewhere we could hear the heavy rhythms of an approaching train. A van dwarfed to toy size by this monster of the deeps moved up to its towering hull and stopped. A platform hung on ropes dropped down the side of the ship; a woman began to unload supplies from the van.

When we found the phone booths, men were already sitting inside, phones propped between ear and shoulder, legs sprawled for long talks. We leaned against a booth and waited. The phone-talkers murmured on and on.

The sun set on this grey world of clanking machinery and stone dust; lights clicked on along the towers and conveyor belts and along the ship. No one spoke to us. We waited. The sailors inside the booths were in no hurry.

Justin took off his camouflaged hat and rubbed a hand through his hair. "Dad, I'm starved. We need to find some food."

I looked at my watch and asked a man standing in line if there were any food dispensers in the plant. He said he didn't know. We waited.

A young man walked out a door in the hull of the ship and down a metal ramp. He stood near the van and glanced over at us. He talked to the woman who was unloading supplies and they both took a look at us. After a few minutes, the man put his head down and walked towards us. His hair was black, his ears hung with earrings; in his blue jeans and casual shirt he looked like a cross between an off-duty yuppie and a pirate. He neared us and looked up. "Did you guys get off the ship?"

"No."

"You work here?" I think he could tell we didn't because everyone in the plant wore hard hats; the only men without them had come down off the ship.

"No, my boy Justin and I are on a canoe trip; we're camped just around that point over there. We came over here to use the phone and maybe find some food."

His face brightened; at least we weren't stowaways on his ship. His name was Tom Wyatter, second mate on the good ship *Wilfrid Sykes*. He said he didn't know about any place to get food at the plant, but he could feed us steak on the ship.

"Steak?" Justin and I asked simultaneously.

"Yeah, we've got all kinds of food. I think there's still some sirloin left. After you make your call, I'll take you on board and show you around."

A half hour passed, and a man hung up a phone and walked out of the booth. I called home. Johanna was out with her mother, but Sqump, Snoof, and their brother, four-year-old Alex, were home. The two sisters were busy making a carrot cake for their older sister's birthday. Each one wanted to talk nonstop, filling me in on the rainstorms that had flooded the streets at home, the trouble Mom was having with my substitute on the paper route, the cake they were making, the decorations they were hanging . . . we talked for twenty minutes. I gave Justin the phone and he talked for fifteen minutes more.

Tom Wyatter had called his girlfriend in Las Vegas. He said he lived there now when he wasn't aboard ship; the company pays travel expenses. The men work sixty days on and get thirty days off from March 15 to January 15.

We followed Tom up the metal ramp of the ship and along a

causeway above the engine room. Tom shouted above the roar of steam turbines explaining how the steam runs the fans that transfer power to a series of gears, which turn the monstrous blades that move the ship. We walked down long metal corridors. He said the *Wilfrid Sykes*, built in 1949, was the oldest ship of the Inland Steel Corporation, but he seemed genuinely proud of it. He took us up a series of narrow stairways and showed us a carpeted, wood-panneled guestroom, no longer in use due to high insurance costs and the threat of law suits. Then up we climbed to the captain's round house.

Surrounded by glass windows, we could see down the length of the ship where gravel was feeding down into the cavernous hold. Tom said this ship could load or unload 21,000 tons of gravel in five hours.

The captain walked over to shake our hands. He was young, tall, handsome, with reddish-brown hair. The first mate, a young man with wire-rimmed glasses, sat at a long counter; he was kidding the captain about some game they had been playing. No one wore uniforms. All three men looked like young college graduates in some highrise office building, but here they were piloting a massive tanker as long and wide as an office building.

They were in no hurry. They would be loading gravel for several more hours, then heading back to Green Bay, which they would reach in about twelve hours. It would take us maybe two more weeks if we were lucky. Tom joked about throwing our canoe aboard the ship and taking us to Green Bay. I saw Justin throw me a hopeful glance—twelve hours and save over two-hundred miles of arm-walking! But of course I declined; I wasn't here to trip around the lakes on a steamer.

We stood in the high, glassed watchtower and spoke of the world beneath us: of the loss of fish in the lakes, of the invasion of cormorants and their destruction of offshore islands, of

Tom's bear hunting in orchards near Naubinway, of the abundant food on board, of the difficulty of keeping off the weight. "We look like apes beside our anorexic girlfriends," said Tom.

I looked down at the still, black forest and the pale beach that ran away toward our little camp and its tiny sliver of a boat somewhere beyond the tip of the peninsula. Up here we seemed cut off, remote. Everything in this realm was outsized, made of steel, and machined for efficiency. In the cockpit all was calm, clean; buttons could be pushed, commands communicated while down below engines roared, great fans blasted air, greased gears intermeshed, steel cables clanked and squealed, and ton after ton of gravel rattled automatically into iron hulls.

Far out beyond the cove, the captain pointed out the lights of another waiting tanker they had beaten into port. "They'll have to wait half the night until we get loaded." He gave a satisfied smile. Speed counts.

Speed, power, size, all count. But they often count against us too. The massive ship breathed and pulsed, it muttered and roared, sweated and stank of hard work while the little figures of crew members down on the decks below stood and watched, and we watched from our high, glass-encased office. It was as if we stood aloof from our own lives watching our mechanical surrogates engaging real life, while we watchers seemed mere phantoms.

A hundred years ago, Romano Guardini was out walking the mountains of his beloved northern Italy. He looked out across beautiful Lake Como and saw working sailboats of a size and construction that had been working the lakes for some 2000 years. But he saw something more: "It grieves me when I see built into one of these vessels, these noble creations, a gasoline engine, so that with upright mast but no sails the vessel clatters through the waves like a ghost of itself." He had seen worse: "Go even further and the sailing vessel becomes a steamer, a great ocean liner—culture indeed, a brilliant technological achievement! And yet a colossus of this type presses on through the sea regardless of wind and waves. It is so large that nature no longer has power over it; we can no longer see nature on it. People on board . . . live as if in houses on city streets. Mark you, something decisive has been lost here. Not only has there been step-by-step development, improvement, and increase in size; a fluid line has been crossed that we cannot fix precisely but can only detect when we have long since passed over it—a line on the far side of which living closeness to nature has been lost. . . . The crew members of a liner are not essentially different from employees on the assembly line of a factory."

We stood on a floating factory, a kind of mirror of modernity, a massive antithesis of little, armpowered Natty Bumpo. This high, glass cylinder, this lofty vantage point, seemed to me a point of deep disadvantage. It was easy. It was comfortable. A man could watch, or play a game, to occupy the mind. But the body was almost superfluous, something to be fed and exercised, but not something of integrated importance. The old Cartesian split between mind and body seemed here to reach a kind of apex; with our machines and our computers, we step away from our own bodies, and that old secular-ethical balance represented by Joliet and Marquette seems to have fallen completely to the pragmatics of progress.

Tom led us down to the galley. It was a narrow cafeteria stacked with shelves of food. Only one sailor sat at table eating; they come when their work allows, their hours dictated by the machines that run them. We loaded our trays with sirloin steak, halibut, fresh cauliflower and cucumbers and tomatoes in vinegar, mashed potatoes and gravy, squares of pistachio pudding, plums, grapes, pralines-and-cream ice cream, and chocolate cake.

The captain joined us, sprinkling diet butter and salt on

a modest helping of peas and corn. We looked at our empty plates, got up, and reloaded: steak, puddings, ice cream, fruits. Tom grinned. "We'd just have to throw it to the seagulls anyway. Those birds make a good living off of these ships." Entrepreneurial birds.

Scavengers that we were, Justin and I kept forking down the food, what Sancho Panza, peasant squire to the romantic Don Quixote, called "belly munitions."

I asked about icebreaking. They said last winter ice had broken a hole in the hull, but they had managed to force passage into port for repairs. He said they used to always quit shipping before Christmas, but that now they regularly ran into January. The pressures of trade.

It was almost midnight when we waddled back up the darkened beach toward camp like a couple of overfed geese. The gravel pit and the long ship behind us were ablaze with lights, still rattling and growling and belching. Gravel was still pouring into the massive belly of the ship; the *Wilfrid Sykes* was still feeding.

Seul Choix

By noon a stiff wind was singing up from the southwest. The waves rose to meet us. These were not the sharp, choppy waves of Naubinway, but long heavy rollers moving with purpose up the length of Lake Michigan. We pulled for the opposite shore, choosing not to hug the coast, but to save time (and risk our lives) by cutting six miles straight across the mouth of the bay. On the far side, the Seul Choix lighthouse stood on a bluff. The place is called Seul Choix, or Sole Choice, because it's the only deepwater bay along this entire northern coast.

The wind blew hard in our faces; waves like hills rolled by

under our little canoe, the crests curling and scratching as they passed. We angled for the distant lighthouse trying to avoid the whitecaps that could break over us, but suddenly a wave snarled into foam and shattered across our bow, soaking Justin down. The spray skirt deflected all but a couple inches of cold water out of the canoe, but it chilled Justin and his hands were already chapped, wet, and cold.

We considered going back, but it is a hard thing on a long trip to retrace your steps and have to face making the same steps all over again. We paddled hard, leaning into our strokes, watching out to sea for the possibility of an approaching tanker; the *Wilfrid Sykes* had left in the night. The sky was a bright blue, the wind came at us crisp and cool, heaving the long, running hills of water against us. Another curling whitecap slapped over the gunwales spraying us both with frigid water.

We kept on rising and lunging into the wind-driven water. I would see Justin's head and shoulders drop deep into a moving ravine then rise right up into blowing blue sky. On the crest he would lift his paddle and hesitate before plunging down the other side, a rough ride for a couple Kansas boys.

We had taken the precaution of wearing our rain jackets and rain pants, but those roaring whitewater crests hit us hard and poured right down through every seam in neck or waist, soaking us and trickling like ice down our legs while the lighthouse stood quiet, remote on the distant bluff, a prim Victorian nurse in long white gown and little red cap. They had an eye for beauty in the old days, even on this remote bluff. Utility did not then, as now, so often translate automatically into ugliness.

An hour and a half of riding the heavy waves had us checking the coast behind us and comparing it to the bluff and treeline ahead. We were maybe halfway across, some three miles out to sea with three more miles to go. Justin slipped his paddle under a bungi cord that held our gear in the canoe, popped the spray skirt open a little and leaned over to sponge water from around his feet, wringing out the sponge over the waves while I kept us on course. He called back to me through the wind saying his hands hurt and were going numb. I took a bearing on the distant lighthouse and dipped my paddle into another passing wave. Justin snapped the spray skirt shut, picked up his paddle with stiff fingers and went back to work, striding over a capricious sea, slow-marching like paraplegic infantry toward that waiting nurse on the bluff.

It is impossible to transmit just how long an hour of such waterhiking drags on. It is like trudging over sand dunes in a desert; each step is forced through sliding sand; every peak surmounted gives out a prospect of countless more. Minutes creep by; the mind is full of waves and wind and motion, of planning the next stroke to achieve the proper angle, executing it, planning the next one, with the knowledge that one erratic wave could slap us over or swamp our canoe. We could do nothing but slog on over ranges and ranges of rolling hills.

An hour later we can hear the roar of waves on a rocky coast. Off the point ahead of us, we see the whitewater: waves crashing and crumbling into white spray along a shelf of grey rock. I steer madly for open water. The elegant lighthouse moves gradually to our right and away.

Thirty minutes later we are off the stony point of Seul Choix battered by whitewater and rocked by thundering waves. They roar all around us like a pride of hunting lions. They bat us over and we barely escape capsizing, they shove us hard toward shore to break us to pieces on the rocks. We yearn for the shore, but we have no choice but to force our way toward deeper water; long broken tables of grey-green rock form a rumbling bastion all along the shoreline.

Around us, green combers rise up sharply in the shallow wa-

ter and shatter across our bows. Twice, maybe three times, we
glance down to see the low troughs scraping over bottom rocks.
We redouble our efforts and fret and struggle through wind and
spray, crawling through chaos, scrambling through confusion.
Still we see no sand ashore, no safe place to beach our canoe,
just a stone-fortified coastland, long white-maned waves, and
that regal lighthouse standing high, white, remote, above a
fringe of grey forest.

Huge boulders begin to break surface here and there, others,
more dangerous because hard to see, wait just below. Up front
Justin begins shouting out instructions, "Go left!"

"What?!"

"Left! Left!—Nevermind, we're already past it. RIGHT!
RIGHT! A ROCK ON THE RIGHT!"

I pull with all my might, bending the paddle with Justin doing the same ahead of me. The prow swerves left. We rise and
fall over six-foot waves, but are only moving by inches around
one boulder after another.

"Another one off to the left!"

"I see it!"

We angle out to sea.

"Why are we going this way?" shouts Justin.

"Deeper water! We need deeper water!"

"Let's get to shore!"

"Where? You see a way?"

He glances shoreward . . . then puts his head down and
thrusts his paddle into a rising wave.

I begin repeating the words of an old poem, speaking to the
stroke of my paddle:

"Here we come a-piping,
    In springtime and in May;
Green fruit a-ripening,
    And winter fled away."

"ROCK STRAIGHT AHEAD!"

"I see it."

"The queen she sits upon the strand,

Fair as lily, white as wand;

Seven billows on the sea,

Horses riding fast and free,

And bells"

"Go RIGHT!"

"WHERE? I don't see it!"

"THERE, just below the waves!"

"I see it.

 "bells, and bells beyond the sand.

Here we come a-piping,

In springtime and in May,"

There is a rhythm in the words and a music in the sound. Say it again. Keep the rhythm going, "Here we come a-piping, in springtime and in"

"ROCKS! TWO OF THEM TOGETHER!"

"Green fruit a-ripening, winter fled, there she sits, the queen she sits . . . she sits upon the strand, "

"THERE! Over THERE!"

"What?"

"Sand! Sand on the shore!"

I see it, but long flat layers of rock and broken waves block our passage through. I hope to find an opening and turn for shore running parallel to the oncoming waves, rocking sharply left and right to keep our balance as a foaming peak hisses under us. We turn to run with the waves; if whitewater breaks over our open stern now, we're sunk. We spot a break in the rocks and lean into our paddles, still dodging submerged boulders. Big rollers heave us up from behind and send us skidding forward. We angle for that slim passage through rock and keep paddling hard.

Our aim is good. We shoot through the crevice and with a few more strokes slide up onto the wide sand beach. No sooner does Natty Bumpo scrape into sand, then a curling wave crashes over his stern. In one second the stern, unprotected by the spray skirt, is full of water. I step quickly out of the canoe into a retreating wave; Justin leaps out and digs his boots into the sand, pulling with all his might as I shove hard; another wave surges in over the gunwales and refills the canoe with water.

We force Natty onto his side to empty the water, but another wave pours in. We keep pushing and yanking to force the canoe above the wash of the waves using the lift of each wave to jerk the canoe higher onto the beach. Then we go to bailing, scooping out the water with our cut-open gallon bleach bottles.

At last, exhausted, we unsnap the skirt and begin lifting out our soaked backpacks and drop them in the sand. We hoist the dripping packs heavy with water and coated with sand onto our shoulders and troop them up the beach and into the forest. It takes several trips. We bring up our duffel bags of clothes, my book bag—some of the books and maps are wet. Fortunately the rubberized duffels with thick plastic bags tied up within have kept our clothes dry. But Justin's fingers are too cold to unbutton his soaked pants. Slowly, painfully, I unbutton his pants for him and strip off his wet jacket and sweater; he lies down in dry pine needles and I untie his soggy boots.

Soon the shrubs and pines are festooned with our wet clothing: wool socks, white t-shirts, flannel shirts, brown wool sweaters, underwear, boots, jackets, all dripping wet. We stoop naked in the chill breeze and pull out dry clothes from the duffels: dry wool socks, dry t-shirts and underwear, dry shirt, dry sweater, dry pants, dry canvas shoes. Even the sea-wind seems warmer now.

I ask Justin how he feels. His lower lip is split and chapped; the chapstick I bought him in Naubinway doesn't seem to be working. His hands have that pale red hue. He tries to flex his fingers, and I promise to buy him gloves in the next town, some kind of protection against the icy wet. He asks for toilet paper— he has diarrhea. I tell him we'll walk back to the lighthouse and find a bathroom. He can't wait. I unstrap the Rude Mechanicals and pull out a roll of toilet paper; it's dry. Then I unsnap the first-aid kit and find the Immodium.

When he walks back out of the pine trees, I hand him the two tiny pills and the canteen. "Let's hope that takes care of it."

He nods and swallows down the pills with a gulp of canteen water.

He's still not complaining. I always knew he was stubborn, but there are different kinds of stubborn: stubborn whiners and stubborn strong. He's never been a whiner.

For my part, I'm feeling a sense of real accomplishment. Just last night, we had been offered free passage across the whole lake, but I had turned away that Faustian offer of delegating the effort of living to a great machine, of relegating the human will and spirit to lazy hours of comfort and consumption. We had risked much, but we had gained more.

That night the moon was on fire. Low thin clouds were running with the wind, trailing like smoke past a glowing disc that would flare up, then sink into white coal, burst into yellow flame to be choked again by flying ash. The wind was pouring through the pines all around us, and I looked at the sky, wondering aloud about rain, but there was no way for us to know whether wet weather was on the way. We sat on old stumps beside our fire watching the embers seethe red in the wind, the flames heeling over and scattering sparks into the night, the coffee beginning to bubble in the blackened enameled pot. We forked down hot pork and beans simmered with onions and canned ham. That's not a remedy for diarrhea, but after such a day's work, men must eat. And after such a battle with wave and rock and wind, it tasted better than the steaks and puddings on the great ship. I wrapped some potatoes in tinfoil and stuffed them in the coals.

Manistique

When we walked out next morning to pack up the canoe, two motorboats were charging around through the waves making noise. They seemed to be going nowhere, just tearing around as fast as they could, bouncing off waves, young men at the helms, "drest in a little brief authority," scaring each other with near misses. Water demons.

Justin recommended we lay the food pack down so that we could snap the spray skirt completely from end to end. Yesterday one good wave over the stern could have drowned our canoe and left us bobbing around in a frigid sea. His plan worked well. Laying the foodpack on its back gave us just enough slack to snap the skirt around the stern, thus enclosing the whole canoe.

The foodpack was a heavy canvas Duluth with leather shoulder straps that enclosed two heavy plastic bags to keep out the water; the plastic contained a woven, ashwood pack basket to prevent the crushing of eggs and the smashing of fruit. Laying the pack on its back increased the chance of water seeping through tiny abrasions in the plastic, but better wet food than drowned us.

The rampaging motorboats were long gone. We had returned to the old world of wide silences. A breeze and its waves had worked around behind us, giving us irregular pushes along our way as the shore stretched out long and monotonous, green with pine, grey with rock.

Far out to sea a nervous loon laughed. We looked for it, but a haze was gathering over the seaward waves, dimming the middle distances. The loon called again and Justin imitated it. . . . it answered, so did he.

Black flies swerved up from the green water and collected in little groups on the surface of Natty's spray skirt. From there they launched their attacks. I would tell Justin when four or five had landed on the back of his white t-shirt and he would flop back onto the covered backpacks killing three or four. We did battle with our paddles, slapping them on the skirt, whacking them on the water, swinging at them in midair; they were easy prey, but there were always reinforcements. Occasionally one would dive through our defenses for a quick sharp bite. After a while we gave up and let them have us. The day wore on.

Far ahead, moving through haze, were seven Frenchmen in two birchbark canoes—just three centuries away.

About midafternoon we rounded a point and saw across a broad bay of grey water the tiny houses, tall radio towers, and water tower of the little lakeshore town of Manistique. It was the first of June, the feast day of St. Justin Martyr. Chap-lipped, sunburnt, sore-muscled, fly-bitten, diarrhea-plagued Justin was feeling the part.

We were tiring of lake travel and hurried across the shallow waters pulling 25 strokes as hard as we could go, then resuming a regular rhythm for 25, then charging ahead again; anything to break the monotony.

A rocky, weedy shore eased up out of the water toward a small park of mown grass, cedar trees, and picnic benches. We stepped into cold water and maneuvered Natty into a stand of weeds hoping to keep him from easy view, then walked up to the park.

Highway 2 curved just beyond and turned east between lake and town. Trucks roared by loaded with cut logs and cars weren't waiting for pedestrians. We hurried across the busy asphalt and into the Holiday Gas Station. I asked the pretty girl at the counter if camping was allowed in the park. She said no, but she said she had seen others do it. I told her I'd call her if they threw us in jail. She smiled.

We stepped out of the station, and I told Justin we'd set up camp about dark; maybe they wouldn't throw us out after dark. We turned for town. The day was warm; we were looking for ice cream.

A half mile of roadside gravel brought us to a little glass-fronted ice cream parlor called Nifty Fifties. Outside, a red-and-white fifty-seven Chevy, the whole car, was perched fifteen feet off the ground on a concrete pole. Inside, an old chromed Wurlitzer juke box hunched against one wall was thumping to the beat of "Wake Up Little Suzy." On the opposite wall a cowboy-hatted James Dean kicked up his boots in a self-satisfied way against the movie set of *Giant*. Marilyn Monroe with metallic blonde hair flirted from five successive photographs, each of her dresses a different shade of pastel. Off to one side Elvis Presley had returned as a lamp, crowned with a lampshade that stuck out the top of his head. Near the door, there he was again, this time as a clock, his blue plaid sportcoat holding the hours of his fame, his hips and legs ticking back and forth the diminishing seconds.

The girl behind the counter looked at the clock. It was almost 5:00. A man in a pinstripe suit stood gnawing impatiently on his Macadamia Chocolate Nut, two dips, waiting for his wife to make a decision. She stood perfectly still, feet together, grey hair smoothly coifed.

An old man with erratic white hair held the door for his ten-year-old granddaughter, then limped in behind her. The

girl went straight for the long, glassed counter and looked
down at the pastel selections in their cardboard containers.
She shifted from foot to foot, wringing her hands at Double
Fudge, Candied Pecans, Very Very Strawberry, Mint Chocolate Chip, Orange Sherbet.

The old man waited. The little girl bounced along the counter and back again. She jumped from foot to foot.

"You could have one dip of chocolate with a drink," the
old man offered.

The little girl looked up brightly and announced, "I'll have
one dip of chocolate with a drink!"

The girl behind the counter had run out of smiles. She glanced
at the clock and leaned over to scoop out the hard chocolate.
The coifed woman deliberated. The pinstripe gnawed.

Then, chocolate cone in one hand, the little girl danced out
of the door to the driving beat of "Tequila" on the Wurlitzer,
the old man hobbling after holding her Coke in a paper cup
and taking a sip or two when she wasn't looking.

I order a malt: cold scoops of vanilla, black syrup, a little milk,
a spoonful of grainy malt, all churned up in one of those old
stainless steel mixers. Justin goes for the strawberry. As we
leave the counter to find a table, I pick up a brochure and sit
down. It's an advertisement for Nifty Fifties, and it's talking
history:

"Visiting the past is like visiting a foreign country. It's a
long way off, a place we remember nostalgically, a place we'd
like to find again. Recapture memories of yesterday as we help
you remember the way things really were in the 1950s—the
automobiles, the movies, the singers, the sport heroes, the
comedians, the cartoons, and—best of all—that happy to be
alive feeling!"

Cars, movies, singers, sport heroes, comedians, cartoons—
sounds like more than the 50s, sounds like "the American
Century." I think of Greek architecture, Roman government,
medieval theology, Renaissance plays, Dutch paintings, Rus-
sian symphonies—and what, oh America, will you leave us in
time? Pop songs? Cartoons? Movies? Cars? Sports heroes?

Throughout our journey, Elvis, Marilyn, James Dean, sometimes joined by Humphrey Bogart, would look at us from cafe
walls. But it's not their actual drug-juiced, ambition-burnt
lives that attract us; it's their theatrical images: James Dean
forever young, defiant, remote; Elvis and Marilyn shaking it
and flaunting it; Humphrey Bogart, yearning, haunted, cyni-
cal, alone. Those images are photo-engraved in our minds.

A man named Feuerbach once wrote that our era prefers
"the image to the thing, the copy to the original, the representation to the reality, appearance to being." Susan Sontag
wrote that in the twentieth century images are the "coveted
substitutes for firsthand experience."

How is it that we prefer these images of imitators, these
famous pretenders, to the men and women who made the history of this region? We saw no Rene-Robert Cavalier Sieur
de la Salle on cafe walls. (With a name like that, he should at
least warrant one square foot on a cafe wall), no Black Hawk
or Keokuk, no Joliet or Marquette.

Now the brochure is talking psychology:

> "Why do we want to step back to another time? Perhaps
> it's because we want to escape from the decisions we must
> deal with on a day to day basis. When you take a step
> back and have a pleasant experience—like the one you'll
> enjoy at Manistique's Nifty 50s—we hope you'll leave us
> with a desire to step forward and carry that good feeling
> throughout your life."

Grab a feeling and take it with you. I sipped at my malt. Marvelous elixir this if it can have such lasting effects.

It's not nostalgia I'm against. The word "nostalgia" just means "homesickness." And it's right that we long for home. A bit of homesickness is a centering thing. Odysseus was homesick on Calypso. It's the need to escape that bothers me, that seems endemic in our lives, a need to escape our unfulfilled lives, or, perhaps, our overfilled lives. But am I not even now engaged on a two-month journey of escape? Yes indeed. But escaping from what to what? I am trying for all I'm worth to walk back into my son's life. I am trying to reengage with work and weather, with earth, water, and fire, with the people of this land and its history—with the real world. I am trying, for the life of me, to come down out of that high, glass cylinder where the world lies remote beneath me. I 'm escaping to a way of life where mind and body and soul integrate and coordinate. I'm trying . . .

I look back at the brochure. Talking philosophy now:

"After all, life is only what you think it is, isn't it?"

Well, no it isn't. My vagrant thoughts never manage to keep up with that leaping mystery we call life, life that secretly pulses through me, and then, this early spring, roars away like a wind off the sea, breathing sap and juice into great forests of oak and spruce and pine, into swarming black flies, into plunging loons and lazy carp, into a chaos of screaming white gulls, into winging formations of black cormorants, into shifting arrangements of argumentative geese, into lordly eagles lifting their wings to the sun, into white swans drifting silent on blue waters—into that mad multiplicity of vital beings that even this second of this spring afternoon are thrusting up and leafing, leaping, honking, yelping, laughing, whippoorwilling everywhere with sounds, scents, sights . . . my meager thoughts will simply not keep up.

But what a grand philosopher I am, sitting in an ice cream parlor debating ontology with an advertisement. Why am I surprised to have a little relativism served up with my ice cream? Relativism is the flavor of the age, the mode of the day: so let's have a little Relativism a la mode.

Four teenage girls are yapping away at another table. Every now and again one glances over at sunburnt, split-lipped Justin. Simmering life casting glances. The girl behind the counter makes a final check of the clock and joins them. It's after five.

Justin and I have time on our hands, a leisure I'm not used to. We walk away from Nifty Fifties and up streets at random. The houses are unremarkable, single and double-storied homes with garages attached to the streets by driveways. A small business district of antique shops, pharmacy, grocery store, occasional churches. A grey spring warmth is in the air, grass is greening, the maples are cascades of tiny green bells. Tulips, hyacinths, and daffodils decorate yards. In front of a porched home, a woman is on her knees hoeing the flowerbed along her sidewalk. Her daughter is pushing a doll carriage away up the sidewalk. The mother sees us, two strangers in a small town, and calls out to her little girl, "June . . . June!"

Indeed it is June, though the tulips and daffodils came up two months ago back home in Kansas.

A little boy charges us shooting with his play gun, a tin badge pinned to his t-shirt.

"Are you the sheriff?" I ask.

"No, that's my brother."

"Are you the deputy?"

"Yes," he grins, "but my gun isn't real."

"Thanks. Glad to know that."

America, America. A small neighborhood at work and play. Boys chasing each other, a girl rolling her doll carriage; it seems like a cliché from the fifties, scenes from my childhood. "The simple, bare necessities,/ Forget about your worries and your strife!" Nostalgia, you say? Yes. And I'm sure the people here have their problems, plenty of worries and strife to go around. But there's much to be said for neighbors you know, streets you can walk, children safe at play. It might have been Topeka, Kansas, fifty years before the rush to suburbia gutted its urban core of shops and homes. Small towns have a hard time competing economically these days, but here there still seems to be a balance of culture and commerce.

But city-bred Justin is bored. The town is small enough for us to walk to a miniature golf course and play a game. I win and Justin demands another game, but I smile and tell him I'll quit while I'm ahead. He grumbles and whispers mutinous words.

We return to the little park and make our way down to Natty Bumpo through a scrabble of weed, dried grasses, and broken rocks. We unload the heavy packs and troop them up to the park, set up the tent under a cedar tree, build a fire in a park grill, and carve up a can of Spam into a bubbling pot of pork and beans. A thin rain begins gusting through the twilight.

Later that night it is still raining. I walk across the highway in my rain jacket to find a phone. The pay phone is outside in the rain, near the highway. I punch in the numbers for home. My wife is out (a friend is having a baby and has called her away), but I talk to Sqump and Snoof and Alexander for twenty minutes as the rain blows down out of a dark sky onto my dripping hat and rain jacket and into my sodden canvas shoes. My mind is watching the home stories Squmper is calmly reporting while my eyes watch the rain falling in little running circles onto the black asphalt of Highway 2. Diesel rigs roar by within a few feet of my feet, their tires tearing to pieces the thin sheet of black water.

I splash back to our tent in the steady rain. Justin is reading a

Tom Clancy novel by flashlight. His sunburnt face looks up and says, "Two weeks is a vacation; two months is a lot of work." I pull off my soaked shoes and socks and stuff them in a corner of the tent.

"Mom was out again," I say. "But I had a good talk with Andrea, Julia, and Alex."

"Do we have to go the whole way?" he asks.

"So you want to give it up?"

"I'm not saying that. It's just that two months is a long time."

"I agree."

"I wish we could have hitched a ride with that ship," he says. "They said they'd be in Green Bay in twelve hours."

I nod.

"Couldn't we just go as far as Green Bay? How long will that take?"

"Maybe a couple more weeks."

"What if we stop there?"

"Then we'll miss all those experiences."

"We've got experiences already."

"But we won't discover the Mississippi."

"It's already been discovered."

"Not by us."

The wind is awake all night, troubling the lake, slinging heavy rain at our tent. Our little grey globe shakes and mutters as the rain sweeps over the thin membranes that protect us.

We sit at our kitchen table, my wife and I. The conversation is typical: What will become of our nineteen-year-old son Justin? "Impulsive as the wind," I say.

"He skips from one job to the next," she says. "He takes off on sudden trips at the last moment and is late arriving. He

misses a family reunion because he wants to help his girlfriend's mother move. We have family reunions, what, once every three or four years? And he skips it in order to spend time with the girl he spends all his time with anyway. And it was the last family reunion we ever had with your father."

I look down into my cup of tea. *"And now he's quit the best paying job he's ever had. How's he going to save money for college now that he's moved into his own apartment?"*

She shakes her head. *"And the car accidents. He's had more than the older kids put together."*

"He's lucky to be alive at all the way he drives—tailgating, speeding, Andrea and Julia are afraid to drive to school with him."

"But he won't listen to me," I say.

"He won't listen to me either," she says.

Icons And Conversations

It's Trinity Sunday, the second of June, and the sun is shining. We're going to church. But our bodies are rank with smoke and sweat, our hair matted and greasy; we haven't washed for five days. Sitting in the tent, we struggle into clean-but-wrinkled khaki pants and clean, wrinkled shirts, then walk across the highway to Holiday Gas. There is no shower, so we shampoo our hair in the restroom sink and dry our heads with a wad of paper towels. We remove our still soaked shoes and put on dry boots. Rather than return the shampoo and wet shoes to our tent, we hide them behind the sink cabinet, then emerge refreshed and cleansed—above the neck.

I'm interested in seeing what's become of the Catholic Church in this Upper Peninsula of Michigan where Marquette the missionary brought his faith three centuries ago. We walk down sunny sidewalks to the square tower and bronzed roof of St. Francis de Sales Church. One thing about American Catholics, not many of them dress up for Sunday services anymore. Except for our wadded, crinkled clothes, and a faint smell of smoked flesh, we should fit right in.

Inside we find a pew near the back. The long strains of a hidden organ begin. Along either wall, tall stained-glass saints look down, transfiguring June sunlight: a young and rather effeminate Jesus observes the gathering crowd without expression, a French missionary with sharp black eyebrows and a long black robe stands in front of a tepee, there's St. Norbert who traded in a life of dissipation and luxury after being nearly struck by lightning, Therese of Lisieux is holding roses. I look at her—that pretty, lively, passionate girl who stands there so solemnly. She saw herself as one of the littlest flowers of the field, but she was much more than she claimed to be. Averse to self-promotion, she wrote down her story only because her superior (her older sister) recognized her gifts and required her to write down what has become a spiritual classic. Her reality transcended her image.

We all stand. The people and organ begin singing. These Catholics need the organ. They don't have an arm-waving song-leader-emcee to hoist their spirits like the Evangelicals of my youth, so they are left to murmur along with the too-loud organ, trying to sort out those odd songs from the seventies or the newly acquired Protestant hymns. They should have stayed with Gregorian chant.

An elderly priest walks to the altar.

"In the name of the Father, and of the Son, and of the Holy Spirit."

Around us there's a motion of hands making the sign of the cross, a murmur of spoken response.

"The grace of the Lord Jesus Christ and the love of God and the fellowship of the Holy Spirit be with you."

"And also with you."

There's something wrong with the priest's chest and the angle he holds his head—some sort of disfigurement. His text comes from the words of the apostle John, "For God so loved the world that He gave His only begotten Son that whoever believes in Him should not perish, but have everlasting life."

We sit down.

I look sideways at Justin sitting beside me, my third-begotten son. I'm praying this trip will not cost him his life. We came too close at Naubinway. . . and Seul Choix . . .

"All creation," the priest begins, "all the past, all the future, and the now, flows from this verse. It is the story of the Trinity . . ."

Marquette was preaching the same message to the Hurons and Algonquins 300 years before. It was, for the tribes of this region, a wholly new teaching. Many of course resisted it, sometimes quite violently (of twenty-one early missionaries in Upper Canada, nine were killed), but the French missionaries did have some success. Marquette tells of the time he arrived among the Kiskakon Indians who had recently converted: The Indians were in the fields harvesting their corn when he walked in. They gathered together and listened to this new "black robe," as they called the Jesuit missionaries. "I baptized the newborn infants, and instructed the chiefs whom I found well-disposed. The head-chief having allowed a dog to be hung on a pole near his cabin, which is a kind of sacrifice the Indians make to the sun, I told him that this was wrong, and he went and threw it down." Intertribal wars devastated some missions, but gradually the missionaries extended their efforts, instructing the converts in the same Creed now repeated.

Then the repeated gestures, the flickering candles, words recited, murmured responses, the water poured over the old priest's hands, bowings, words, the people kneeling and repeating, "Holy, Holy, Holy Lord, God of power and might, heaven and earth are full of your glory . . . " words spoken, words sung, his hands moving from white cloth to golden chalice and plate, candle flames moving with the words—then, with simple sign— the bread the wine made transcendent, a little bell rings . . .

After the service, the old priest tells everyone to sit down again. And I think, a delay? Are these not Americans? Are there no roasts in the ovens? Are there no ballgames already in the bottom of the first inning? But we seem to have no choice.

He announces a fiftieth wedding anniversary and invites the elderly couple forward. They get up slowly and walk down the aisle, their hair so white they might have already returned from heaven. On our two-month journey Justin and I are to witness three fiftieth wedding anniversaries. I thought that rather marvelous until I remembered this was June, fifty years after the boys came home from the Second World War. Still, it *is* marvelous.

A little boy suddenly runs up the aisle to the priest. The priest leans over to shake his hand, but the little boy loudly proclaims that he needs to go potty, then wheels about and flees down the aisle with his mother in close pursuit.

The priest straightens up smiling and reads a poem by Elizabeth Barret Browning on enduring love: "I love thee to the level of every day's/ Most quiet need, by sun and candle-light."

He looks up and pronounces a blessing over the blessed couple. Though I sensed a restlessness, a kind of vacancy in the congregation, I felt a certain peace there too, a certain righting of a balance. Without the moral ballast of religion, the individual rights so loved by Americans could run away with them. That perceptive French traveler, Alexis De Toqueville, recognized this in 1832. He noted that the moral constraints of religion counteracted the centripetal force of individualism and materialism which, even in the 19th Century, he saw running away with

American culture. Put differently, every personal journey needs its Marquette and its Joliet.

The congregation stands and sings the song of the poor man of Assisi:

> All creatures of our God and King
> Lift up your voice and with us sing
> Thou burning sun . . .
> Thou silver moon . . .
> Thou rushing wind . . .

I left the service glad that Marquette's faith is still here, pursuing the young, sustaining the old, still integrating the life and commerce of a small community.

Justin and I walked through bright sunlight to a nearby grocery store to replenish our supplies. Then it was a mile walk back to the tent toting armfuls of oranges, cans of corn, bagels, cheese. We were getting a taste of the life of the poor. To rub that fact in, when we returned to Holiday Gas, our shoes and shampoo were gone. We asked the woman behind the counter. She had just come on shift and didn't know anything about wet tennis shoes or a half-used bottle of shampoo. We needed those shoes.

I hurried outside to the garbage shed in back and started opening plastic sacks of garbage. The smell was rich. I started rummaging through wet paper towels, befouled diapers, wet coffee grounds, candy wrappers, bites of hotdog, clumps of mustard-soaked buns. In the fifth bag, I found shoes and shampoo. We needed those shoes.

Late that night a foghorn began sounding incessantly. I kept waking through the long damp night to its mindless calling. Justin lay beside me, sleeping fitfully. He was close, yet somehow still remote. I wondered if we would ever reach that communion of mind with mind and heart with heart that is the source and fuel of friendship. He tended to drift away into his thoughts and books, I into mine. He didn't like walking around sightseeing; he didn't like long hours of paddling. He was impatient of history. He wanted out; he wanted escape. But I thought we were gaining ground—or is it water?

Monday morning I crawled out of our tent into a thick fog. I could hear the low lapping of waves fifty yards away, but I couldn't see them. The foghorn kept repeating its one hoarse word. I crawled inside and said, "Looks like we'll be staying a while." Justin turned over on his hard mattress and went back to sleep.

Later in the afternoon, the thick fog, folding and refolding in layers, lifted a few feet above the surface and retreated a hundred yards from shore. Justin and I were impatient to leave. We wondered if we could travel a few hours beneath that low roof of shifting cloud while staying close to shore, but we decided we were too inexperienced to outguess a fog. An hour later, having failed to seduce us, the heavy mist moved back ashore and enveloped Manistique.

As evening dyed the fog black, we decided to spend money. We walked to Big Boy's Restaurant and ordered chicken-fried steaks and mashed potatoes.

A man in a white knit shirt and his wife, both of them in their sixties, walk in and sit down at the booth behind Justin. Six diamond rings of different sizes and shapes clasp the woman's fingers. After their meal, the man places a hairy, freckled forearm on top of the seat behind Justin and turns a balding forehead to us. He looks at me and asks, "You from around here?"

"No, just passing through."

"Us too. You been to the casinos?"

"No, we're canoeing."

"Oh . . . well, we've been to all of 'em around here." He names four or five casinos.

"Having a good time?"

"Oh sure, but they just don't give back enough. Too damn stingy. When we find out they've set their intake rate too high we move on."

"You mean they set a kind of percentage for winnings?"

"Oh yes. The government regulates it, you know. They've got to let us win *something*". He looks annoyed.

I nod. "That's a lot of diamond rings." I point to his wife's bespangled fingers.

She smiles and starts giving us an animated history of her rings. One of the diamonds she found in a field in Arkansas.

"Arkansas?"

"Oh yes. They have a field of diamonds there. You pay so much to go out in this field and dig around. They plow up the field every now and again and you just go out and see if you can find one. People find diamonds all the time. I just walked out there and there it was. It had rained, so the place was all mud, just all mud! I had to slog through the stuff. Got mud all gummed up on my shoes. But maybe that's why I found this one. I think the rain had washed the mud off and it was just sparkling away right there in the mud! Pretty good sized, huh?" She holds up wrinkled fingers.

I look at the odd-shaped sparkle and nod, remembering the diamond waves at Naubinway.

"Well, here's our waitress," the man says.

I think she wants to relate more of her ring cycle, but he is already placing his order.

A phone is on the wall. I call home. Joy is there at last. We talk for 140 minutes.

* * *

Justin is reading his book when I return. I ask him if he wants to return to the tent. "Nothing to do there but sleep," he says.

"Might as well have some more coffee then," I say.

Waitresses come and go, I think of Joliet and Marquette and their five companions sitting out a fog around smoky little fires. Marquette never mentions such things in his account of the voyage. Hardship and waiting were ordinary fare for such men. Four years before his exploratory voyage to the Mississippi, he had accompanied some Indians on a 500-mile journey along the southern coast of Lake Superior. They left in mid-August but had to fight sleet, snow, high winds, rain, and floating chunks of ice for a month in open canoes. Marquette recounted the journey thus: "after a voyage of a month amid snow and ice, which blocked our passage, and amid constant dangers of death, I arrived." So much for description.

These were men who expected hardship. Marquette wrote that one must not hope to avoid hardships in this country, "and the best means to live there contentedly is not to fear them, and to expect from God's goodness, while enjoying the small ones, to have much heavier ones." That's not a prayer I repeat. But hardship is the test of any real journey and the measure of its triumph.

An aged man in a dark blue work shirt and thick, black-rimmed glasses is sitting behind me. His name is Kenny. He has eaten a bowl of chili. Now he's sipping coffee and talking to his friend Henry. I hear the voices behind me.

Henry says, "Ya know that magazine contest? Not *Reader's Digest*, but ya know what one I mean."

"Yeah, that Clearing House."

"Yeah, that's right. Clearing House. They say ya might win a million dollars . . . What a farce!"

"Yeah, I don't want a million dollars. I don't have much, but I'm satisfied."

"Yeah?"

"I like the chili here. I eat a lot of it. I don't like Sonny's chili. He throws everything in it every time he walks by it."

A long pause behind me. I reach for my cup of coffee.

"Well it's June already. I need to go home and tear off my calendar. Ya know June, July, August, then September, October and you're into winter again."

"Yup."

"No, I enjoy myself. I work my puzzle every morning. Then I hear the cat saying, I need to eat. I get up and open her a can of food. At night I listen to the news and she gets up into my lap and just purrs and purrs. She's quite content."

My cup is empty. The waitresses move here and there. It's getting late.

"I wish I could see some of my friends from the old times that are gone. Old Joe Scott. He was in real estate ya know. We'd follow him when we was kids, follow him down the sidewalk and we'd find money. Yeah, that's right. Money right there on the sidewalk, maybe a nickel or sometimes a dime. We'd call out, Hey, Mr. Scott! We found some money! He'd say, Keep looking; you'll find some more . . . He was a good old man."

"I went to see Buffalo Bill in the old days. I even knew two old guys was in the Civil War."

A waitress walks up to our table and refills our cups for the tenth time.

"Thanks."

She moves on to Kenny and Henry.

"The movies in the old days was good. The new ones don't have no talent. Don't have no good music neither. And all they sing about is dirty stuff. . . It's a dirty world. That's why I'm glad I lived in the world I lived in. Old folks should be glad they lived when they did."

I stir in the sugar. The voice behind me seems to have neither age nor youth, but floats on, dreaming of both, an aimless wandering of half-remembered lanes and by-ways—an old man driven by time into a sleepy corner, measuring out his life with coffee cups.

"Well this is a good way to pass part of the evening. It only costs six cents more to sit here than at the other place. And it's worth it. More comfortable here.

"Old Johnny married a woman had two kids already. Now he's got all that trouble. He says to me, Ken, don't ya wish you was married? And I says, No. It wasn't meant for me, so the hell with it. I'm satisfied the way it is. Aren't ya glad we come from the nice years, Henry?"

"Yeah. Nice years."

Coffee, nostalgia, and contentment—or maybe it's just limited options. A cat could be content with food and a warm lap. I'm not. If a man has his wits, his strength, his will, he can still launch a journey to the new world.

It's getting late. The coffee's cold. The waitresses have given up on us. Justin is still reading. "We'd better get back to the tent," I say. "The fog's gone. Looks like a long day tomorrow."

He shuts his book and stretches. He has a handsome face, straight nose, firm jaw. He looks out the window into darkness.

We pay our bill and leave, taking the long walk together through the night air. He's strong, agile, sauntering along with his hands in his pockets, his book tucked under his arm. I ask him about the story he's been reading. It's an historical novel about the Revolutionary War in the state of Maine. He gets into the description, telling me the details of snowshoeing through a Maine winter lugging a heavy musket while Indians try to chase you down. It's good to hear him tell his story. I've had too little time in my busy life to listen to him, to live with him.

Twice one winter, he had gone bottle hunting down by the Kansas River with two brothers and their father. Each time he had broken through thin ice and fallen waist deep into freezing water. They had built bonfires to dry out. I remember him coming back with old bottles in hand, flush with the excitement of adventure. He stood in my office turning a blue, antique bottle filled with river mud over in his hands. I had wished to join him on those adventures, but a poor man putting himself through college works a lot of overtime. Now at least, for a time, the adventure was our own.

A Long Day Toward Christmas

Grey day. Constant wind. Occasional seagulls winging over us. Black V's of cormorants drop down to wave level and skim the surface from one end of a three-mile bay to the shore, then sweep round and cover another swath on the way back; eight or nine black, long-necked birds flying in formation, their wings missing the wave crests by an inch. Living nets trolling the air.

We have been paddling for hours and hours. Each time we pass another stony point of waves clattering onto a shingle beach, another broad, grey bay opens behind it. The mind sends the eyes scanning back and forth across the long horizons of waves and distant forested shorelines yearning for some point of interest to break the monotony: an eagle floating on the wind, a leaping fish, something. Adventures are full of monotony. Marquette's journal completely skips over the first 250 miles of their journey. Long, hard days of paddling were just a given necessity, not worth mentioning.

At least the wind is behind us, breezing past us, shoving us along with the endless waves. Earlier we tried making use of the following breeze by wrapping our tent fly around our two spare paddles. Justin thrust them up into the wind. But the nylon fly was too slippery; it flapped off of one paddle, then the other. In the frustration of trying to hold onto the billowing sail, Justin lost one of the red plastic gardener's gloves I had just bought him to protect his hands, and somewhere my rolled up rain pants slipped out of my pocket and into the lake. One glove left for Justin's sore hands, no rain pants for me.

Occasionally we hear the tremolo of a loon as we pass into its well-patrolled waters. Our eyes scan the seaward waves until they focus on the black, upturned head, the speckled body. One of us points. The nervous calls grow more frequent until suddenly another loon has materialized on the grey waves, just up from a deep dive—companions on a lonely sea.

V-tailed terns ride the wind watching and waiting, occasionally dropping smack into the waves.

At Manistique we met a tall tanned man with a yellow canoe strapped to the top of his van. He told us the next stretch of our journey would take us back into the wilderness, a forty-mile peninsula of jagged coastline that drops down from the Upper Peninsula. (On my map this peninsula looks like a brief version of Italy complete with an island or two off the end of the boot, only this boot looks like a Persian slipper with a long pointed toe. Where Italy boots Sicily westward into the Mediterranean, this Persian slipper is swinging east and seems to be stepping over a whole series of islands that step-stone down toward that long ragged finger of the Door Peninsula that points up from Green Bay, Wisconsin.) The man warned us about the cliffs of Burnt Bluff around the end of the peninsula where the waves bounce off the cliffs, refractory waves, he called them. He warned us about waves that curl over and capsize canoes. He warned us about crossing Big Bay de Noc where the shallow water can turn quickly into a sea of steep, running waves. A friend of his in a kayak almost "bought it" there once. "But if you've made it all the way from St. Ignace, you don't have anything to worry about," he said.

I smiled.

* * *

Bored. Grey water. Grey skies. Wind. Ceaseless waves. An end-less shoreline. Unremitting labor. Motion without movement. Sore butts.

We need a song, music. Justin had wanted to bring a radio, but I had chosen to part from that world of chatter and noise and late-breaking news, but these interminable hours require something.

Unfortunately, one of our cultural losses since the advent of radio is that a father and his son do not know the same songs. The songs of my youth are not his songs.

We do know a few Christmas carols.

It's June 4. "Let's try some Christmas carols."

Justin shrugs. Why not.

"God rest ye merry gentlemen.

Let nothing you dismay . . ."

We do them all. "O Little Town of Bethlehem," "Hark the Herald Angels," "O Holy Night," "Of the Father's Love Begotten," "Angels We Have Heard on High." The songs are therapy. The constant pain and tedium dissolve into words and melodies. We pull through the waves bellowing to the seagulls, "Glo--o-o-o-o-o, o-o-o-o-o, o-o-o-o-o, ria! In excelsis Deo!"

An indifferent gull passes over without pause. They are a pagan race, and they all sing like maniacs.

But Christmas only carries us about a mile on our way. We can't remember much more than a verse or two of each carol. We fall silent.

It's a sad thing we know no work songs. I recall a few words of "John Henry" that steel-driv'n man. Bits and pieces of Stephen Foster: "It rained all night the day I left/ The weather it was dry." Are there no songs all Americans know? We try "America the Beautiful" and manage a verse. Then there's the Kansas state song: "Home on the Range." One verse of that.

We repeat it a time or two out of loyalty for the old home state.

The skies are still cloudy.

The French voyageurs who paddled twenty-five-foot birch-bark canoes along these waters for two hundred years used to sing from before dawn to sunset. Those hard-muscled little men would rise at three in the morning, load their canoes with a ton-and-a-half of 90-pound bales of furs and equipment, then, before eating breakfast, launch into the predawn darkness and start singing their way through the black waters, their long narrow paddles beating out the rhythm of a stroke per second. Two or three hours (and how many songs?) later, as the dawn began to color water and shore, they would rest on their paddles and the cook would scoop up cups of thick cornmeal or pea soup boiled with pork fat and pass them round. Then a few puffs on their little clay pipes, and it was back to the paddles and the songs: multi-versed songs from France and Brittany, native songs of the French-Canadians, songs religious, songs bawdy, songs romantic, songs of loss and of home and of lover abandoned, long, repetitive songs, music for the miles.

But having few songs to help us wait, the waiting is hard. Even the seagulls are silent. Only the wind sings its long, dissonant song.

"Old men ought to be explorers," said Eliot: "Here and there does not matter/ We must be still and still moving/ Into another intensity/ For a further union, a deeper communion/ Through the dark cold and the empty desolation,/ The wave cry, the wind cry, the vast waters . . ."

Poems. We do know some poems in common, I think.

"Let's recite poems," I offer.

Justin shrugs as he paddles.

So we do.

"The world is too much with us; late and soon,
Getting and spending, we lay waste our powers:
Little we see in nature that is ours;
We have given our hearts away, a sordid boon.
This sea that bares her bosom to the moon;
The winds that will be howling at all hours,
And are up-gathered now like sleeping flowers;
For this, for everything, we are out of tune;
It moves us not—Great God! I'd rather be
A pagan suckled in a creed outworn;
So might I, standing on this pleasant lea,
Have glimpses that would make me less forlorn;
Have sight of Proteus rising from the sea;
Or hear old Triton blow his wreathed horn."

That's a poem I memorized in college. My children learned to recite it from their schoolteacher who had taken the same class I had. After a try or two, Justin and I could sail through it. We worked our way through several more poems: Sir Walter Scott's "Breathes there a man," and Yeats's "Lake Isle of Innisfree." Poetry, like music, is an ordering of sound, a cry against chaos. "To find my home," says Czeslaw Milosz, "in one sentence, concise, as if hammered in metal. Not to enchant anybody. Not to earn a lasting name in posterity. An unnamed need for order, for rhythm, for form, which three words are opposed to chaos and nothingness." Yes indeed.

We take the shallow water around another rocky shore looking for sand to beach the canoe and set up camp, keeping an eye out for bad weather. But the wind today is steady. No sand on shore. Rocks and more rocks and nothing but rocks, and dark thatched firs and pines, and water by the mile. A long day of "the grinding wave and the gasping wind": Point Aux Barques, Pillows Point, Hiram Point, Point O'Keefe, Little Harbor, Nameless Point . . . maybe it takes 10,000 strokes over grey waters on a grey day to begin to end a father's too-busy ways, 10,000 strokes to recover the adventures of our ancestors, 10,000 strokes as payment to purchase an evening beside a campfire.

Deep inside the next bay we see a strip of sand and stroke for shore. The sun is setting through thinning clouds. We have traveled maybe twenty-five miles, twice the distance we had been averaging per day. Nine hours without stepping out of the canoe. When we finally slide into shore, our backs are so cramped we can't straighten up. Ah, adventure.

That evening, as we set up the tent in white sand behind a ragged line of spruce trees, we looked up and saw the tree line across the bay gone red in the sun's last light. The sheltered waters of the bay lay still, opalescent, like pale ice in moonlight. A white shoulder of sand circled our side of the bay like a snowdrift, but the long line of green pines and balsam firs beyond were singed orange and red in a straight shaft of sunlight. Christmas trees in June.

Within minutes the clouds closed and the fire at our feet gathered up the colors of sunset. Cold, wet, and stiff, we huddled over the heat waiting for the soup. Suddenly the air was full of beating wings and the honking of twenty or thirty geese that swung over the treetops and glided out onto the bay waters. They settled a hundred yards out, gabbling, occasionally honking. Old Triton sporting with his birds.

Another World

Next morning we saw blue sky above, but out to sea a white fog was blowing in. We ate fried eggs and bacon as the thick white hair of the Old Man of the Sea blew ashore. Before long the Old Man turned the world grey and ancient like himself, and the face of the sea wrinkled in a southeast breeze. Near shore gulls were stepping through black weeds, rocks, and standing water feeding on leeches; for them there was no fishing from above in this fog. We decided to delay our departure and followed a trail into the woods, winding back through brushwood and tall trees. I pointed to deer prints in soft mud. Justin knelt to examine them. A bald eagle flapped suddenly from a branch just overhead. Later, a ruffed grouse exploded from undergrowth and went careening between tall trunks at great speed. How it missed smashing into a trunk or defeathering itself as it blasted through tangled undergrowth is beyond me.

About noon the fog thinned and tore away in places; the Old Man was going bald again. Sunlight reappeared, cutting long shafts through the shadowed fir trees and into the new-leafing brush below. We returned to our already loaded canoe and set out across the bay. Lake travel is flat: flat water, bordered by a single row of trees, often distant. Sometimes you pass a rocky isle that gives footing for a fir tree and a little brush, or, if you're lucky, you see a single line of low hills. It's not mountaineering with long vistas up-mountain and down-valley. But the sky is deep and variable and you're moving on a transient floor, sometimes transparent, sometimes translucent, sometimes opaque, but always catching and commenting on the hour's sunlight.

Fish shadows broke away and shot through shallow waters, others in deeper water wove slowly between stones of ochre, broken stones of red and brown, over rough, pebbled floors that dropped away into boulder-furnished rooms twenty and thirty feet deep but still clearly visible. Ducks tan and brown with inked lines drawn over their heads and down their necks were cruising the clear waters ahead of us, trying to outswim us. We were skimming between two worlds, afloat on a single membrane of light.

As we rounded a point, The Old Man of the Sea had a surprise for us. He turned and covered us with fog. Trees and rocks faded away. According to my map, we must cross the mouth of Kregg Bay, a distance of about four miles. I tried to hold a straight course, and within minutes we'd lost all sight of shore. We were reduced to seeing only ourselves and a dematerializing surface of rolling grey.

"I don't like this," Justin said. "I think we'd better head for shore."

I agreed. Strange that my sixteen-year-old would hold the voice of reason and caution. After some time, a dim wash of faded trees appeared through the gloom. They were not where I had expected them to be. I had evidently been steering us straight out to sea. We hugged the shore after that.

Rounding a long rocky point in late afternoon, the air is full of the sound of small waves chattering onto a gravel beach. The fog is gone. Just off shore we see a stooped figure messing around in the shallows. A raccoon. A rather large one. We stop paddling, then carefully, quietly dip our paddles through the waves. The raccoon pays no attention. His eyes seem to be gazing out across the bay away from us, though his concentration is on the work of his darting little prehensile hands beneath the water, feeling for minnows, grasping at crayfish.

As we circle toward him, the southeastern breeze comes round behind us. Suddenly he lifts his nose and without even a glance in our direction turns and splashes ashore and runs for the forest, a big galloping ball of grey-brown fur with a ringed tail bouncing along behind.

We look at each other and grin.

Within another hundred yards we see his mate. She's smaller, but is hunting supper in the same way as husband (it's a two-income family) masked head just above the waves, hands darting over the surface of the little rocks. Our scent must be blowing beyond her, for she doesn't notice us. We stop paddling and the waves rock us toward her. Suddenly she glances up. Stock still she stares. We don't move. The gentle waves rock us back and forth. She stares disbelieving. We float nearer.

She still seems uncertain, but then she's had enough of that long green log with its very odd branches not thirty yards from her. She turns and clatters up the gravel shore, through weeds, and into thick forest.

In the curve of the bay we see an old, abandoned house half submerged in sand dunes. We paddle toward it over a broken world of grey-green boulders, a rocky moraine, fifteen to twenty feet below us, until we find sand and grass where we beach the canoe and walk up through deep sand to the house. Doors and windows are long gone. Bullet holes crater the white stucco as if it had been caught in a war zone.

Inside, the sand has drifted in through a window and fans across weathered floor boards. An old counter made of ply-wood runs along a back wall. Rusted nails protrude from cast-off boards. A ladder of pine limbs nailed to two pine poles ascends to a loft. From up in that loft, we begin to hear something shuffling and whining. I climb slowly up the homemade ladder. As my eyes rise cautiously above the loft's floor planks, I see black excrement scattered about the floor and piled up in hard lumps in the eaves. There, where roof meets loft, I see three sets of small eyes peering from the shadows. The white-tipped ears become visible, then the white noses and black-masked little faces. I climb on up onto the floor planks of the loft, reporting, "Baby raccoons!"

The little raccoons whimper and huddle together. Justin clambers up the ladder and is beside me. He's delighted. He brushes aside the dried excrement and reaches out to pet the furry heads. One of them whines. Justin murmurs something to them and the one in the middle gives a sharp growl. Justin's hand jerks back, then ventures out again. Its small mouth hisses and snaps, and Justin's hand retreats. But soon Justin is softly stroking the snapper's fur. He picks it up and cuddles it. It struggles a little but doesn't seem unduly upset and soon settles down and begins nosing around for food. They must be less than a month old, soft grey balls of fur, uncertain whether to fear us.

"It's just like Rascal," says Justin, recalling that wonderful children's book by Sterling North I had read to each of the children when they were young. As a boy in southern Wisconsin, the boy adopted a baby raccoon his big Saint Bernard dug up from an old tree stump. A friend's mother taught him how to feed it by warming milk in his own mouth and letting it pass into the raccoon's mouth through a wheat straw.

And now, once again, our storybook life has become our own reality. Except for one thing. We can't take the little snapper with us, much as we both would like to. How would he survive on mixed powdered milk? Besides, I have no heart to take it from its mother.

After a few minutes, Justin reluctantly puts him back.

The forest here is tall and thick; there's no place for a tent. An old forest service road runs rutted and sandy near the house, so we set up the tent in the road, between the dusky trees, hoping no four-wheeler will come banging through here tonight; it appears the road hasn't been used in some time. As I hang up our wet clothes to dry and begin chopping wood, Justin wanders off to explore.

I carry the wood back to the tent and arrange small sticks for the fire. Just then I see something moving my way up the shadowed road. Something is moving toward me out of the black cave of forest. My first thought is that it is Parent Raccoon, but as I squat down to watch, I see that it is a porcupine, head down, muttering to itself, sniffing quickly at a root here, a stick there, paying no attention to the world of long distances, or even middle distances. I sit perfectly still. On it comes, sniff, sniff, mutter, mutter, "not worth eating, no, not worth the trouble, keep going, how about this little root? no, not this time, move along, move along, oh, something good here, no, didn't think so, move along."

It shuffles through patches of sunlight, changing colors: black to burnt brown to a rich reddish brown as its quills move from shadow to light. Long quills thatch the first half of the little animal, but the second half and tail are trimmed in short sharp quills. An extravagant hair do, worthy of a teenager. It approaches Justin's rain pants hung from a pine limb. Sniff, sniff. "Hold it." sniff, sniff. "something strange here." It looks up, its little wet nostrils fairly vibrating with an effort to understand me. Black beady eyes glance about camp, then return and fasten on me. "Trouble, sitting right THERE. Head for the trees!" It scrambles clumsily off the road and through some brush, snapping limbs as it goes. Then I hear it hunch its way up a long pine trunk, breaking twigs, snapping small limbs, scratching bark all the way up. Then all is silent again.

I lean down and strike a match. The twisted handful of dried grass smokes, and catches, yellow flame whispering up through thick smoke, tiny twigs lighting up, burning bright orange and whisking out, other twigs catching, snapping, spitting sparks, warming to the living flame. I slide in a handful of brittle twigs, they break into fire, dead matter stirred suddenly to extravagant light.

Meanwhile, Justin was walking the silent trails into the dark forest with sunlight high above in the needled branches, deepening shadows below, carrying his rifle. One trail turned away, and he followed it. The shadows grew strong. After a time, he felt something was following him in the half light, something watching him. He fingered the rifle and walked on. Crowded trunks right and left, a twisting trail, the world going grey and black but for the high lights far above. He couldn't shake the feeling. The trail was not his trail, the feet that formed it were not of his kind. Then in faint light he spotted tufts of scattered fur. He stopped, then stepped closer. Big black flies buzzed up, circled, and dropped into a thickness of fur and hooves. Fur, colored like the forest floor, the hide folded and wadded in the brush, the body completely eaten away, even the bones gone, pieces of white underfur ripped away and scattered like flowers along the needle carpet, among broken, rotting logs. A deer once.

He glanced about him. The feeling strong. The forest silent. He grabbed a hoof and tugged. The hide broke away from the shrubbery. He hurried back up the trail, dragging hooves and skin behind him. Hurrying. The hard skin scraping and catching in brush behind him.

He came at last into camp still dragging the remains of the animal: that childhood desire to show a father his discovery. I walked over and poked at it with a stick and listened to his story. After a time, he dragged the remains of the carcass down to the beach and away. We wanted no scavengers in camp tonight.

I told him about the porcupine. And so we exchanged stories, and were granted the gift of living twice.

Late that night, in our tent, we heard a snapping of branches. We sat up in the darkness and listened. The rifle lay next to me. More twig-snapping. Something out there. Something near. Then I remembered the clumsy porcupine. It seemed to be backing down the pine. We lay back down, still listening.

Hades

We awoke to rain pattering on our thin roof, the air chill and damp. We dug into our clothes duffels for dry sweaters, put on our hats, and crawled forth to find our rain jackets still hanging from limbs, dripping wet. The tall, dark forest of spruce and hemlock stood quietly about us in the grey rain. Down a small slope of wet sand we could see something of the bay, grey waves lapping into sand, a fog drifting in, the shore-side conifers dying away into blowing mist. We reached for our rain jackets and pulled them on. Justin set about looking for dry wood beneath the tall old forest. I squatted down, reached for a wet stick and stirred soaked ashes. An inch down, the ashes were still dry.

We cooked up oatmeal and ate bananas and drank hot coffee.

I wanted to round the point of this forty-mile peninsula and position ourselves to cross Big Bay De Noc the next day. To do this, we would have to circle the long slippered toe of that southeastward-pointing foot, a place called Point Detour because here a voyageur could cut off miles of his journey to Green Bay by taking to the open sea and stone stepping from Summer Island, to Poverty Island, to St. Martin's, to big Washington Island, and finally to the tip of the Door Peninsula. But even if I had been inclined to take this route, the weather made the decision for us. Fog. A heavy mist blowing up from the southeast dissolving forest and rocky shore in a watery tea. Visibility between fifty and a hundred yards. It was not weather in which to go island hopping in a little canoe. We repacked our gear and shoved off, keeping within sight of shore.

It was a slow, featureless journey into a wet breeze over ceaseless waves. A limited world. The self-centering sphere that seems to place each of us in the center of the world had grown small, vague, and turbulent, a "point of spacelessness." We had no idea when we would round that last long point of solid land and turn northwest. It was like paddling to the end of the earth, like Odysseus's voyage to the Place of the Dead: "They came to the limits of the world, to the deep-flowing Oceanus. There is the land and the city of the Cimmerians, shrouded in mist and cloud." The limits of the world. Hades, the Place of the Dead. For the ancient Greeks, it was a joyless region of disembodied souls who had nothing to look forward to, a realm of grief, full of the consciousness of lost pleasures, lost friends. As the old Anglo-Saxon poet, The Wanderer, said of life on this earth: "Here wealth is fleeting, here friend is fleeting, here man is fleeting, here woman is fleeting—all this earthly habitation shall be emptied." Long before death, Hades cast deep shadows in the mind.

Ashore, through the mist, we can see the faint images of white seagulls scattered like lost souls among the rocks, the waves washing in among them. We paddle on. Patrols of black cormorants are the only sea birds flying in this fog. They pass us at wave-top, searching the sea for the shadows of fish, winging by in formation like demon patrols on the coasts of the dead.

Sky and sea and land merge and mix together. Dim trees and insubstantial rocks fade into view then liquefy as we pass. Pale seabirds flutter up into the blowing mist, then melt back into white surf. The air is loud with waves crashing on rocks and faint with the cries of gulls. A nescient world. Nothing remains for us but motion and change—and the endless tedium of our work, pulling the waters by us with a continuous motion, moving through a mazy world. Hungry cormorants materialize and as quickly dissolve into blowing rain. The wind and the work take our voices away. We say little. Once, in a trance, I let my paddle slip out of my hands; taking my spare paddle, we circle around to lift it from the waves.

At times, the shore is completely lost to us and we are moving through an active void, the mists blowing over and around and between us, fading the waves, fading the canoe, fading my son. With some fear, I steer for shore, listening for sounds of surf, hoping we have not yet passed that last point of land.

At the end, we were paddling directly into the wind, the oncoming waves stubbornly shoving us back. On shore we could make out a few stunted fir trees twisting out of long tables of wet rock and bent away from the prevailing winds. Then across the broken tables, we caught sight of open water. We had reached the tip of Point Detour. We worked our way around the point through rising combers that slapped hard over the gunwales and broke over our spray skirt.

In time, we had wind and waves behind us, and we began to move with speed. We noticed that every seventh wave seemed to mount up and run for the shore with unusual energy, crashing along into shallow water in a surge of foam. Then we caught one. Natty Bumpo lifted with the wave and suddenly we were surfing down the far side of a curling wave, white water hissing and crackling all around us. Justin shouted his joy and we paddled like madmen, racing toward the rocky shore.

Fortunately the wave outran us or we might have wrecked on this abandoned shore. We quickly turned left to avoid the bedrock rising fast beneath us and paddled hard to ready ourselves for the seventh wave. It came. We felt the swell lift us. We churned the water with our paddles and flew, racing along with a running sea, skimming down the glassy wave, laughing and shouting in a wild ride: surfing the coast of the dead.

But as we passed the sole side of the slipper's long toe, the forested headland blocked the wind; the sea grew still, the shores preternaturally silent. Tall trees stood solemn watch behind rock buttresses, the forests behind dissolved into fog. The silence silenced us. We paddled hard and fast through dead waters, watching the mist-soaked forest. Ducks lifted into the air, rose above the tree line, and catching the wind, fled away overland.

The Roman vision of the underworld was, if anything, worse than the Greek. As wandering Aeneas approaches the gates of Hades at night, the slopes of the forested mountains begin to rumble and shake. There is a howling in the night and shapes like hounds appear, just visible through the shadows. Someone cries out that a god is approaching. Aeneas presses on and passes into Pluto's "substanceless Empire," past lifeless homes, yet he can discern figures there at the gates of Hades, terrible shapes: Grief, Resentment, Diseases, Old Age, Fear, Evil Counsel, Poverty, Pain, Insane Strife, War, and even Death itself. There are beasts: fierce centaurs; half-human Scyllas; Briareus a giant with a hundred hands groping about in the shadows; the Chimaera coughing bright fire—part goat, part lion and dragon. And monstrous Gorgons—wild, winged, contagious, clawing, snake-haired females, and there "in mud and murk seethes the Abyss, enormous and engulfing, choking forth all its sludge" into the river Cocytus. He meets dreaded Charon, a ragged, filthy figure in a dirty robe with wild white hair and beard and eyes of pointed flame, the ferryman who gathers the dead like falling leaves into his boat and poles them across the dark Stygian marsh and past the giant, three-headed dog Cerberus.

Justin said it looked like a battleship. He pointed with his paddle. A ghost ship in the fog. As we made our way through mists, it slowly emerged into a long L-shaped dock constructed of rusted I-beams. The seaward end of the dock had been smashed into the sea; rusty beams buckled and the broken walkway sloped steeply into cold water. Long lines of white gulls, hundreds of them, stood silent watch along cold steel rails. Other gulls perched on iron-hulled commercial fishing boats, a whole fleet of Cimmerian ships. All around us the gulls watched with eyes like empty pits. Suddenly a white gull gave a strangled cry, a strange, creaky gurgle, like the grating of a rusted hinge, a sound we never heard elsewhere on our journey. Another gull lifted off a trawler, giving the same wretched cry. A thousand empty eyes turned to watch us paddle inside the decaying dock and toward shore, dipping our paddles through silence, sliding over still, clear water, passing over a rusted row of huge iron teeth slimy with green algae—as if years ago a dragon had died.

We looped our yellow rope over a rotting post and climbed painfully out of the canoe. Our pants were soaked. We were cold. Taking our thermos and our sack of bagels and cheese, we walked the dock's planking to shore. We had food, but we were hoping for a café—hot coffee, hot soup.

The smell of fish was strong in the foggy air. Not a soul in sight. A nearby metal building's concrete floors had been washed clean, but the fog smelled of fish.

A rough street rose steeply from the water and passed away into the mist, houses lying on either hand. Suddenly a little demon motorcycle shot out of the fog, growled down the steep hill, made a sharp turn spitting gravel, and roared back up the street. We followed the little demon, climbing the steep street. In the yard of the first house a large red dog lay in the grass gnawing on the long haunch bone of a deer, eyeing us. The deer's cloven hoof was still attached to the bone. A low rumble came from his throat, as we hurried up the hill.

Hands in pockets, a wary eye on the big dog, we walked through heavy fog. A burly man with white hair and a ragged grey sweatshirt appeared, walking toward his mailbox. Mailboxes in Hell? We approached him and asked for a place to buy a cup of coffee. He looked at us suspiciously. "No coffee shop here," he muttered. "Used to have one. The woman died of cancer. No store at all anymore . . . and that's the way we like it." He stared at us for a moment, then turned and passed back into the mist.

We returned to Natty Bumpo and drained the last of our thermos of lukewarm coffee.

Plastic bottles had washed ashore, ropes rotted to old posts, rusted cables snaked through weeds or lay curled among jumbled rocks and wet soil. Paint peeled from iron hulls: "filthy, limb-strewn, and most lonely world's end." We chewed on cold bagels and felt the cold seeping into our bones. Justin was shivering.

"Let's get moving," I said. "Maybe it'll warm us up a bit." We paddled away from the ranks of silent watchers, into the Cimmerian mists. Iron fishing boats lay in still water: *Proud Maid, Maybee, Cassandra*. Out in the water and here and there on shore stood strange devices shaped like huge Y's mounted on old tires, evidently used to roll the fishing boats from the water for cleaning and repair; they lifted corroding arms to a hopeless sky. Along shore, beside every mist-shrouded house in Hades, a satellite disc pointed skyward, contracting mass-entertainments into little black boxes.

Once, cold hours later, a lively fish, a startling red-gold in color, leaped into the air. Like marigolds on a rainy morning, like fireflies in a wet night, that leaping fish seemed too gaudy for this grey world, bright life leaping from a dead world. It seemed a hopeful omen.

But as we turned the point of land, we found ourselves gliding over a giant's causeway of large, flat stones. On the steep, forested hills to our right white dogwoods stood up like sudden ghosts among the dark oaks, and a crabapple flamed pink fire among smoky firs. High up, a pale slag heap scarred the forest floor. White limestone cliffs began to climb the hills above us, jagged promontories of white blocks stacked layer upon layer, creased horizontally, breaking off in rectangular pieces that lay shattered along the shore below; trees clutched the crevices of white stone, their trunks swaying up the sheer cliffs. Above, a somber forest covered the high round hill.

Sky and sea were grey, but the mist had passed away. We drifted over the flagstone pavements and rounded the slow bend of the high bluffs. High up on the white wall we saw two large black caves side by side. The entire bluff was a huge bone-white skull staring vacantly across a barren sea: broken white jaws and teeth below, black hollow eyes above, the rounded head a mess of unfamiliar, forest-green hair. I pointed this out to Justin and he said, "Let's explore those caves!"

We slid the canoe into flat stones and climbed ashore. He ran ahead, pulling himself up the stone cliff by roots and young trees. After I roped the canoe to a rock, I scrambled after him. Wet soil collected in rock crevices, pungent with rotting pine needles, but spring was alive even in these regions of the dead; green cascaded from every tree young and old, white flowers crowned a bush of many-fingered leaves.

Climbing thirty or forty feet up, we side-stepped along a ledge and made our way into one of those caves. The walls were black, as if cave-dwellers had long used them for their fires, but the blackness came from a fungus that grew wherever water seeped down. A dead tree trunk had fallen into one of the caves and protruded horizontally. We stepped in, but the cave was shallow, so Justin moved from one cave to the next, then on, following a pathway along the cliff into broken galleries thick with moss where water dripped and trees arched skyward. At one point he climbed up and investigated an old eagle's nest long unused.

I remained behind, sitting in the giant's pierced eye, staring out across a pale sea. The light was flat, there was no horizon, sea and sky slept together. But within that vast union of air and sea, what dreams? Dashing fish flashing gold vermilion, moving now in their great migrations to their breeding grounds; birds in their millions and millions winging north night and day, soaring, diving, then mating, nesting on low rocky islands, on high promontories of limestone or granite, stacking jumbled sticks in tall fir trees, wrapping their broods in prairie grasses, daubing huts of mud and stick and hair, burrowing into oak trunks or clay banks, hanging thread-like spheres from high cottonwoods. Life so powerful—rooting through dead stone, seeding every crevice, each tree exploding slow-motion into leaf—and multiplying, multiplying. Even the black fungus in the eyes of that great death's head was a form of life, full of light, its very blackness evidence that it absorbs the whole spectrum of light. Death, be not proud.

Justin was calling me. I stood up and edged out of the cave, then clambered over rocks, ducked under limbs, picked my way along a cliff-edged trail. When I found him, he was standing in a great cavity broken back into the rock by life and time. Topped and surrounded by soaring trees, we were standing in a tall, rock-walled pavilion halfway up the cliff, a meeting place for the gods.

But time was wasting away. The day was dying. It was time to find a camping place.

We slipped away from the staring eyes of Burnt Bluff in our canoe, and paced over the giant's stone courtyard. Ahead the trees came down to the water in the perfect silhouette of a great bear watching the sea. No sooner had we paddled past this giant sentinel, then heavy waves began rolling against us, the breeze picked up, carrying, again, a light mist. Erratic waves began shoving us from different directions, tipping us one way then another. These were the refractory waves the man in Manistique had warned us of. It was difficult going, and the sun forsook us, stepping over the edge of the world.

The near shore was a scramble of round rocks, gravel, and driftwood backed by as thick a forest as we had yet seen. We went ashore hoping for a clearing behind the line of trees, but this cold, wet jungle was impenetrable, a choked thicket of trees, fallen logs, and strangled brush. No resting in Hades.

Twilight. A grey mist blowing. A darkening sea. Anxiety strengthening our strokes. The map marked a tiny bay some two-and-a-half miles up the coast with a campground. I was worried about being caught out after dark, so we cut directly across the bay. We pulled hard over the blackening waves. The coast slipped away, weakening into mist. There were times we could see nothing shoreward through the heavy mist.

Night was near. Rain began to fall and a cool wind blew from the northwest. A seagull, burning white against the murky sky, accompanied us like some silent angel. But what remained of light was leaching away, seeping into a dark, steady rain, and I was afraid.

We angled for shore, searching for shore lights. I kept asking Justin if he could see anything. He said he thought he could still make out the outline of a black hill. Rain and mist were blowing in my face, fogging and dripping from my glasses; all I could see were the dim waves around us and the blurred image of my son before me. This was bad planning; we had spent too much time on the cliffs.

We allowed ourselves no rest, double-footing through a dark sea under a blind sky. The night and waves were one, everything a fluid black; we couldn't judge the oncoming swells in the darkness. If the wind picked up, we'd be in real danger of capsizing.

"Can you still see the hills, Justin?"

He looked to his right. "I think so."

"Are there any lights over there?"

He stopped paddling and stared. "Not anymore."

We bowed our heads to the blowing mist and pulled hard on our paddles. I began angling back in toward where the hills should be.

And then a bell was ringing. A ringing bell far away. Again and again. We were rising and falling through a murky twilight. Again and again, a bell ringing erratically. I steered for the sound. The ringing grew louder. Ahead of me Justin searched the water. Clanging again and again. I steered blindly toward it.

"There!" said Justin. "Over there. It's a bell out in the water!"

A bell buoy, nodding and swaying like Macbeth's drunken porter at the gates of Hell. I was hoping it marked the entrance into that tiny bay I'd seen on the map.

We swung past the incessant bell. In time a dark hill materialized on our right. We turned into a sudden opening in the hills. Pallid cliffs beyond dropped straight to the sea—a long palisade with no possible place to camp, but here was little Snail Shell Harbor curled around itself like its namesake. We stole into it like a wave-battered hermit crab finding an empty shell. And then a strange sight. Grey, weathered buildings scattered about in just the ghost of the day's light. No lights in their windows. But directly ahead of us, vaguely, we could make out a long stone building with two high towers. We seemed to have found our way into some medieval castle with its central fortress and a number of storm-beaten outbuildings, a ghostly citadel of the dead. The remains of a dock ran along one shore, old black posts protruding from still water. No one in sight. A lonely place, isolated . . . No sound but the muffled waves on the far side of the hill.

"Some kind of abandoned town," I said to Justin.

"Look at those towers," he said quietly. "What are they?"

"Looks like a fort or something," I said. "I don't know; we'll have to wait till morning."

"I don't see anybody," he said.

"Me neither."

We peered into the darkness. It was almost impossible to see now. There was a suggestion of another dock, but we didn't want to climb onto rotting boards. We kept moving. Ghost town or not, we were glad to be off the night sea.

We curled clockwise into that snug shell, past the rotted posts, on into water as flat and black as crude oil, until we slid ashore among reeds. We climbed out and searched the darkness for six feet of level space for our tent and our tired bodies. Feeling the crunch of an old gravel road beneath our soaked boots, we followed it into cut grass, then worked our way over to a stone wall and there pitched our tent, hurrying through the routine: unrolling the tent, attaching the poles and sliding them through the hoops, staking it out, popping it up, a little half balloon against the miserable rain—doing much of it by feel; going for the pack of sleeping bags, unrolling them in a tent as dark as a wolf's mouth—glad for shelter with the rain still coming down—returning to the canoe, hoisting up the heavy pack of Rude Mechanicals while Justin heaved the heavy food pack to his shoulder. We stole rocks from the old wall for a campfire, searched the nearby forest for wood by flashlight, then tried to strike life into dead, damp grass, but it wouldn't catch fire. We tore pages from the early pages of the *Odyssey*, pages we had already experienced, and lit the fire with old tales.

An hour after eating, I awoke to a stiff wind shaking our tiny tent and the rain roaring down. Through the darkness I said to Justin, "Do you hear that wind?"

I heard him move near me.

"Can you imagine being out there now?" I said. "We just made it."

I heard him murmur his assent and turn over, pulling the

sleeping bag up around his ears. Rain slashed against the sides of our little half sphere; the tent fly flapped and strained at its ropes as if it wanted to fly us away in the gale. I sat up and wrapped my wool blanket around the feet of my thin sleeping bag and lay back on the hard earth, pulling the cover over my head.

Hades Still

"Who's in there? Hey! Anybody in there?!"

A voice harangued us from just outside the tent. The rain was falling, the wind blowing, but the pale light told me it was already morning.

"Hey! Wake up in there!" A woman's voice. Angry. Imperative.

"We're here. What do you want?" I responded.

"You've got to move!"

"In the rain?"

"That's right!"

"Why?"

"You're camped illegally!"

By this time I was pulling on still-damp trousers. I jammed on my wet hat and crawled out in bare feet. A short, thickset woman in a yellow rain slicker confronted me. Another woman stood behind her.

"We'll move on as soon as the rain lets up," I offered.

"No. You're camped in the middle of our historic town! And you're going to have to pay the camping fee."

"And we have to move now?"

"Yes. And we are staying right here until you do." Implacable.

She stood pointing the way we must go. I glanced out through the opening of the little harbor. The wind was blowing hard, the grey waves crashing in.

"I don't think I want to venture out on that sea until the wind dies down," I said. "All we've got is a canoe."

Her jaw set with a click. "You can load up your stuff in the back of the pickup here, and we'll take you to the *official* campground."

I looked at the pickup. A pretty young woman was at the driver's wheel. "Well, all right."

"And look at this campfire!" The ranger kicked at the blackened ashes. "That's illegal. You've got to clean this up right now. And the rocks!" She was incensed. "Where did you get those rocks?"

I said we'd put them back.

"Everything must go back exactly as it was."

Her sharp eyes then spotted the ultimate outrage: a leaf. Yes, I hate to admit it, but there was a green leaf on the end of one of the branches we'd hauled in for our fire in pitch darkness.

"Don't you know it's illegal to break off limbs in a state park?"

"Well, we came in after dark, weren't sure where we were."

"Well, we can't have that."

"It looked dead in the dark."

"Do you see the leaf on that branch?"

"I see it."

"It's not dead wood."

"Apparently not."

"We're going to have to charge you for camping here. Pay the woman in the pickup."

Eight dollars. The pretty one wrote us a receipt.

Rain drizzling down, we replaced rocks, raked wet ashes into a pan and poured them in a trash can, repacked and loaded everything in the pickup, including Natty Bumpo (their trophy fish). The ranger stayed behind with her lieutenant, as there wasn't room in the pickup. I climbed into the cab while Justin rode in back to keep Natty from falling out. We followed a bumpy, muddy road around the bay, past brick and limestone buildings 150 years old.

I asked about the place. She was courteous and considerate, willing to talk about matters other than rules and rents. She told me it was an old pig-iron factory used during and after the Civil War. Iron ore was shipped in from up north and smelted in furnaces fed by stacks of white pine cut from the nearby forests and catalyzed with limestone from the cliffs beyond the bay. That explained the two-towered building; it was a blast furnace (a proper industry for Hades). There was a blacksmith shop, houses for the doctor and management, stables for horses. The men who worked long hours when the furnace was blazing lived in barracks beyond the town; when the furnace broke down or the ore was delayed, they were not paid. A grim life.

All is silent now. The "old works of giants stand idle." Later in the day, Justin and I walked inside the two-towered building. Odd tools lay labeled for observation, marking the hands that made them, marking the men who shoveled and cut and hammered and lifted. And there. . . there were the sepia photographs of the men: brown shades, last shadows of living men long silent, reflected light burnt long ago into photographic plates, their shadows lingering in the sunlit world long, long after the spark in their eyes went to ash.

The pickup pulled away from the empty town and rolled through wet grass and wildflowers. The conversation moved on to canoeing. She told me of days canoeing on Lake Superior with her husband. We bounced along through taller trees. "If you came a week later, you could have your canoe blessed," she said.

"By a priest?"

"Yes. There's a blessing of the fleet every spring."

We didn't have a week to wait of course. Besides, Natty Bumpo would probably have to go to confession first. I take that back, O faithful barque! Young Natty Bumpo had journeyed like a missionary saint. Crashing up and down through wind and wave, skimming through interminable calms, even surfing the quick wave. We had scraped him over rocks, hauled him onto gravel beaches, tied him up among boulders. All in all I was thinking he might be a candidate for beatification. Saint Bumpo. Does have a thump to it.

She steered us into a campground of tall trees and mud, a mile from the historic town. Large mosquitoes drifted everywhere among the wet leaves. She stopped and I climbed into the pickup bed to begin unloading our gear. Justin pulled on Natty's prow and I lifted the stern, taking a wide step down from the bed of the pickup. There was a loud rip. The back of my pants had announced their openness to the ways of the world. I shrugged at the smiling ranger. What can you expect from a sojourn in Hades? A little humiliation, perhaps.

Escaping Hades

We left that place with the wind still blowing against us, high waves driving us back to the land of mists and mortality. We struck out for Round Island, five miles away. At least the rain had stopped. Heavy waves, dark grey like pig-iron, kept rocking hard against us, flicking foam in our faces, splashing ice water down our necks, numbing our hands.

But why complain? We were alive! Full of sea and air and a late cup of coffee. "Never are we in half a gale of wind," says sailor Hilaire Belloc, "but we pray crapulously for calm. Never are we in a calm but we whine peevishly for wind. What, Dog, would you have the weather cut out for you like a suit of

clothes? Is all the universe to arrange itself simply to your convenience, as it does for the very rich—so long as they keep off
the sea?"

We were not rich, nor were we off the sea. We must take
what comes. What came was another long, hard passage whose
destination was as stench-ridden an island as I ever hope to eat
a late lunch upon. Long before we arrived, the seagulls rose
screaming into the air, mad clouds of demented parents, insane
with fear for their young. The green waters fifty yards from
shore rumpled with black, floating guano, the shores beyond
were plastered white in the sticky stuff. If it wasn't Hades, it had
to be Purgatory Island. Thousands of small, downy gulls, just
hatched, huddled together on their nests like suffering souls. As
we stepped ashore, a frightened one would raise its neck and
run for cover under a patch of weeds or a scraggly bush that
somehow had managed to survive the fecal assault. Above us,
absolute screaming pandemonium.

We stepped on through weeds and scattering chicks, trying
to find a log or a rock unbespattered to sit upon and eat our
lunch. Herons were nesting too, their rough nests blotching the
higher limbs of fir trees. We waded through raspy old stalks and
stinging nettles, through soggy turf, and out the other side of
the island to more nests scattered about the rocky shore—more
furry little gulls and their furious parents. We sat down on a log
and cut slices of cheddar to lay between halved bagels. I took
the squeeze bottle of mustard and aimed for the sandwich but
splattered my wool sweater. It was one of those days.

After escaping from Round Island, the weather cleared for several hours. Strips of sky were a clear, tender blue, newborn; the
water fresh and clean again, clouds above us laminated ivory
and gold. Seagulls burned white against the dark, retreating
cloudbank ahead of us; the waves began to follow us, lifting us

on our way. After days of slowslogging through rain and fog, we were feeling exuberant. Justin would call out, "Look how that seagull shines against that cloud!" and I would respond with "Look how green that meadow is over there!"; things we'd seen a thousand times were suddenly breaking into sparks igniting our joy.

As evening neared, we drifted through shallow water along an emerald shore of reeds and new grass. A deer grazed below the tree line, raising its head to watch us from time to time. We coasted slowly, looking for some way to approach shore through the scattered rocks, but the water was too shallow a hundred, two hundred yards from shore. We paddled on.

On our left, seven or eight miles straight across the bay, the sun picked out the cliffs of Burnt Bluff in a reddish-yellow hue; that old death's head come alive in sunlight.

Seeing a green swell of land ahead, we moved toward it, hoping for a convenient camping place. Then I saw something running along shore, something like a dog running flat out through tall grass, weaving between young pines, sprinting through brush, heading straight for the line of rocks ahead of us that pointed out toward Burnt Bluff. "Look, Justin!" He saw it too.

We lost sight of it for a few seconds, then an antlered deer shot out of the trees bounding across low weeds and rocks and then, in a burst of spray, charged straight into the lake, running full out toward Burnt Bluff miles across the bay. Two brown wolves were snapping at its heels, splashing in its wake. Deer and wolves ran exactly along our horizon, silhouetted against the last light of day. Fifty yards, a hundred yards and still racing through only knee-deep water. Against the light, the flat black outline of the fleeing deer cut the water into crystal spray and the wolves leapt after like dolphins born for the sea chase. Another fifty yards and still leaping; they looked like they had every intention of water-running straight across those eight miles to Burnt Bluff. The deer was now bounding heavily through deeper water and the two wolves slowed, up to their necks in cold water. They gave up and stood panting, ears erect, watching the deer struggle out another fifty yards. It finally turned to face its pursuers almost a quarter mile from land, well beyond their reach.

We drifted slowly toward them, lost in the intensity of the moment. The buck turned and made its way toward us through deep water paralleling the shore. The brown wolves turned back for dry land. The deer maneuvered through chest-high water, carefully placing its feet, still not seeing us. Then suddenly, it broke for shore. The wolves cut through the shallows to meet it, catching up to its slashing hooves just as it scrambled ashore. It leapt high and bounded away through juniper trees and brush with the wolves in close pursuit.

After a few moments, Justin turned and looked at me, taking off his hat. I shook my head in wonder. It's one thing to see such a sight on a twenty-one inch black box of electronics, quite another to be a part of the land and sea and air and light as the chase erupts before you.

We paddled on in, removed our shoes, and stepped out into frigid water thirty yards from shore to pull Natty over the shallow rocks. Rocks cut our feet and once I slipped into a hole to my waist and gasped. Justin laughed, "Cold enough for you, Dad?" I stepped out of the hole. "Cold enough," I said.

We pulled the canoe near shore. Clouds were gathering again. We lifted our packs and tent from the canoe and hauled them through shallow water, then a hundred yards over rocky weeds to that green swell of grass. After several trips, we returned for Natty and carried him ashore.

We stopped. There, far out in the water was a female deer. How had we failed to see her? Had she run into the water after the buck drew the wolves away? She was watching us and began moving away through the chest-deep water. The water was cold, we wondered how long she could stay out there, but then she began moving toward shore, choosing her way through shallower water toward the place the male had charged back ashore. She was frightened, stopping every few steps to look at us, then to scan the shore with her eyes and with those long, catalpa-leaf ears. After stepping into shallow water, she bounded away.

Then we looked back across the bay. Far out on the horizon a huge shaft of red light rose straight up into the air. I have never seen anything like it. It had to be thousands of feet tall. We stared at it for a few minutes. Was it a rainbow? If so all its colors had gone red. A single blade, wider than a rainbow, thrust straight up into the dusky air. For some reason it reminded me of a vision recorded by one of the first Jesuit missionaries. His name was Brebeuf, a powerful man, strong and determined. In the winter of 1640, while living with the so-called Neutral Nation, a tribe that remained neutral during the vicious war between the Hurons and the Iroquois, he saw in a dream a great cross slowly approaching from the Iroquois country. When he told the vision to his friends, they asked him what it was like, how large was it? "Large enough," he responded, "to crucify us all." Within a few years, Iroquois war parties had decimated the Huron missions. During a raid on a village, they captured Brebeuf and several of his companions, then tortured them slowly to death.

I hoped this red shaft, this blade thrust up from the northern horizon, did not portend a similar fate for us, or for this pristine landscape of forest and fresh water.

We gathered stones for our fire, and by the time our stew was bubbling, cool evening had darkened and dampened our world; a light rain falling once again. Our boots stood near the fire steaming, our wet wool socks lay on rocks propped up to reflect the heat. We had been more or less wet for four days now and before the rain began again we had hoped to dry out our foot-gear, but weather rarely waits on travelers.

I poured out the stew into Justin's pan. The rain increased; we hunched over our food as the rain dribbled off our hats. I was telling Justin about the coyotes I used to hear as a boy while hunting the hills of Kansas:

"We had been out hunting until after dark. My friend Mark says, 'Listen to this.' He throws back his head and starts yipping and howling and squealing. I look at him kind of crazy, but he stops and listens. Then far away we hear a pack of coyotes start yipping and barking. They stop. Then we both begin howling and whooping and barking like banshees. We wait. And pretty soon we hear them again. We were standing on a kind of cliff above a two-lane blacktop. Beyond a creek and across the little valley, we could hear them. Just yipping and yelling and car-rying on. They don't sound like the lone coyotee of old Hol-lywood westerns; you always hear them together, running in a pack, yipping and singing. Their voices kind of swoop up and down and mix all up with the others. It's hard to describe."

I shook coffee into the well-blackened pot, poured in water, and slid it on the grill. Red coals hissed in the falling rain. I slipped in more sticks and blew them to life. For the water to percolate, you need a live flame, not just coals. But now we were beyond the coasts of the dead, and the fire leaped up around our pot. We rinsed out our eating pans with canteen water and put them aside for the rain to finish washing and crouched down over the fire.

"Out in Africa, when I was a kid, there were lions. Once we heard a pack of hyenas fighting a lion somewhere out in the head-high elephant grass beyond our compound. Now that was a noise. They were tearing up the night with roars and hyena screams and that funny laughing hyenas make when they're ner-vous. Lions hate hyenas.

"And then sometimes you don't hear them. Once we found tracks of a big lion that had walked through our compound in the middle of the night. And us sleeping on a screened-in porch. That was enough to make you think twice about walking out at night. You never walked out at night without a good flashlight. Not with scorpions running around in the dust and those huge centipedes. You ever see a centipede?"

"The ones with all the legs?" Justin squinted up at me through the rain.

"That's right, only these were three times as long as the ones in Kansas. We always heard their legs were poisonous, that they'd sting you if they ran across your hand or foot, but I don't know if that was true. But there were cobras, all different kinds of cobras. And they'd kill you if you stepped on one. Once my dad encountered a puff adder."

Justin was staring into the fire. "A what?"

"A puff adder. It's a kind of cobra, I think. Anyway, he was wearing khaki shorts when he walked into our storeroom to get some grain. He felt something wet on his leg. Didn't think much about it. When he walked out of the storeroom, he felt something wet on his other leg. Well, he was busy, so he just kept walking, his mind must have been on something else. He came back for another bag of grain, and there it was again. He stopped and looked down. A puff adder was curled up in the shadow of the door. Every time he walked past, it'd spit a little ball of poison at him. They're deadly. They use the poison to blind a rat or mouse, then strike. It's the strike that kills you."

I turned the boots around and Justin flipped the wool socks over on their rocks to dry the other side; the rain had let up a bit, but we had little chance for dry footwear on this night.

"Once a British game hunter drove a jeep onto our station. He'd shot a big male lion. But his boot was all torn up and his foot was bleeding when he drove in. He'd been out hunting alone and came on this lion, shot it, then walked over to kick it, to see if it was dead. Big mistake. The thing lunged over and grabbed his foot. He shot it again, but he could *not* pry that thing off his foot; the teeth were clamped down hard. Well, he tried using the gun barrel to pry open the teeth, but all he could manage was breaking a tooth or two; maybe rigor mortis had set in. Now he was in a fix. All alone on the big savannah and a lion with a real attachment for him. Lions tend to hang out with their families, so he was worried about being invited to a family dinner. He starts to drag this thing, and believe me a full-grown lion is a load. He somehow makes it to his jeep and climbs in, turns the jeep on and drives over the grass and down the rutted, pot-holed road dragging this monster on his foot. By the time he gets to our station, the lion has given up on the relationship; it tore off his boot. Somehow he managed to lift it into the back of the jeep. But the man had a case of the nerves. Post-carnivore stress syndrome or something."

I saw Justin shaking his head under his hat and knew he was smiling.

It was late. The rain was falling. There was the smell of wet wool and coffee. Justin had his hands to the fire, his hat pulled down low against the rain. I poured him a cup and he shook in the sugar. He lifted the cup under his chin and held it with both hands trying to absorb a little heat from the coffee.

And then the wolves began. Just as in my story. A family of them, yipping and barking and singing to the night rain. We wondered if they had caught their deer or if they were just feeling the enthusiasms of youth and spring. They were not far off in the darkness, somewhere beyond the meadow in the trees or along that wild shore. They must have known we were there, but they sang anyway, free, joyous, a wild spring nocturne.

I poured my boy another cup of hot coffee. After a few minutes, the night was silent again, except for the steady sound of falling rain on the meadow grasses.

Cigarette Burns

The clouds had run away with the night. The morning sky held that brisk, rinsed, after-rain blue, as if we were living on the inside of a newly polished sapphire. The water all around us was spilling lights: blues and greens and mauves all rippling together in long sheets that changed color with the depth below or the breeze above. That little breeze, young and indecisive, was hithering and thithering over the little waves, unable to decide what to see, which way to go, what to say to us as it scurried by. But Justin was paddling with his head down, seeing none of this. He was bored with constant paddling and had retreated into that historical novel about revolutionary Maine, the book propped on his lap.

I was breathing in the day, listening to the light ripple of our wake, and looking far away to the clear circumference of that half sphere we move within. After long days of cloud and mist, I was dazzled by the lights, sun-struck, and centered like a tiny prince within a diadem of forests and flashing waves. On our right was the Hiawatha National Forest: "by the Shining-Big-Sea-Water." Pines ashore shone brittle green, their needles precisely articulated in a morning light that cut out the rocks, glanced over bright sands, and flooded the chameleon waves upon which we always ride.

Justin kept his head down, reading, his thoughts caught up in the past of his historical novel, his back turned to me as his arms automatically pulled his paddle through the water. Silent hours of paddling seemed to carry him away from me. There he was, a dozen feet ahead of me, but still a mystery moving in and out and away, lost in his own world.

We'll sing, I thought. I began practicing a song. Sqump and
Snoof had learned it in school and had given me the sheet music.
It's an uncomplicated humorous gospel children's animal song
from the south. The song begins with the refrain:

> *All God's critters got a place in the choir,*
> *Some sing low and some sing higher,*
> *Some sing out loud from the telephone wire,*
> *And some just clap their hands, or paws, or anything*
>   *they got now.*

Justin and I had already learned the chorus and the first verse.
This morning I wanted to work on the second verse:

> *The dogs and the cats they take up the middle*
> *Where the honey bee hums and the cricket fiddles,*
> *The donkey brays and the pony neighs,*
> *And the old coyotee howls.*

As we rounded the point of land we had camped upon, Justin
closed his book and we went rollicking through the song in our
usual cacophonous way. I repeated the second verse to Justin a
couple of times and soon we were belting it out. You incorrigible
skeptics (who won't believe anything you haven't seen on television) can call me a liar, but no sooner had we shouted through that
last verse, then our wolf family on shore took up the refrain. It's
true I couldn't make out the words from where we were (wolves as
a rule are a little weak on consonants), but they did their polypho-
nous best—in broad daylight, which is the first time I have ever
heard wolves, or their smaller cousins the coyotes, howl and yelp
in daylight. Without doubt they had been moved to rapture by our
fine singing (as well they should have been), and we were as delighted with theirs, especially by the fact that they knew their cue.

* * *

Late that afternoon, I was sitting in a real chair next to Harold Ogren's shower and laundry building. Justin was inside taking a hot shower as I sat waiting my turn. Mr. Ogren, owner of a lakeside campground for RVs, "The Park Place of the North," had allowed us to use his facilities: six bucks for two showers. We had not had a real shower in fourteen days, so I was content to pay for the privilege. The washing machine behind me was churning out the last two weeks of mud, pine soot, sweat, and ashes. I was feeling good, chomping corn chips, scooping salsa, and waiting my turn. Justin was taking his time.

Tall pines sheltered Ogren's campground. After a warm day of paddling under a bright sun: miles down the Hiawatha Peninsula and several more miles across not-so-Little Bay de Noc, I was glad for the chair in the shade. Harold Ogren himself was sitting not far away in front of his mobile home office talking to an old friend, tossing an occasional log on the fire that burned in a metal ring at their feet. He had generously offered us a free camping place on his beach, but I had turned him down. We had already found a little backwater near the mouth of the Ford River where we could hide Natty Bumpo. There we had unloaded our packs and set up the tent in long grass next to a willow tree surrounded by tall weeds and bushes. Our chosen spot was full of spiders, ticks, mosquitoes, a city of insects—the beach would have been much better—but we were too tired to set up camp all over again.

Justin finally emerged from his shower a young man reborn, clean and hungry. He took my corn chips and I took a long, hot shower and reappeared, a middle-aged man refreshed, if not quite reborn.

It was after midnight. We had walked for miles and miles trying to find a place to eat, but had finally ended up back at a bar directly across the highway from our hidden tent. A thick-necked man with tousled hair sat spread-legged on a barstool; he was talking to Justin. A beer gut sagged over his belt and rested on his thighs like a sack of barley. He squinted sideways through cigarette smoke at young Justin and rubbed a muscled arm that was cross-hatched with long straight black hairs. He looked to be in his fifties. "Here," he said to Justin. "Hold out your arm."

Justin looked at him warily.

"No. Just hold out your arm." His voice had gone gravel rough. He took a drag on his cigarette; the smoke curled out his nose.

A younger man down the bar a few stools said, "Don't do it."

The big man threw back his head and laughed, then pointed at his forearm with the hot end of his cigarette. "See this? Know how I got these?"

Small white scars, some of them thick and sworled, pushed up through the black hair of his forearm and wrist like emergent toadstools. "When me and my buddies was drinkin' too much we used to have this contest. See who could last the longest. You just take the cigarette, see? and hold it to the skin. You don't push too hard, cause you don't want it to go out. Whoever gives up first loses." He lifted the lighted stub from his arm, looked at us, and grinned. "Crazy, huh?"

Justin agreed.

The man held the smoldering tip a few inches from his wrist. "See this one? I was blasted drunk that night. I could smell the hair burning first, then the skin started to burn. I held it right through the pain. Pretty soon it all went numb, and I still held it. After a while, I felt the pain again because the skin around it was burning. Burned it right down to the bone."

He shook his head. "Yeah, I was pretty crazy then. I guess it was some kind of test of manhood. It all seems crazy now." He shook his head and put the cigarette to his lips. "The wife had to come pick me up from the bar and take me home. Next day I got delirious. Don't ever do that kind of shit, son."

Justin needed little convincing.

Someone asked what we were up to in these parts. We told them. The young man came over and sat down on an adjacent bar stool. He was from Texas.

"That's good," he said. "You're doing the right thing. You ought to feel lucky," he said to Justin, "your Dad taking you on this trip."

I raised my eyebrows and smiled at this, but Justin only shrugged. A teen doesn't like to be told that something's good for him.

"I wanted to go into psychology after high school," said the young man. "Help kids your age. I feel like I needed those years: eleven to eighteen—with a father. My father left when I was eleven. That's a tough time for a dad to pull up stakes. I didn't hear anything from him for years. Meanwhile my mom remarried. Then one day I pick up the phone and it's the mortuary calling. My father had fallen out of a second-story building. He'd knocked his beer out of an open window and then took a swipe at it trying to catch it. Landed on his head on the sidewalk.

"My mom's new husband tried to be a father to me. A great man, willing to give if I did, but I never gave him a chance. At sixteen, Mom said, 'If you won't live by our rules, move out.' So I did. Wish I hadn't now. But I drove up here to think about life. I remember driving all night, up through Oklahoma, Kansas, Missouri, saying over and over, Everything matters, everything! And it does.

"In the big city you don't see that. You say something nasty to someone and you'll never see him again. Here it's different. People talk about the little things here. You see that man over there in the corner? He just keeps on digging himself down deeper and deeper. Tries to buy his way into relationships with women. But around here, word gets around pretty quick. To lessen his guilt, he tries spending more.

"Once he ran for sheriff. Couldn't even get the 126 signatures in order to get on the ballot. Now he's got to dig out of that hole. Up here, people are more basic and connected. You say something or don't show respect, the talk's going to get around."

He tipped his mug of beer to his lips, then shook his head. "You guys are doing the right thing. Father and son. My dad did take me fishing once. One of the best days of my life. We drove out to this pond there in Texas and caught ourselves a mess of bullheads and channel cats. I never caught so many fish at one time in all my born days. I remember Daddy holding up that stringer full of fish and smiling just as big as a Texas highway."

The young man shook his head. "Happiest day of my life."

A Dark Dash Of Life

Sunday morning. A day off. My feet were sore from walking back and forth through Ford River the day before, so I told Justin the night before when we had made our way back to our weedy camp after midnight that I wasn't walking five or six miles to the nearest church. But somewhere in the high halls of Heaven, some angelic accountant noted my sloth and arranged to send me a little gift: aching ribs. Through two weeks of hard paddling, I had never suffered from aching ribs, but this Sunday morning I could not sleep. I rolled over, stuffed a t-shirt under the small of my back, and closed my eyes. The ribs throbbed. I tried left side, right side, stomach. I was determined to sleep. But there was a second gift already in place. While flopping from side to side, I happened to glance up at the top of our tent. A spider. A very large spider, hanging its bulbous body from a neat little net above us. I sat up, found my two canvas shoes, poised them on either side of the invader, and slapped them together.

Splat.

Justin sat up.

"What was that?"

"Just a spider."

"In here?"

"It's okay, I got him . . . a big monster."

The fat martyr had done his duty. We were both wide awake. "I guess I'm going to church," I told him. "I can't see walking all that way; I think I'll try hitchhiking. You can stay or come. Whatever you want."

Hitchhiking sounded interesting to Justin.

I showed him how to walk backwards with thumb extended while I regaled him with tales of my youthful adventures hitch-hiking. I told him the only people you could expect to pick you up were poor people in rattle-trap cars. See a recent-model car, you can forget a ride. We walked backwards, thumbs out. I hadn't hitchhiked in twenty-five years and had little confidence we'd catch a ride. Times have changed; people are afraid to pick up strangers. "Look for young people in old cars," I said. "Old people in new cars don't pick you up."

Just then, a new car swerved into a quick U-turn and pulled over across the road. A grey-haired man rolled down the window and said, "We're going right by that church you're going to."

Say what? I stared hard at the driver. It was Harold Ogren, that generous soul who owned the campground. I had asked him for the location of the nearest Catholic church the day before.

"Absolutely!" I cried, scrambling across the road to his car with Justin close behind.

Mr. Ogren and his gracious wife were on their way to a Protestant church. He turned back up the highway, and off we flew
on the wings of angels.

We're sitting in the back of St. Anne's Church. The priest is en-
ergetic. The place is full of well-dressed suburbanites: businessmen and women, lawyers, doctors, successful entrepreneurs:
Joliet's children. It is the Feast of Corpus Christi.

This priest has recently led a group of pilgrims to Lanciano,
Italy, scene of the first Eucharistic miracle (one of eleven the
Catholic Church affirms as authentic). Not everyone, I realize,
is comfortable with the idea of miraculous interventions, other-
worldly inveiglements. It has taken me time to get acquainted
with these conundrums to reason myself. But the stories are
there.

The priest begins:

In the eighth century, a priest is wrestling with his doubts.
How is he to really believe that this thin wafer of wheat, this
sip of grape wine, actually changes beneath his own hands into
the body, blood, soul, and divinity of his Lord? It's one thing to
believe that Jesus instituted a sacrament a long time ago, but
to believe that here in modern, eighth-century Lanciano, he
the priest, imperfect soul that he is, can speak words and make
Christ present? He could see no change in the bread, no change
in the taste of the wine after pronouncing the requisite words.
Surely Jesus meant that the bread and wine *signified* his body
and blood, that this meal was simply a *memorial* of his death
and resurrection—or worse, was this a ruse played upon the
people to keep them loyal, to siphon off their money?

Yet how could he continue as a priest and not believe this
central sacrament of his faith? It was a problem. A serious problem. It was tearing him apart. How could he go through with
another liturgy if he could not bring himself to believe?

Then, says our Escanaba priest, before the eyes of the Lanciano priest and his congregation, the bread changed to flesh and blood. They took the wafer of flesh and put it in a glass case. In all these centuries, it has never deteriorated. In 1971 and again in 1981, scientists ran tests. They found it was made of human heart muscle; the blood was type AB, the same type as in all ten of the other Eucharistic miracles scattered over the centuries and accepted by the Catholic Church. What are the chances of that?

A strange tale. Here in modern Escanaba, U.S.A., I am surrounded by people of business and the professions, but none of them seem to bat an eyelash at this story right out of the Dark Ages. But of course it could have been a simple magician's trick. Cut a piece out of a cadaver, have the priest slip it out of his sleeve. But then, it doesn't deteriorate in twelve centuries. Strange. Like St. Anthony of Padua's tongue, like the body of St. Innokent of Siberia, buried by the Communists after 200 years of incorrupt rest, then disinterred 60 years later still uncorrupted, the Lanciano wafer of heart muscle doesn't deteriorate.

In a society that hurries the dead to the mortuary to put the body safely out of sight, this public display of bodies and body parts seems grotesque. I am new to all this, but the Catholic Church has always accumulated bone splinters, teeth, and stray fingers. Very odd. But I do understand the principle. It's right out of the Apostle's Creed: "I believe in the resurrection of the body, and the life everlasting." Incorrupt tongues seem to be whispering something about bodily eternity; shriveled fingers pointing out an age-old principle about the union of body and soul.

There's something more here too. I see it in the people. A girl gets up to announce a fund-raising dinner to support the youth group. You know these people will do it. Whether they need the calories or not, they'll eat and pay and pray to support

their young. There's a community here, an interactive, support-
ive group of men and women and children who have managed
to integrate faith and business into everyday life. Those early
French-Canadians saw little conflict between faith and business;
Joliet and Marquette were both a natural and necessary part
of that exploratory journey. The same, I suppose, is true of the
church the Ogrens attend, and many other congregations scattered about these little towns, integrating faith into everyday
life, recognizing the twofold claims of body and soul.

It is past noon, and we are walking past a graveyard looking for
a place to eat. There's a used bookshop across the street. Justin and I are drawn as to a magnet. It's a small stone shop, the
door is standing open. We walk in. Hardback books, paperback
books on shelves. More books in boxes. Stacks of books chest
high on the floor. Justin goes looking for westerns.

    A thin man sits sprawled on a chair behind the counter. He is
loosely dressed in a maroon t-shirt and paint-speckled, maroon
sweatpants, yellow leather moccasins literally down-at-the-heel.
He looks up from a book, scrapes a hand over a two-or-three-
day growth of beard, and opens his mouth. He tells me he's
written newspaper columns, books, screenplays: "Meryl Streep
comes over one day and sits down beside me and says, 'You
ought to write screenplays.' So I did. Hallmark Hall of Fame,
some movies. Have you seen *Primal Fear*? I know the writer."

    He rambles on about his ten children and five wives. "One
son's an actor. I told him when he went into it, son, let me pre-
tend I'm not your dad now and let me give you some advice.
Son says okay. I tell him, Three things you need and one of
them is not talent. One-hundred-thousand actors out there who
all look like Brad Pitt or Julia Roberts and have loads of talent.
Three things: one, discipline, because you ain't got it now; two,
get a second job to pay the bills; three, plan to stay with it at

least five years. Well, it worked. He does TV, commercials, movies. Making pretty good money.

"Another son of mine made 47 million last year."

I tell him I think I'll look around the store a bit. He gets up and says, "Come on back here." He leads me into a small back room: more books, a computer and monitor on a table. "Look at this." He hands me a small newspaper entitled, *Peninsula Press*. On the front page are two pen-and-ink drawings of priests dressed in black robes, one of them speaking to an Indian boy, and a brief article with the title: "Louis Jolliet, Father of the Upper Peninsula."

"We publish that right here," he says.

I begin to page through it. "Keep it, " he says.

He breaks off to attend to two women who have walked into the store.

I skim through the article on Joliet. It mentions his birth in 1645, his five years in the Jesuit college of Quebec and five years working as a merchant, his great exploratory journey with Marquette, his map making. The article concluded that Joliet "must be considered the father of the Upper Peninsula for his many explorations, maps, and other activities throughout the area." Not a lot of detail, but at least here was an acknowledgement of Joliet's role in developing this area. He was in fact a man of many talents. He was known at the college in Quebec as a musician. He was a good debater, having been chosen to represent the college in a public debate. At some point, perhaps in his 1667 journey to France, he learned the science of hydrography, a subject he later taught at the college in Quebec. After leaving college, he borrowed money to purchase a dozen ells of cloth, wampum, hatchets, small bells, coarse cloth, canvas, forty pounds of tobacco, and a steel forge and canoed west to join his older brother Adrien as a fur trader, establishing a trading post at Sault Sainte Marie. There he became business partners with two of the men who would later accompany him on the search for the Mississippi: Pierre Moreau the Mole, and Jacques Largillier the Beaver,

Fifteen minutes later the bookseller finds me sitting outside on a bench in the sun, paging through a faded Graham Greene hardback. He sits down on the bench opposite. "This used to be an old mortuary during the Civil War," he says, looking up at the building. "You know Hemingway? He used to drink down at a bar just a couple, three blocks from here. Wrote 'Big, Two-Hearted River' about this area. His editor wanted him to call it 'Fox River.' Said that people all over the country have associations with Fox rivers. There's 160 Fox Rivers in this country. Call it 'Fox River,' says the editor. Hemingway says to him, But 'Big Two-Hearted River' sounds like something somebody'll want to read." The man smiles.

Justin wants to buy a Tom Clancy novel. The man tells him he can have it free, and I'm wondering how Joliet's child here makes a living. I start to put the Greene novel back on a shelf, "Take it." I look at him. "Free," he adds. We thank him and move on down the sidewalk.

We found the bar: peeling rust-colored paint on a short building of concrete block and brick. Inside, a line of men sat at the bar knocking back whiskey or nursing beers. I glanced inside. Ernest Hemingway: rough, plain-spoken, lover of courage, of the expert movements of the bull fighters, lover of iridescent grasshoppers and mottled trout, of coffee on the boil, of brandy in a clean glass, of red blood on a black bull's hide. . . but in the end, lover of less, lover of losses, lover of nothing.

Bright sun. Flowers blooming in a lakeside park. Down on the water, two young men on noisy jet skis speeding around and around in circles like bees caught in water. Justin and I are walking. How few the times we have walked anywhere together.

The town of Escanaba reminds me of Topeka, Kansas. Same wide streets and storefronts. Like Topeka, the stores of the old downtown are closing. There must be a mall somewhere out there siphoning off the people and their cars. The easy walk along storefronts of local businesses where you had a chance to meet your neighbors is dying all across America. They call it the malling or mauling of America: "Ill fares the land, to hastening ills a prey/ Where wealth accumulates and men decay."

I stop to read an historical marker, but Justin grows impatient. "Come on Dad, this is boring. Let's go find a movie."

"But it's a beautiful day," I say.

"We've seen lots of beautiful days. I haven't seen a movie for a long time."

We step into a little store to ask directions. I buy Justin an ice cream cone and me a cigar in honor of sad Ernest. Outside the store, I strike a match and light up. How can such fierce loves turn upside down and leave a man like Hemingway hooked like that grasshopper in "Big, Two-Hearted River," stabbed through the chest, and walking on nothing but air? It distresses me.

By the time my cigar had burned down to a wet stub, we were walking across a wide, vacant lot with fast avenues on all sides and shopping malls scattered among vast parking lots. We were in the land of the automobile: few sidewalks, dangerous sprints across multi-lanes of concrete, a long walk along glaring sidewalks to the movie theater. Little Escanaba on a fast track toward the global economy? Apparently so. As that old prophet Wendell Berry says, "The global economy does not exist to help the communities and localities of the globe. It exists to siphon the wealth of those communities and places into a few bank accounts. To this economy, democracy and the values of the religious traditions mean absolutely nothing." Progress, progress, to what unknown sea are you carrying us?

In honor of our counter-current journey, we take in the movie *Mission Impossible*: thumping music, high-tech gizmos, improbable feats, betrayals, a high-speed train chased by a helicopter through a tunnel, explosions: the usual. Justin liked it a lot. So did I.

Afterwards, we wander through shopping malls that look the same as the ones in Topeka. Sunday shoppers drifting like fish through air-conditioned reefs of bright attractions, moving trance-like as if to the old blues song: "All I want is plenty . . . but I will take more."

A long walk back along Highway 35 slow-footing the roadside gravel. My wool socks are eating into the soles of my feet. My cheap canvas shoes are little protection against the concrete and asphalt and gravel. I walk on the sides of my feet. I walk in the grass. I take off my shoes and go barefoot. I put them on again.

We decide to try hitchhiking again. Car approaching—thumbs out—car passing away into smallness. Repeat exercise fifty, a hundred times. Keep walking. An evening of white lilacs and purple lilacs fragrant in the quiet air. An evening of sore feet. Every step hurts, but walking like paddling gives the mind time to think. Why do objects grow smaller with distance?

Thumbs out. Cars passing. The people in the cars are listening to the bouncy DJs calling out the latest pop, their minds impatient for home. I'm wondering why things grow smaller with distance. We'd be in a real fix if distance didn't diminish the apparent size of things, but just why did a car's tail-lights draw together as it hummed away? And what a strange thing it is that purple lilacs are actually rejecting the color purple; it's the color they reflect that we see; all the other colors of the visible spectrum they absorb, so that we might say they contain every color but purple and a purple lilac is therefore anything but purple. It's the color they sacrifice that attracts us—like the attraction of a saint.

Justin's feet are fine. His lips are still chapped, his hands dry and red, but the feet are fine. He dances around me, punching the air. He shoves his head into the small of my back and pushes me along. How can he have so much energy after a day of walking?

Car approaching. Thumb out. Whoosh of tires and diminishing whine. Justin walks well ahead, then circles back, throws a few more punches, some just missing my head. I grumble, and he skips on up the road. I'm still carrying my free book: *A Burnt Out Case*. Justin is carrying his: *Without Remorse*.

We walk by a church. Evening services are just over. Cars move out of the parking lot and onto the highway.

Come on, Christian folk! Practice what you preach! Notice our thumbs! The thumbs! "I'm just a pore, wayfarin' stranger! A-travelin' through this world below!" Whoosh. Whoosh. Whoosh. Gone with the wind.

Headlights begin appearing on the long highway.

Still walking.

We wonder if our tent and canoe are still hiding beneath that willow tree. Clothes, food, fishing gear, books, notes, a roll of twenty-dollar bills stuffed in a vitamin C bottle, maps, paddles, Duluth backpacks. Are they still there? Or have some young demons confiscated the lot?

A one-eyed car drones by, then pulls over onto the gravel. "Justin, let's go!" We're running. A white, rattle-trap beast of a car is belching exhaust into the gravel. I jerk the front door open and slide in. A young woman inside! A young woman picking up strangers at dusk? But I'm not asking questions.

"Thanks very much!" Justin climbs in the back. "We really appreciate this!"

She's a heavy-set young woman with a pleasant face. She pulls out onto the highway.

"You just getting off work?" I ask.

"Oh no. I've been to church." I notice Christian folk-rock

music coming from the speakers. The engine doesn't sound too good either. The door handle is broken on my side, stray wires wander out of holes in the dash and disappear into the glove box—but we're speeding by hundreds, thousands of sore-footed steps, and I'm elated.

"What church is that?"

"Agape Fellowship." She pauses. "We're kind of Pentecostal." She hesitates again. "See that finger?" She holds up her bare ring finger. "I had a wart right there. I put wart medicine on it, but it just got sorer. Then last week I went forward at the church service and had it prayed for. It's almost gone now. Doesn't hurt anymore either."

We're driving into Ford River: sweeping away a million footsteps.

She's still talking warts. "I had 'em pray for another lump on my leg tonight."

I'm thinking I could use prayers for my sole: the left one and the right one.

Following our directions, she pulls off the highway, down a gravel road, and into the parking lot for the boat ramp. A street lamp illuminates fishermen hooking boats to boat trailers for the trip home. She stops. My door handle is broken. I reach outside and lift the handle and step gingerly onto hard gravel, lean down, and thank her again. Her taillights weave away like fine rubies through boat trailers and men.

We walk up a worn trail where late fishermen with pressure lanterns are still watching Ford River's dark water, still hoping for a quick dash of life on the end of an invisible line. We feel our way back through high weeds to the willow tree. Natty Bumpo and all his household goods are waiting beside the tent. Pleased and exhausted, we unzip the tent and crawl into darkness.

*Two semi-trucks blasting through night rain, the left one swerv-
ing hard right, the right one standing on his brake and rumbling
onto the asphalt shoulder to miss the crumpled red car in the
left lane, the left semi shouldering up against the right one and
braking hard . . .*

    *That same night, two hundred miles east along that same
Interstate 70, in Columbia, Missouri, my wife awakes in a
sweat, her heart pounding. The storm front is moving in. Rain
is pounding on the tarred tin roof of the trailerhouse where she
is caring for my ailing mother. She listens. The electric fan on
the dresser near her head whirrs through the darkness. She is
gripped by a terrible worry. She listens. Outside, violent winds
thrash through the hickory trees; rain drums on the tin roof.
Her mind is fixed on Justin. She cannot stop thinking of him.
She does not know why. She cannot sleep.*

    *All night long the rain comes down, lightning darting across
her open eyes, prayers moving across her lips . . .*

Zeus

Slow waves. A grey, warm haze. We have been paddling for hours,
south southwest now, down the long, forested coast of western
Michigan toward Green Bay, Wisconsin. Bugs flitting around my
nose, eyes, and ears. Eyes heavy. I want to sleep. Paddling trance-
like through a world scarcely felt. Justin is reading his book, head
down, arms moving automatically—in the same boat as his father, but his eyes and imagination are roaming a different world.

    I'm surprised by how well we're getting along; I've had no an-
gry outbursts; he hasn't retreated into stony silences as we sometimes do at home. I enjoy his company, and he seems to be doing all
right with me, but at this point, ours is an active relationship, not
a conversational one. We cut wood, stake the tent, cook pancakes

or soup, shoot, fish, and hour after hour we work the paddles. We don't talk politics or philosophy or religion. Maybe we should, but I don't think he's ready. I wish he were, but there's something out of sync between us. I love books too, but for him they seem to be a way to shut the door on the present and escape into the world of imagination. I like the books that open a door onto reality, that make me think and reconsider. A Robert Browning poem has the painter Fra Lippo Lippi listing things of the world: forms, colors, lights and shades, towns, landscapes, human bodies, and saying that "we're made so that we love/ First when we see them painted, things we have passed/ Perhaps a hundred times nor cared to see." Paintings, sculptures, and books open our eyes on our own world. An artist lends his vision to the rest of us and for the first time we see the pallor of death in a painted hand, the arrogance in a man's sculpted shoulder, the mystery of a river and the power of grief in a single paragraph. Art need not be an escape, but an invitation into a world planted thick with wonders. For Justin, and perhaps for his generation, books and movies and television and video games seem to be a diversion or a departure from a world that bores them.

Somewhere, seaward, through the sluggish air, I think I hear a rumble. My head turns and I gaze lethargically out across pale waters into a pale sky.

"Was that thunder?" I ask Justin.

His head comes up slowly. We both look out through a white haze indistinguishable from cloud. Not hearing anything, his head returns to his book.

Weary. Sleepy. Two loons are bobbing in the waves near the point where they lose substantiality and become air and water. It's a phantom world and we only are left alive.

"There it is again. Did you hear it?"

Justin looks up. "I heard something."

"I can't see anything out there."

"Maybe we ought to get closer to land," he says.

* * *

The thunder is louder now. Muffled detonations coming from somewhere out there: Zeus the cloud-gatherer veiled in mist. I'm still not convinced the storm is moving our way, but we both begin watching the shore for a landing place in case something blows up. We don't want to be caught in a squall.

Twenty minutes later, I point with my paddle. "There it is."

Justin sees it too; a low, dark frown of clouds building and deepening in the east. "Let's go for shore," I say. "See the sand beneath those pines?"

A warm breeze moves through the haze. We are paddling fast; the sand is maybe half a mile ahead, the shore is a hundred yards to our right, so at least we're close if we need to run it in. We see our first flash of lightning through the scudding haze and count the seconds. Zeus is maybe a mile away. A cool breeze hurries by. Quite suddenly we are rolling over two-foot waves that run by us and eventually snarl into shore sand.

By the time we slide ashore, a cold wind is blowing hoarsely through the pines and chattering through the lower bushes; we can smell the rain. The crack of thunder is loud and raw. We jump out into a wave and heave Natty up the beach. Justin grabs the tent and runs heavily through deep sand. A big spider jumps out from his footprint and scampers away. I pull out my book bag, camera case, and the folded brown tarp and hobble after him through the ankle-deep sand, my feet still very sore.

By the time we slide the tent poles through their channels and pop the tent up, heavy drops are spattering dark dye across gold sand and shattering wet crystal through pine needles overhead. Successive lines of waves are crashing ashore. We run for the heavier packs. I love this violent weather: lightning ripping down through woolen clouds, shadowed winds whirling showers along the sand, the clean smell, the fresh-swept air.

Our timing is perfect. We stuff the last packs under the tarp and scuttle into the round tent as heavy rains rush toward us across the waves on millions of little feet, charging ashore like a Greek infantry. We are pleased with ourselves. We lie back and relish the shaking and pounding of Zeus's army. The double membrane of tent and fly above us snaps and flutters. Such a solid defense.

We unzip the back window to watch the storm at sea. Grey waves are thundering ashore, torrents of rain sweep over the seas, and the clever winds whip beads of rain through our screen and shower our faces. We zip up tight.

Now, with the rains drumming the tent, we have time on our hands. I reach into the book bag for my bag of tobacco, tap a little into my pipe, light it, then reach for *The Odyssey*. My teenager flops back and puts his hands behind his head as I read a couple chapters. Outside old Zeus roars and shouts all about us. Inside, the smoke curls about the tent like a contented cat and we breathe deeply of safety and security—however tender and transitory.

After reading together, Justin pulls out his Tom Clancy and I decide to try my Graham Greene:

Greene's man in this novel has lost all relish for life. His name is Querry and he is indifferent, anomic: "cold the sense and lost the motive for action." His only goal is to go to a place where he needs no goals. His only contact with ethical values is a nagging sense of remorse. He has arrived at this mental state not through the suppression of his desires, as Freud predicted, but through a lifetime of self-indulgence and a successful career as a creative architect. After success, fame, and the conquest of other men's wives, he concludes, "I've come through to the other side, to nothing." Sounds like Hemingway.

He has left Europe and is moving away to the end of the world, to a leprosarium run by Catholic brothers and an atheist doctor far up the Congo River. It's a harsh world: vast jungles, heavy heat, a muddy, sluggish river, fierce storms, mosquitoes, tse tse flies. The man finds no romance in strange places, just vast, empty forests, exhaustion, and disease.

"You have to give pain a chance," says the Father Superior, for Querry no longer feels his own pain, not even his psychological pain; he says he feels only discomfort; he is a spiritual and emotional leper. Later the atheist doctor tells him, "Discomfort irritates our ego like a mosquito-bite. We become aware of ourselves, the more uncomfortable we are, but suffering is quite a different matter. Sometimes," says the doctor, "I think that the search for suffering and the remembrance of suffering are the only means we have to put ourselves in touch with the whole human condition. With suffering we become part of the Christian myth."

"Then I wish you'd teach me how to suffer," Querry says.

The rain passed. My son and I walked out in bare feet through wet grasses to find wood for the fire. The air was cool, rinsed, pure, reborn. Every spray of long pine needles held its dripping beads of light, galaxies of little stars, each bright drop a tiny mirror to our passing.

Refugees In A Rich Man's Yard

All morning long we were fading into fogs and rematerializing in bright sunlight. The forests ashore came and went.

Moving around a peninsula into sunlight, we saw three men. They stood like herons, peering fiercely into tea-colored water. One leaned from the low shore, two others stood fixed, knee deep in cold water. Each held a bow with its arrow drawn. They stared into the water. Complete concentration. We drifted toward them. They stood in a triangle perhaps thirty yards apart. Slowly, with extreme caution, one of the waders lifted a leg and eased one step forward. They had no eyes for their own images floating on the rippled surface; they were looking deeper. We drifted nearer. They paid us no heed. Precisely machined arrows were slung from their backs, they gripped sophisticated compound carbon bows with pulleys, arrow racks with black-pointed barbs attached to belts, there were spools and lines, hip-waders, camouflaged vests and hats: all that gear, and tackle, and trim. What were they after that they would go to so much trouble? Enlightenment? Beauty? Truth? God? Carp?

Late afternoon. We see the rich man sitting alone on his back deck. Tall pines and firs shade his huge, new, tudor-style house. He seems to look up as we paddle by, but we are phantoms of another age and soon lost to his view. The sea has never been so calm, not a breath of a breeze, just the slow, easy, lift and fall of silken waves, as if the sea is breathing in its sleep.

We paddle around a stony point into a tiny bay. Willows overhang a rushing little stream that washes foaming into the lake. A few frogs have begun their evening prayers, a regular choir of Tibetan monks, basses and baritones all, except for one falsetto yooper who seems wildly out of place. Fish are hitting the surface all over the quiet water. We have been passing houses and kept yards all afternoon and have wondered where we'll find a vacant spot to camp.

We beach the canoe and take a little walk. We are in the rich man's yard, but his house is hidden by a thick stand of trees. He, or rather his hired mowers, have mowed around gnarled old apple trees that still lift white blossoms to the evening sun, cut around young blue spruces and thickets of knee-high ferns and perfumed lily-of-the-valley that hang their carillons of tiny white bells in dark green foliage.

It is a long yard that lies between highway and lake; a mowed track winds back through the tall forest toward the house we cannot see. Boulders have been dropped along the shore to prevent erosion and a rectangular harbor for a boat has been cut back into the forest, but this has silted in; nature is a democratic force that spurns the rich as well as the poor.

We decide to take our chances and throw up our tent near the rushing stream at the very end of the man's yard, surely he will not begrudge us, little fleas that we are, one night's sleep in the tail end of his yard—or better yet, perhaps he will not find us here at all, for how often do the rich make use of their many acres?

Justin fishes. I sit on a rough boulder and gaze upon a sea of undulating Chinese silk: pinks and pale blues blending near shore with subtle green teas, and, in the far sky, a few fragile clouds pink against a satin sky of palest blue brightening toward a phosphorescent orange horizon—a long sarong of silken orange. I'm caught in a mandarin spell. The slow minutes stain the land to umber and then to black while the colors of the sea intensify and the long horizon goes orange vermillion. Justin's dark silhouette is still fishing, winding a silver spoon through perfect silk.

But Justin caught no fish.

That night he tried sleeping outside among the lilies: young Adam in the Garden. Yet, though Eve had not yet found him, the mosquitoes did. He zipped the hood of his sleeping bag around his head, but the tiny demons, who have no pity on the poor, found the small hole he left unzipped in order to breathe. He returned to the tent and absconded with my pipe, hoping to puff them away, but with marvelous courage, they kept on diving like fighter planes into the smoking hole and doing their damage. No rest in Eden. He soon fled to the tent, young Adam driven from the garden by sword-wielding angels.

Refugees In Menominee

Joliet and Marquette stopped in Menominee to visit a tribe Marquette called the Nation of the Wild Oats, after the wild rice which, he said, "grows spontaneously in little rivers with slimy bottoms, and in marshy places." He informed the Indians of his intention to go west:

> They were very much surprised, and did their best to dissuade me. They told me that I would meet nations that never spare strangers, but tomahawk them without provocation; that the war which had broken out among various nations on our route, exposed us to another evident danger—that of being killed by the war-parties which are constantly in the field: that the Great River is very dangerous, unless the difficult parts are known; that it was full of frightful monsters who swallowed up men and canoes together; that there is even a demon there who can be heard from afar, who stops the passage and engulfs all who dare approach; lastly, that the heat is so excessive in those countries, that it would infallibly cause our death.

Marquette thanked them for their kind advice, but assured them "that I could not follow it, as the salvation of souls was concerned; that for them, I should be happy to lay down my life." So they paddled on. And so would Justin and I, though we were to find many of their warnings quite true.

Unlike Joliet and Marquette, we knew no one in what is now the city of Menominee, so we hid our canoe in a thick stand of tall dry reeds at the end of a peninsula called John Henes Park. We were famished. All morning and well into the afternoon, we had bucked a head wind and now I felt weak and exhausted, though Justin was in good spirits—hoping, of course, to see a movie.

We walked out past a beach where children shouted and splashed and a pretty life guard with perfect skin in a neon-orange swim suit sat on her perch waiting for a young man to begin drowning. We walked past a small zoo: ducks, deer in a meadow, a black bear slumped behind bars on a concrete floor, a trickle of urine finding its way to a rusty drain. Outside the park, we turned up an old, busy highway: Everywhere the roar of machinery on the run: the guttural blasts of semis picking up speed, cars revving up, motorcycles ack-ack-ack-accelerating, the clamorous hiss of hurrying tires, all of them rushing toward the stop lights; car brakes squeaking, squealing, air brakes gasping, yelping. A warm wind blew gritty sand in our faces. We walked by an old furniture factory; we could hear the snapping of pneumatic staplers. The high-pressure, nerve-snapping urban life all about us.

Late that night we walked back into sweet darkness beneath the tall, silent trees of the deserted park. I was hobbling on blistered feet. We had eaten fast food twice. We had walked through old neighborhoods, past countless small businesses, past faded billboards: Welcome to the Beginning of the Ending of Your Pain (an ad for a chiropractor). Down by the lake we had found a good bookstore, but the poems of Seamus Heaney were too high for my billfold's reach and Justin couldn't find the Louis L'Amour book he was looking for. At Spies Athletic Field, built in 1937, we had stopped to watch a little league baseball game. There was much to recommend this city: small businesses still working, little league baseball with its ardent parent fans and its volunteer coaches still at play in the historic field. But suburban spread was at work too, driving the big retailers and theaters to the suburbs (We couldn't find Justin a movie).

Then we had found our way into Charlie B's Extra Innings Bar to watch the Chicago Bulls lose the fourth game of the play-offs. Justin had been suddenly depressed. But there was nothing for it but to step out into the night and take up walking again.

For Justin the day had been a flat loss. No movie. Too much walking. Bulls defeated.

For me it was no loss at all: a new, old town observed, a memory earned, time, however ordinary, spent walking with my son: a long seam stitched together with our footprints.

At the entrance to the peninsula park was a sign declaring the place closed at eleven. It was after midnight. We stepped around the sign and walked on in, following a little trail beneath ancient trees. Here all was still but for the quiet gabbling of two ducks on a small pond we passed. There was the good smell of quiet things: mud and grass and old pines.

When we reached the end of the peninsula, we broke our way through tall dry reeds and spider webs in the dark, over a jumble of broken rock, to where faithful Natty Bumpo lay waiting. We pulled out flashlights, jerked out our pack of sleeping bags and our rolled-up tent, and stumbled back out to a dark place under the trees.

Sleep at last? Not quite. After I placed my rolled up pants under my head for a pillow and was stretching out my raw feet atop my sleeping bag, I heard mosquitoes. I played a flashlight around the inside of the tent and, with my thumbs, began methodically pressing mosquitoes against the nylon, leaving rich smears of blood. Without complaint, Justin sat up and leant his thumbs to the task. After several kills, I sent my searchlight across our small grey cosmos a final time, then rolled up my sweatshirt and placed it under the small of my back and lay down to sleep with my aching ribs and blistered feet. But this was not suffering. All that we had gone through this long day of paddling, of hunger and weakness and walking was at the most mere discomfort, what the poor of most nations experience as a matter of course every day of their lives.

A little after six the next morning, I shook Justin awake and told him we needed to move; park crews would probably show up around seven, and I didn't intend getting caught; refugees avoid the law. As we slipped back into blue water, we saw a park pickup truck with a couple men sitting backwards on the tailgate drive up the road toward our vanished tent.

We followed some seagulls across the bay, past an island where they and their now half-grown young screamed at our passing, and onto a gravel beach behind a Howard Johnson's Inn.

After picking up a quick breakfast at a Burger King, we returned to Natty Bumpo where we met a well-dressed, grey-haired gentleman pacing the gravel beach. He kept leaning over his round stomach and picking up bits of driftwood, examining them, and dropping them. As we snapped up Natty's spray skirt, he wood-picked his way over to us, and we fell into conversation.

As a boy, he had lived on the peninsula we had camped upon; his father had been the park caretaker. "They close that park at night," he said. "Used to have a policeman on duty there all night, but not anymore. I guess they're trying to save money."

I smiled. (Blessed be stingy taxpayers and their strained city budgets.)

"They don't keep it up like they used to," he said. "Of course I know that's just an old man talking."

"What's that you've picked up?" I asked.

"Just pieces of driftwood. I carve them into little birds: finches, sparrows, little birds. I retired thirteen years ago; I was in school administration. See that water out there?"

The waves washing in were dark green, speckled with blonde bits of sawdust. "The sawdust used to be so thick and dirty from the sawmills and factories around here, we kids used to wait for an offshore breeze to push the scum away from shore before we could swim. Or we used to go out to the lighthouse over there where the river pushed the scum away enough for us to swim."

A light, cool breeze ruffled the waves. The air was clear. I asked about an island we could see floating in light haze to the northeast.

"That's Chambers Island, about fifteen miles away. When we were kids, we used to ride out there on iceboats. You could go a hundred miles an hour on one of those."

He reached down and picked up a couple pieces of driftwood to demonstrate how they constructed an iceboat. "Just home-made affairs," he said, "a sail attached to a platform with metal sled runners underneath." Handmade successes. As he talked on I began seeing this Midwestern town in the thirties: sawmills ripping through billions of board feet of northwoods lumber, smoking factories, desperate men going out on strike at the Lloyd-Loom Factory during the Depression when labor unions were fighting hard to get organized, semi-pro football played on freezing fall afternoons at Spies Athletic Field, and boys bundled in caps and coats and scarves skimming fast beneath stiff canvas sails across miles of snowy ice, flying fast before a winter wind, the smokestacks and factories growing small behind them, their noses and cheeks going numb and their eyes blearing until all they can see ahead is the pure joy of unlimited possibilities.

"Nothing to stop you from here to the island on those ice-boats," I remarked.

"Nothing to stop you," he agreed. I saw him gazing across the water.

He leaned down and picked up a flat piece of time-worn

driftwood. "You see? This would make a good perch for my finches."

Candied Copper

The sun was strong, the afternoon warm. White gulls floated high beneath scattered puffs of white clouds; a tiny silver airplane hummed higher than the clouds and away. Looking east, the Door Peninsula was clearly visible now. We were forty miles, on a straight line, from the city of Green Bay, and were looking forward to getting off Lake Michigan and onto a river, though I was concerned about finding a place to camp in the city of Green Bay, and we were both wondering how we would fare paddling upcurrent on the Fox River after the recent rains.

After rounding Peshtigo Point, the shoreline swept east and almost out of sight into a wide bay miles and miles across. Our path lay straight across to Oconto, but where that little town lay along the thin penciled shoreline across the bay, we didn't know. I took a compass reading and headed out toward a tiny bump on the horizon.

The water here had turned dark green and still carried tiny specks of sawdust; after Menominee, we would never again be able to look down through twenty or thirty feet of clear water to the rocks below. We began spotting dead fish floating by that the gulls had passed over. Dead fish. Fewer fish. Every old timer we had spoken to about fishing had told us the fishing was nothing compared to the fishing in their youth. This is more than the nostalgia of old men. Fish stocks in the Great Lakes are not reproducing like they used to. In fact, all across the world, the major fisheries are crashing, and this is certainly true of these Great Lakes. Even the yellow perch—that used to be so common that lakeside taverns and bars fried them up and gave them away free—are now being regulated. Most of the commercial fishermen have gone out of business. The only way fish stocks are kept up at all is through artificial restocking: growing huge batches of fingerlings in special ponds and releasing them.

Some argue that overfishing is the problem, but recently scientists have been saying that the main problem is chemical buildup in the water. Farming methods that contradict the patient evolutionary way of change are devastating the waterways. Chemists have tried to control, rather than manage the land, and now their insecticides, herbicides, fungicides, and organochlorine chemicals that were designed not to break down and don't, are building up in the water and silt of the lakes and oceans. Meanwhile, paper mills and other industries still pour mercury and dioxins into the waterways.

It is a national problem. In 1996, government officials issued 3500 warnings not to eat the fish in various waterways across the United States. This included all of the Great Lakes, 5% of all river miles in the U. S., and 15% of all lakes. In thirteen states, all of the lakes and streams were under the warning.

These chemicals stick to algae. Then the microscopic water fleas, called Daphnia, and other tiny animals absorb them; larvae and small fish eat the Daphnia, and so on up the food chain to larger fish and birds where the chemicals accumulate, and eventually to us. Theo Colborn, senior zoologist for the World Wildlife Fund, says many of these contaminants "mimic or interfere with female and male hormones, thereby modifying development and reproduction." Stanley Dodson from the University of Wisconsin and Takayuki Hanazato of Japan have concluded that the "Reduction or removal of Daphnia from a lake food web may result in a greener lake that produces fewer fish and has a greater tendency toward winter kill."

We have dumped over 200 kinds of PCBs and 75 kinds of lethal dioxins on our farmlands since World War II. Even after the regulation of DDT in 1988, the problem has not gone away. Brent and Sylvia Palmer of Ohio University in Athens, Ohio, and other scientists report that bald eagles surrounding the Great Lakes are still in trouble: "Adult bald eagles that migrate to the lake shore develop reproductive difficulties associated with contaminated food. The Great Lakes is acting as a sink for bald eagles migrating from reproductively fit inland populations . . . . These local populations of long-lived species may be heading for extinction . . ."

It's late afternoon and that pencil line of a distant shore has gradually sketched in a faraway smudge of trees and a small water tower. We are moving along painfully, groaning like exhausted animals, our backs hurting, our butts aching; a lot of effort for so slow a progress.

Long before we see it, we hear the drone of an approaching motorboat. After a while we see it slap-skipping across the waves toward the water tower, the water tower I've been watching grow from the shore at about the same speed as a plant grows. I think the tower indicates the little town of Oconto, so I want to observe where the motorboat enters that vague wash of afternoon grey that resembles a shoreline.

But suddenly the motorboat heels over to starboard and turns toward us, coming to a rocking rest scarcely thirty yards away. One man's at the wheel, a second young, bearded man stands up and takes a look at us. "You guys need a tow?"

Justin jerks up his head like a startled horse.

I glance at the shoreline. "Maybe another half hour away, Justin. We can make it without a pull."

"WHAT?" Justin is in shock. "They're offering us a ride!!"

"I know, but I want to take this trip without rides."

"WHAT?!"

I start trying to explain my romantic wish to do this trip the old fashioned way, to achieve an adventure without the aid of machinery, to . . .

"WHAT?!?!" Justin is desperate.

"We're only about a half hour from shore," I say in a soothing voice.

"A HALF HOUR?! We're two hours from shore!"

"No, look over there. Maybe a little more than a half hour."

"Dad! You always underestimate."

"Justin, you always overestimate."

"Dad! Come on!" He looks pleadingly at the voice of tyranny. "Dad! Come on! A ride!"

I'm thinking fast. I've read of how you can tie the prow rope to enable the pulling of a canoe, but it's a touchy thing; you can drown a canoe if it's not done right.

I look at the two young men in the speedboat. "Thanks. I really appreciate the offer, but I think I want to do this on our own."

"WHAT?" Justin flops onto his back in despair.

The man in the motorboat shrugs and smiles, and sits back down. The one at the wheel eases the throttle forward. The water boils to life under the powerboat's stern, and it roars away.

Justin is angry. He lies on his back staring up at the sky and mumbling mutinous words.

The droneboat diminishes over the waves.

I begin paddling.

Justin lies there staring up at the sky.

I keep paddling.

Ten minutes later, he sits up shaking his head and begins plying his paddle again. The water is heavy on our paddles. The late afternoon sun is hot.

An hour and a half later we paddle into the mouth of the Oconto River. Trees and bushes on the left; a heaped stone sea wall on the right. Two black men fishing off the sea wall. A tall motorboat rumbles quietly by us as we flat foot it up the smooth green current.

At the first boat dock, people are sitting in lawn chairs in the shade. They tell us we can't camp there, but maybe upstream a ways.

"Upstream?" Justin gives me a disgusted glance.

On we go, fighting upcurrent. A tangle of trees and bushes on the left. Mown grass and tall cottonwoods on the right. We pass boat marinas, homes. A motorboat buzzes by pulling four young girls on skis. We pull over to the right bank and climb stiffly out of the canoe, watching their bent-legged, ungainly progress downriver. A young man nearby tells us they're practicing for the weekend water show. Tomorrow this little peninsula we're standing on will be thick with people here to take part in Oconto's annual Copper Culture Festival. Copper, because Indians using copper tools once lived hereabouts. The young man shrugs and says, "Don't know why we do it, but we do."

Copper was a serious concern for the early French-Canadians. Before Joliet and Marquette's journey, a Jesuit missionary, Claude Allouez, had discovered copper on the shores of Lake Superior. This had precipitated a 1688 expedition by none other than Louis Joliet's older brother Adrien. He found no copper mine, but the royal court of France then appointed another expedition to seek out iron, lead, copper, and tin mines, admonishing the leader, a Saint-Lusson, to consider this work "as most important for the prosperity of Canada."

But copper was not our concern; camping was. We decided it was better not to ask if we could pitch our tent there, expecting an answer in the negative. I stepped out of our canoe and noticed sharp pains running up my legs each time I took a step. I leaned over and observed two dark and very painful spots about a handbreadth in size on my shins. In the heat of the morning, I had rolled up my khaki pants and the sun slanting over Natty's gunwales all afternoon had basted these oblong spots to a dark reddish brown. We had been careful to use sunscreen on our necks and arms, but I hadn't noticed the sun on my legs.

We unloaded our packs and carried them beneath a huge, double-trunked willow tree that certainly shaded lumbermen a hundred years ago if not the copper-culture Indians before them. Black ants three-quarters-of-an-inch long were foraging along exposed roots and running up the trunks as we set up the tent in the shade. We were hungry too.

The four girls came plowing back up the river as we left our packs inside the tent and took the blacktop toward town. I was now limping on still-sore soles and newly-burnt shins.

It felt like the first day of summer. There was heat in the early evening air; after weeks of growth, trees were thick and complicated with leaves; tufts of foxtail sprouted from the roadside gravel, bending to the weight of swelling seeds.

Oconto is another sawmill town gone to seed and come up again as a highway town between Green Bay and Menominee. Once it was rich. You can see that in the old stone churches and the lovely county courthouse. It has lost the screaming saws, the roudy lumberjacks, the ships coming and going, the teams of working horses—all that sound and smell and fury of early success—for quiet, well-kept lawns, a line or two of shops along main street, and a weekend of annual remembrance. The town carries a mature beauty, and apparently some honest folks.

A car pulled up and a woman asked if we'd lost a billfold on the corner. Money being at the heart of trips to town, Justin and I both slapped our butts. His wallet was missing. We thanked the carload and Justin headed off at a run for the corner we'd just passed. The carload pulled away. "See," the lady shouted, "there's still some good people left!"

Yes indeed.

Justin found his billfold beside a lamppost while I counted my money. We were spending too much money eating. I hadn't foreseen all these camping places that prevented us from cooking our own food over open fires. We entered The Brothers Three café and devoured a large pizza and downed a pitcher of iced lemonade, then walked out to take a look at the town.

Teenagers everywhere, Justin's own tribe, loitering along the sidewalks in pairs or threes, the girls flashing quick glances at the passing cars, all the girls clean jeaned and white t-shirted, flowing together at street corners, swirling in complicated currents around each other at the lampposts, laughing, squealing, shouting across streets, and rippling away again, all eyes for the passing faces, all ears for the radio rhythms of the loud cars and the boys inside them.

We followed a current up an alley and into the loud, tinny music and glittering lights of an amusement park hastily staked out in the parking lots between the main line of stores and a railroad track. Leather-faced men shouted for dollars to throw a ball at stacked bottles; rouge-faced women held up darts for balloons, darts for paper hearts. The merry-go-round swirled to the sounds of a recorded calliope. Candy-colored lights flashed lemon, orange, lime, and cherry-red. Cheap stuffed animals dangled from tent tops. Justin wanted to win a stuffed bear for his little sister Julia. Back in Manistique, he had already bought a small stuffed Smoky Bear for little Alex. He tried the BB machine gun shooting out the print of a red star. The BBs burst out of the air gun in short pressurized rattles. I watched him. He shouldered the gun again, leaning forward in his camp-stained white t-shirt and his camouflage hat, concentrating on the chewed up red star. He fired again, but winning would take more practice, or luck, than Justin had dollars to spend.

We trailed away from the winking lights, the restless teens, the noise, out past homes whose windows flickered the blue TV lights of the evening's entertainment, out the hard road to where the cottonwoods stood tall and easy in the night air and the first fireflies of summer drifted away from the shrubbery and out over the black river.

We lay exhausted in our tent atop our sleeping bags. The air was warm and still. Justin's face and lips burned. My shins ached, my feet hurt. We tried to sleep. But suddenly several cars roared by and screeched to a stop in a parking lot twenty yards away. Car doors slammed. Boy voices loud, radio music pumping power chords, bass guitars low-beating the rhythms, shouts, laughter, popping beer cans, more cars, more teenagers, raucous laughter, smell of beer, cigarette smoke drifting over, an aluminum can kicked along asphalt, laughter uproarious—shouting away the insecurities, laughing for acceptance—another car now and loud girl voices, radio DJs triggering short, pressurized bursts of radio talk, pounding radio rhythms, boy-girl-boy shouts—then suddenly a girl is peering into our tent.

She squeals and scrambles away, "My GAWD! There's a DOG in that tent!"

I look over at Justin who has sat up. "Well, it's not me," I say.

He laughs.

Out there loud, beery laughter. Justin chuckles. I see him sitting there, a shadow on the mosquito net, peering out at the figures sprawled across car hoods or shuffling restless in groups. He stays there a long time, gazing, longing for members of his own species.

Two hours later I am dozing. Car doors slam engines roar tires squeal shouts fading radio rhythms . . .

Six A.M. I hear the metallic rattleroar of a big diesel truck engine rolling right up to our tent, then a gasp of air brakes. I lean over, unzip the mosquito net, poke my head out, and ask the truck driver if we need to move. He says no. I go back to sleep. There's the crash and noise of equipment being unloaded.

Eight A.M. A man is shouting. "Anybody in the tent?"
I respond.
"Did anybody give you permission?" comes the voice.
"Someone told us about this place."
"Who was it?"
"Don't know. Someone we met coming in. We're leaving in a few minutes."
"Okay."
At least reason prevails in good Oconto.

When we dress and crawl out of the tent, we discover twenty portable toilets lined up next to our tent. Our little grey tent is in line to be the twenty-first. A few feet away, a long trailer is backing into position: Oconto Trailblazers painted on the side. Twenty men and women are unfolding tables, unloading supplies: small town volunteers setting up for the celebration. No one worries about us.

We forgo our breakfast, pack up our equipment, and slip back into the river. We'll not linger for the Copper Culture.

Simple Complexities

Eleven miles later, beneath willow trees, sitting on a washed-up log, we ate almonds, oranges, cheese sandwiches. The flat pale lake rippled slowly away beneath a hot white sun. A carp was rotting in the sand on the other side of the log; the maggots busy beneath the scales. The place stank, but we didn't move from the shade until we were finished eating our oranges.

The sun has set. We sit in the cooling sand beside a blowing fire gazing across the darkening water toward the indigo hills of the Door Peninsula. A wind has come up and is roaring hoarsely through the tall cottonwoods and willows behind us. Natty

Bumpo is rocking to the wash of incoming waves. Our tent sits humped on a strip of sand a few feet from the water. Behind us, in a marsh, a red-winged black bird trills, a goose honks repeatedly, then falls silent. Warm, south wind blowing. Sky darkening.

Far out across those deep blue hills we have been watching distant fireworks begin blossoming against the sky like night flowers. It takes maybe a minute or more for the distant detonations to tap our eardrums. It's Flag Day. Some little town over there is celebrating.

I'm sipping strong coffee and thinking of home, missing even the arguments of life together. Our oldest sons, David and Seth, will both graduate from college next year. David has taken a summer job near the university in Iowa; Seth is home—perhaps his last summer home. Johanna will be heading off for college in Texas come fall and I am missing her smile as she comes in the door after work, and missing her troubles too.

A minute will pass with the faraway sky black, lit only by the still light of farther stars. Then, out of the depths, a flash and a scatter of silver fishes. Then a burst of goldfish surfacing over the hills, then sinking away. Bright species red and green leaping to life and as quickly fading into the reefs of night.

My back aches. I stretch back on my elbows in the sand and extend my burned shins toward the waves as if the proximity of water can soothe the deep pain. And I am loving this place, this night here, now, the sky that an hour before was a pale violet but has slowly deepened into dark infinity stung by the stars we will never know. And I am missing my wife and the way she lays her head on my chest with my hand lost in her thick hair. And I am looking at Justin, the firelight washing amber across his bare arm and back as he props himself on an elbow and peers into the night. "Look at that one!" He points to a blue-white flower's briefest spring.

A summer wind is in our faces. There's the heavy swash of

the long waves, and the steady passage of wind in tall trees, and the wet smell of breaking lakewater, and the coals blowing bright near my elbow, and the sharp-scented smoke swirling up and away with the snap of a vagrant spark whirling into darkness, and far away, far away . . . the sudden tap. . . tap, tap, of the vanishing flowers.

"Nothing is simple which is presented to the soul," says the French philosopher Pascal, "and the soul never presents itself simply to any object. Hence it comes that we weep and laugh at the same thing."

Green Bay

The French called this Fetid Bay (not a name loved by chambers of commerce). Marquette tried to ameliorate the negative name by explaining that in the Indian language the name was really Salt Bay, "although among them it is almost the same." The Indians hated the taste of salt and equated the word "fetid" with salt. For that reason, Marquette and Joliet searched the area for salt springs but found none, concluding that the name had been given "on account of the slime and mud there, constantly exhaling noisome vapors which cause the loudest and longest peals of thunder that I ever heard." Justin and I had noted small eruptions in the lakewater near the mouths of rivers, evidently caused by the decomposition of vegetable material carried down the rivers.

On the day we entered the city of Green Bay, the bay lived up to its more ancient name. The air was stagnant and warm. Huge mosquitoes, three times the size of any I'd seen before, were stationed at intervals on the water surface and, like the black flies before them, would swerve up and strike as we passed. They had a vicious bite. I later learned these were Asian mosquitoes, brought over on container ships from Japan and China—global trade, globe-trotting insects. We stopped to dab on the repellent, but they kept on attacking, singling out the sunburnt areas along Justin's ribs. His constant slapping of sunburnt skin was driving him (and me) crazy. He could hardly paddle three strokes without stopping to fend off the kamikaze mosquitoes.

We pulled hard for the city. A tall smokestack flashed its strobe light next to a bridge that arched over the Fox River, mindlessly repeating its announcement of our entrance into the mechanized world. We passed two islands denuded of trees by crowding black cormorants, and passed a rocky manmade island whose signs warned of unstable materials; it looked like some kind of toxic waste dump. Dead fish kept floating by. We headed for a grove of trees on shore where we hoped to camp, but the shore was rocky and littered with wreckage: rusted engine parts, a jumble of nails rusted together, broken glass, corroded sheets of metal, slimy rocks rank with the smell of rotting fish, a tangle of broken trees and brush. We turned and paddled away.

It was carp mating season. Hundreds of them swirled the green waters around our canoe, paying little attention to us, sliding alongside each other, twisting, breaking water, curling over and under each other, then suddenly, as we came within a paddle's length, flipping away: a carp orgy in the warming mud-bottomed water. Big fish white-red and gold-green slammed into the bottom of our canoe, others, with a panicked slap of their tails, splashed water in our faces. Heavy, scaly bodies, gaping mouths, and ever-open eyes bright with the moment's passion swirled around us in fluid knots of three or four or five fish. Carp sex in Fetid Bay.

Natty Bumpo, part fish himself, was slightly distracted by the row, and ran a-ground, or a-muck as the case was, and we had a bad time trying to pole out of the smelly slime, shoving our paddles into a foot of mud and heaving together to move a few inches. Eventually we pushed free and paddled back to the mouth of the Fox River. There we beheld a similar distraction. Powerboats of every size and description were moving down the river and out onto the lake. Tall cabin cruisers, wide-bodied racers with massive engines, one-person jet skis, everyone was headed for open water on a warm Saturday afternoon. We threaded our way through them, a solitary arm-powered craft amid the snuffling, sputtering, grumbling, buzzing, roaring world of leisure machinery.

The women had donned their bright, florid bikinis and assumed their perches on the various highpoints of the boats the better to invite the sun into their diet-thinned bodies; the barechested men were slathering tanning lotions over their own considerable chests and bellies. Everyone was in an ebullient mood: sun, wind, water, speed, noise, cold beer, sexual attractions on every perch, the boats weaving in and out and around each other. But as soon as they passed the mouth of the river, they shoved the throttles forward and charged out across the water in a furious spray, breaking huge wakes. Chins up, hair flying in the wind, the boat people scarcely gave our bedraggled selves and our anachronistic craft a cursory glance as we dutifully rolled over their wakes and turned upriver, beginning the long hard pull against the streaming current.

But we were pleased to be there. After three long weeks on the broad lakes, we were finally on a river where we could see both banks. It was a milestone on our journey, a goal attained. The Fox was no longer the river "very beautiful at its mouth . . . full of bustards, duck, teal, and other birds" mentioned by Marquette, but it had its own interest for us. We paddled under the high arched bridge we had seen for miles across the bay and on between commercial buildings and large hotels.

We found we could make steady if slow progress against the current. We passed under many bridges, some that broke in two and lifted to allow passage to the taller cabin cruisers, others that turned sideways on rusted cogs and gears. Cars and trucks rumbled over the bridges. Three black children peered down at us from a bridge; an old man shuffled along a nearby sidewalk, but it was a world for mechanized conveyances. Tug boats sheltered under a bridge; long, sea-going tankers docked against a paper mill. Electrical lines webbed the shores and the bridges, and occasionally large signs warned of cables beneath the water.

After four or five miles of brick apartments, industrial plants, old churches, steel-truss railroad bridges, shops, warehouses, a reinforced concrete overpass, and homes along the bluffs to the left, we discovered trees and grass in a little inlet on our right. We camped above a stony dike in an abandoned and badly deteriorated miniature golf course: unmowed grass, rusted rebar protruding from broken concrete walkways, corroded nails poking up from ripped and weathered sheets of plywood and strips of wrinkled green carpeting, hardly the green meadows and rich forests that had greeted Joliet and Marquette.

We ate hot dogs at a gas station and asked about the location of a movie theater and a church, our usual weekend priorities. The woman behind the counter flicked through a phonebook for us, looking for Catholic churches while she told us where to find the nearest cinema. Then she sat down with us in a booth and began talking.

"Don't tell me you can't work two jobs and raise kids as a single mom," she said. "I did it. You just have to give up your social life for a few years, that's all. I raised my kids; now I've got all the time in the world.

"I was raised in a big family. All of us kids, eight of us, got together fifteen years ago for a reunion. We shot off all kinds of fireworks in the back yard. The cops, they start goin' door-to-door to find out where them fireworks is comin' from. Illegal you know. I already told all the neighbors about it, so they just tell the cops they don't know. Then the cops come to my door and my brother, the minister, goes to the door and there's the cops! And you know what he does? He lies to 'em! Paper and fuses and stuff all over this fire pit in the back yard and smoke hangin' in the air and he LIES to 'em!

"You're goin' to hell, I tell him. Just like he's always tellin' us: You lie, you go to hell. I'm splittin' my sides laughin'. My minister brother lying to the COPS!. Course the cops already knew what was goin' on. I mean they could just look around and see it. So I go to the door and explain the whole thing to 'em and they remembered my brothers. They said, It's been ten, fifteen years since they was around these parts."

She watched us finish our hot dogs. "And now it's been fifteen more years," she added.

"Time passes," I said.

We found the Catholic church before we found the theater, but I was disappointed. It was one of those modern abstractions that religious people build so that they can impress others with how relevant their faith is to the modern world. It was set among tall, beautiful, blue spruce trees, but the building itself looked like a plane had crashed through the roof of a brick factory. It was called the Church of the Nativity, and I suppose we could say it was some kind of metaphor for that rough cave for goats and donkeys where the Christ child was born. But why build a metaphor? Body and soul need a quiet refuge pleasing to the eye and elevating the mind, not an architect's abstraction.

Of course people can pray in caves; they can pray in prisons, slums, and concentration camps; they can even pray in plane-wrecked factories, but given a choice, I decided I'd walk five or six miles into Green Bay and choose one of the older, lovelier structures we had observed on our way up the river.

Graham Greene's burnt-out character Querry was an architect of churches before he lost all interest in life. He says he built churches as a matter of self-expression; he was not concerned with the people who occupied the space—only with the space: space, light, proportion, those were his driving motivations. He despised the people who cluttered up his finely lit spaces with cheap plaster saints and replaced his plain windows to put in stained glass "dedicated to dead pork-packers who had contributed to diocesan funds."

The atheist doctor tells Querry, "I am not a religious man, I don't know much about these things, but I suppose they had a right to believe their prayers were more important than a work of art."

Yes indeed. I shall take the long walk.

Father's Day

The next morning threatened rain, but we put on our best wrinkled shirts and rumpled slacks and began walking the back roads that paralleled the river. We walked past the paper mill, along streets lined with old homes where American Indian children played and oriental women sat on the porches, past shops selling pornography, past neighborhood bars and small industrial buildings. A light rain began falling. We crossed the Fox River on a bridge, and finally walked into St. Francis Xavier Cathedral, a tall brick building with twin towers surmounted by bronze cupolas.

We sat down damp and looked around. Behind the altar hung a huge painting of the crucifixion: black sky, women weeping, the Son of God in mortal pain. On the walls were paintings of Biblical events and scenes from the preaching of the Jesuit missions. The cloudy light outside soaked through stained glass where carefully nuanced figures in rich colors told the stories. It was a church rich in story.

Afterwards we walked. In front of City Hall, a great domed building that looked like the capitol building of Kansas, we found three stone sculptures labeled, "The Spirit of the North-west." A grim Indian stands there. He is given no name. This is unfortunate, for one cannot trace the stories of a man with no name. And the secret of statues is that they come alive only when you know their stories. The Indian is, I suppose, repre-sentative of all those tribes who lived hereabouts whose stories have so often been lost.

Beside the nameless Indian, is Father Allouez, that early Je-suit missionary who had discovered copper on Lake Superior and was a friend of Marquette; he had explored the Fox River and founded the mission at Green Bay. Several years after Joliet and Marquette's journey, Allouez and two Frenchmen set out near the end of October to travel south to a mission Marquette had founded on the Illinois River. They were stopped by frozen waters on the lake. After waiting until February for the water to freeze solid, they contrived a sail for their canoe, and "un-dertook a very extraordinary kind of navigation, for instead of putting the canoe in the water, we put it on the ice, on which a favorable wind carried it along by sails, as if it was on water." When the wind failed, they pulled the canoe over the ice with ropes "as horses do a carriage." A seventeenth-century iceboat on Green Bay.

On this journey, Allouez was called to comfort the mother of a young Pottawatomi convert who had been killed by a bear. The young man had found a hibernating bear in a pile of fir branches and had emptied his quiver of arrows into the animal. Wounded, the bear had risen from his nightmare and attacked, ripping the scalp off the Indian and tearing out his bowels. Af-ter discovering his body, the young man's relatives and friends declared war on the bears, hunting them down all winter and killing, they said, some 500 bears "to make them atone for the death of this young man who had been so cruelly treated by one of [the bear's] nation." It seems to me the bear was acting in self defense, but then, wars often have an irrational beginning.

It was Allouez who had first heard details of a water-route to the mighty "Mes-sipi" river and had passed on the information to Marquette. It was also Allouez who journeyed to Green Bay to denounce unscrupulous French traders who were deceiving the Indians. The conflict between dishonest French mercantile interests and French faith persisted.

The third statue in front of City Hall is of Nicolas Perrot who, like Joliet, was a fur trader and explorer. But unlike the French traders of Green Bay, Perrot was well respected among the numerous tribes that bordered the Great Lakes. He managed to settle a major dispute between the French and Indians at Oconto, and, in the summer of 1670, intervened to stop a riot near Montreal when a dispute had erupted between a large band of Hurons and Ottawas and French traders over a bit of stolen property. He was a man who combined integrity and commerce, the concerns of soul and body.

Three figures: the Indian, the merchant, and the missionary: fathers of the Northwest.

We stepped into a little corner shop. Justin was running low on funds, but he insisted on buying me a good cigar for Father's Day. Then we began the long walk back upriver to camp. "The Bulls play tonight at eight," he said. "We've got to find a place to watch the game."

"We'll find a place," I said. A light rain began to fall again through the light-soaked clouds as we made our way over a bridge and back through the working-class neighborhoods. Justin had his head down and shoulders hunched against the rain; we had forgotten our rain jackets.

I hobbled after, puffing away on my cigar like an out-of-repair steam engine.

The light had gone when we passed a little corner bar and stepped inside.

As the Bulls played, I kept one eye on the game and one ear to the bartender. He was talking about one of the hazards of modern fatherhood. Eight years ago he'd been living with a girlfriend in Florida. After a couple years, he had proposed marriage, but she had turned him down and developed a relationship with another man. So he moved back up to Green Bay. Six years later he got a notice from the government telling him he owed five years of child support. He hadn't even known she was pregnant when he left. But he was uncomplaining. "Hey, that's the way it is. You get the girl pregnant, you take responsibility for the kid. That's why I work nights at this bar. I never even seen the kid, but I ain't goin' to let him grow up with no support."

The Bulls won the NBA championship. Justin was pleased.

We walked out of the bar and into the night rain. Justin skipped on ahead of me. I limped along after, stepping over a streaming gutter, crossing a street, making our way along miles of puddled sidewalks. Everywhere there were sounds of night rain, pattering through leaves overhead, gurgling from downspouts, swirling into streetside drains. Sunday evening, no one around, but the occasional passing car. Rain, as John Graves says, "Even in gray heaped cities it has a privacy and a sadness."

Since Justin had given me that cigar, I'd been thinking about my own father, afflicted now with Parkinson's Disease. He could barely walk these days, the man I'd followed on walks along the Nile River, who had slogged through a mile-and-a-half of mud and knee-deep water during the rainy season to bring back mail from the riverboat, who had pushed a mower for hours on end to cut an airstrip for the incoming biplane, was now sitting out

his days in a wheelchair. My mother was still caring for him in
their little house trailer in Columbia, Missouri.

I wondered if it was raining there on this Father's Day. I
would have to find a phone and give him a call.

An hour after leaving the bar, we arrived at our tent thoroughly soaked. There we discovered we had left the tent window unzipped, so the foot-end of my sleeping bag was also
thoroughly soaked. No matter, a little more discomfort. I told
Justin I needed to call my dad for Father's Day. He wanted to
come along. We changed into dry clothes, pulled on dry socks
and boots, shouldered into rain jackets, grabbed our rain hats,
found a flashlight, and headed out through the rusted nails,
ripped plywood, and broken concrete of that miniature golf
course.

Justin's got a good heart, a kind of stubborn affection which
he gets, I suppose, from his mother. I'm too reserved when it
comes to displaying affection, as was my father and his father.
Old Grandpa Faulkner had been a bricklayer, and he could be
hard and mean. His son, my father, was never mean, but was
reserved and quiet. And that quietness sealed up within him the
stories of his life: his journey to Africa at the height of World
War II on a blacked-out merchant-marine ship running the risk
of being torpedoed by German U-boats, his near death of malaria one night on the banks of the Nile, the time he had three
flat tires within fifty miles of Khartoum while driving a load of
supplies back to our remote station; it was 350 miles of thorny
waste and rutted roads back to the mission station (a three-day
journey), but he had decided to go on, 300 miles more, without
a single spare tire. Was that rashness or faith? Slowly the stories
have surfaced after such a long time.

Rain was falling heavily as Justin and I walked along deserted streets, across empty fields of soaked grass, through a line
of brush, over a railroad track, jumped over flowing ditches,

hurried across a highway, and made our way along streets still splashing with traffic on a Sunday night. Rain was still falling when a cop pulled over and asked us where we were headed. Rainwalkers in Carworld warrant suspicion these days. We told him we were looking for a restaurant. He told us to get in. He clipped through the usual questions as he drove the mile-and-a-half to a Perkin's Restaurant: "You guys from around here?" "No, we're canoeing up the river." "Where abouts you camped?" "Over on the river." "Where you from?" "Kansas." "Where you headed?" "The Mississippi . . . if we get that far." "How long you staying?" "Just until tomorrow . . . if the rain lets up." "Well, you guys take care of yourselves." He let us off.

We ate and I called my parents. "Hello Dad. Happy Father's Day."

"Hello, Steve. Where are you now?"

"Green Bay, Wisconsin. Do you remember how I loved the Green Bay Packers when I was a boy?"

"Yes I do. I remember that you cried once when they lost a championship game."

"I remember."

"So how are you getting along on your trip?"

I filled him in, then asked how he was getting along with the Parkinson's. The answer was not too well. His medication sometimes gave him hallucinations; he would see fourteen people in the room and begin conversing with them. Once he saw African warriors attacking his trailer.

"Maybe they should cut down your medication," I suggested.

"We're working on it."

I talked to my mother for a time, getting more information about his medications, then said, "Well, Justin's happy, the Chicago Bulls just won the championship. You want to talk to him?" I handed the phone to Justin.

"Hello Grandma." I saw him smile. "Yeah, we're doing all right. Except it's pouring rain here right now . . ."

It was a long wet walk back to our half-dry tent wondering what this rain would do to the river. I was kidding Justin about the dove the previous day that had so perfectly timed his shot that Justin had caught a splat of bird crap on his head. "Smart bird," I said. "A real marksman."

Justin said the bird was a lousy shot. "What do you mean? It was a perfect shot!"

Justin looked at me from under his hat. "No. Totally missed. He was aiming for you."

I smiled and shook my head. We crossed the railroad tracks, leaped the flowing ditch, and hurried on through the night.

What is it that love seeks? What did I want from my father? What does this boy slopping through puddles beside me want from me? I think it begins with that first step beyond indifference: that constant naming of the boy, the naming of the sleepy-eyed child stumbling downstairs on a grey winter morning, the turn of the head and acknowledgment as he steps into my office, the naming as he's tucked into bed as a youngster—to know this boy as that individual he is, to name him a thousand times through the scattered and busy days.

Then to see. To really see the boy who glances at me as he leaps from the picnic table, whose look invariably turns to his parents as his seven-year-old hands dribble the ball down the court. To see him in his own particularity, and in the seeing to delight in him again and again. And he, seeing the delight which cannot be disguised, will know that he is somehow worthy of an adult's love.

And then to approve that which deserves approval at his age—and to disapprove of that which deserves disapproval, for this too (given patience) is also a kind of knowing, a recognition of a child who will not always please me, but whose presence must somehow be completed by my nod, my smile, my frown, my hand on his shoulder that now, this rainy night, has become his hand on my shoulder. A word, a look, a touch; it's not too much to ask. But it's the repetition that counts, so that the word that touches and the touch that speaks are not rare, but again and again are woven into the fabric of our ordinary days. A lot of those threads have been missing over the years. I was trying to stitch things up now, but hand stitching takes time.

The rain was still falling and our feet were still falling along a dark deserted street that led through an abandoned golf course to an old grey tent. By that time, neither of us were feeling much like words.

Next morning the rain was still coming down. The river was roiling along, high, swift, and muddy. We slept late, waiting for a break in the clouds. I was still sleeping when Justin woke up, pulled on his cold-wet running shoes, and jogged off in the rain to see another movie. What is it about these movies? I rolled over and pulled a book from my book bag. Try a little Socrates.

The rain was still drumming its slow song on our little faded dwelling when I heard Justin walk by through the wet, knee-high grass outside the tent, stoop down, and unzip the door. He had brought me a huge cinnamon roll that he had bought with his own money at a shopping center. He said he had already eaten his, so he settled back on his side of the tent with a satisfied smile to watch me make my way through layers of creamed sugar and white bread, black raisins and brown cinammon. It was an excellent thing, a kind of Father's Day communion between him and me.

But the rain continued, and the river was rising.

PART THREE

GREEN AND GOLDEN

And as I was green and carefree, famous among the barns
About the happy yard and singing as the farm was home,
In the sun that is young once only,
Time let me play and be
Golden in the mercy of his means,
And green and golden I was huntsman and herdsman, the calves
Sang to my horn, the foxes on the hills barked clear and cold,
And the sabbath rang slowly
In the pebbles of the holy streams.

—*"Fern Hill," Dylan Thomas*

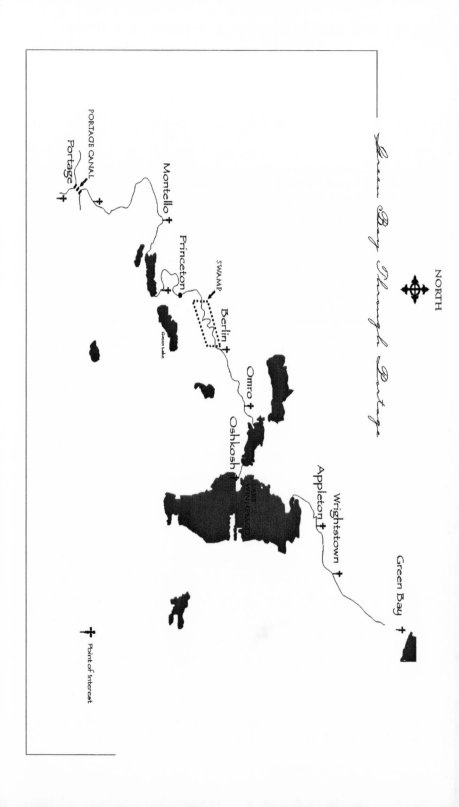

Up The Fox

The next day the river was running high, brown, and choppy, the current strong. But fortunately for us old Boreas the north wind had a notion to fly up the river that day and visit his relatives in the south; its cool bluster sent long rollers against the current, and we found that we could ride those rollers upriver, not without effort of course, but we had rested our arms for two days and were ready for the struggle.

We paddled under the high concrete bridge that rushed Interstate Highway 43 over our heads. Everybody in a hurry. Two miles up the chocolate river, we stopped in De Pere. There we passed through the first of many locks set up on the Fox River a century before to facilitate river traffic around the river's notorious rapids. Unfortunately for us, river traffic has been replaced by road and rail, so in recent years the government closed all the locks except the one at De Pere and one thirty miles upriver near Lake Winnebago. Our National Oceanic and Atmospheric Administration maps said the locks would open May 1 and close

October 31, and that the U. S. government would maintain a channel six feet in depth over that thirty-nine miles. It was not to be. The dams were still in place, maintaining river depths, but fifteen locks had been welded shut for several years.

The passage through this first lock was simple enough. We paid five bucks and paddled into a 144-foot-long by 35-foot-wide rectangle enclosed by stone walls on right and left and by iron gates on either end. Inside we hung on to ropes thrown over the wall while the lock master let in water from upriver until we rose to a level with the upper river. Then the gates opened and out we paddled, following four or five mallards into the main current of the river.

On either side of the river, elaborate lawns sloped steeply up to large, elegant homes. These were the homes of the wealthy, surrounded by carefully cultivated flowerbeds, terraces shored up by stone walls and planted with ferns and groundcover. We saw an occasional grounds crew hoeing flowerbeds or mowing grass, taking advantage of the break in the weather, but no children. Strange America: the larger the house, the fewer the children. Go to a poor neighborhood and you'll see all ages of children skateboarding, bouncing basketballs, running, shouting, playing the old traditional games of tag and hide-and-seek, inventing new games. Go to a rich suburb and where are they? Even the young ones must be holed up with their video games or developing relationships with television actors. Automatic games and artificial friendships.

Blue spruce, oaks, maples, ash trees, and a few birches shaded the long yards. We were largely beyond the firs and pines of the northwoods now and into the hardwood forests of central Wisconsin.

In time the houses gave way to green pastures and forested hills. A mist was blowing over the river floating the shoreside trees into vague colors, stirring them into the pastels of a distant barn and silo. The going was hard against the current. We learned to maneuver into eddies and take the quiet water near shore—trying to outfox the Fox.

Sometimes a mother duck would paddle nervously out of reeds or undergrowth trailing six to nine brown and yellow ducklings, all of them paddling like mad to stay with Mom. As we approached, the mother would quack and swing wide into our path while her brood ducked under overhanging limbs or huddled in shoreside grasses. If there was no shelter, the little ducklings would make a run for it, literally getting up on their big flat feet and flap-stepping across the water. From behind, they were little comics, Charlie Chaplins: all feet and wagging tails slapping along the surface ahead of us. If we got too close, the little ducklings would dive and pop to the surface like corks a few feet away.

Six miles from De Pere, we came upon our first closed lock, the Little Kaukauna Lock: a vestige of old industry gone to rust. We tied Natty Bumpo to a railing and climbed the steps for a look. There was a boarded-up house where the lockmaster used to live. The iron gates of the lock were closed and rusting, water streaming from a small opening. A sidewalk ran the length of the lock (about 150 feet) along mowed grass, and then descended in steps on the other side.

We jerked our packs out of the canoe, and eventually carted our whole heterogeneous mess up the rise and down to the water on the other side. Then we returned for Natty Bumpo, hoisted him out of the water, and carried him over. Using the ropes tied to each end, we lowered him over the handrail and into the water. Then we reloaded everything, snapped down the spray skirt, and pushed off. It was a process we would repeat many times in the days ahead. This artificial solution to river travel, the lock and dam system, had lost its usefulness, but its effects are, like old factories and toxic wastes, still with us.

We fought the rising current for five more miles until we came by a collection of houses and a handful of stores on our left called Wrightstown. The river was running fast, rising over the left bank and seeping up through the mown grass of a vacant lot that lay between an old stone warehouse and a couple of white houses. We steered the canoe up a water-filled depression beneath some trees that divided the vacant lot from the houses, then began setting up the tent in the vacant lot, trying to keep out of sight.

"There you fellows are!" A voice hailed us from the neighboring yard. A bearded man in dark blue work clothes ducked under the trees. I was afraid we were going to be ordered off private property, but on the contrary, he had come to make sure we were comfortable. He told us he had watched us canoe in from a restaurant window. His name was Bill Fritsch; a custom cabinet-maker, and his shop, Country Cabinets, was at the end of the yard. And a fine host he was.

"Here, come on up here to the high ground," he boomed, "The river's on the rise." He pointed to a spot in the back yard of his shop. "The bugs were so thick over at the park you could cut through them with a knife. They're not so bad here. And look, we'll start a fire. Them bugs don't like that." He walked into his shop and returned with two big boxes of wood scraps: oak, white pine, pieces of walnut and cherry. He threw the armful into a fire ring, poured on some thinner from a screw-top can, and threw a match. Whoosh! Flames erupted and the dry wood was merrily burning.

"That was easy," I said, thinking of former efforts to start fires after heavy rains.

"The bugs won't like it either," he repeated. He showed us where to fill our water jug, offered us the use of his shop restroom, and generally made us feel very welcome.

"What's the forecast?" I asked.

"The paper said rain tomorrow, very likely the next day, clearing on Friday, then more rain for the weekend."

I looked at the river.

We talked for a time. He had three sons, and now one was taking over the family business here in Wrightstown. I don't know the details of his relationships with his sons, but it seems to me a singularly satisfying thing to pass on years of hard work, a successful business, and valued skills to a son, to see the efforts of a lifetime carried on, especially when the product is something beautiful worked in wood. And how many sons take up satisfying jobs anymore? So many work in an industrial and service economy where the labor is tedious, empty, repetitive, devoid of personal meaning. A hundred years ago the tedious, repetitive work accomplished in sunlight and open air resulted in six-foot-high corn crops or acres of gold-bearded wheat: something beautiful, something you could eat, something your family could sell. Hard work, wise choices, and good rains gave promise not only of survival, but of personal accomplishment. Simplistic nostalgia you say?

Maybe. But hard realism will show you too that today's cashiers stand for hours both day and night under artificial lights punching in the numbers, punching in the numbers, punching in the numbers while repeating, "Is that everything?" "Is that everything?" to faceless consumers, and waiting hard for shift's end. Computer secretaries peck peck peck away at keyboards at all hours watching their lives tick down on the clock's digital numbers. Factory workers repeat their repetitions repeatedly and long for Friday, Tuesday, or Sunday—whenever their week ends, for we have shattered the natural order of night and day, and the sacred order of weekday and weekend. These droves of drones—and I am one—who undergird our service economy are goaded on by heavy threats and light raises. Where's the payoff in such work? Even in terms of crass economics, the cost is disproportionate to the benefit.

Old *Small Is Beautiful* E. F. Schumacher had it right when
he said, "to organise work in such a manner that it becomes
meaningless, boring, stultifying, or nerve-racking for the worker would be little short of criminal; it would indicate a greater
concern with goods than with people, an evil lack of compassion and a soul-destroying degree of attachment to the most
primitive side of this worldly existence." Right as Wrightstown,
but who will listen to the old prophets?

Night was rising like river water through the valley, drowning
the sunlit leaves of a nearby cottonwood. We threw more wood
on the fire, took off our boots and wool socks and propped them
near the fire. I brought out my wet sleeping bag and drooped
it over a log near the flames. The socks steamed—a rich smell
of wet soiled wool. Nearby, the river ran beneath an iron truss
bridge. We could hear the river pushing around the piers, and
see it seeping inch by inch up into the yard.

The fire crackled and snapped.

Two ducks and a dozen half-grown ducklings drifted up the
watery depression between Fritsch's yard and the vacant lot,
paddled past Natty Bumpo, and took cover in the bushes below
us, the mothers clucking, the young peeping.

We heard a train coming, rumbling along, occasionally blasting its triple horn. It roared by on the opposite side of the river
shaking the ground and shoving its way on through the darkness, three diminishing blasts at every crossing . . . three more
. . . three . . . no one on the train saw the ducks, no one heard
their young.

In time quiet returned. Our fire burned a small sphere of
warmth and a wider circle of light into the surrounding darkness. We stretched our feet to the warmth and watched the
flames cunningly work jewels into the sticks of cherry and walnut and oak.

Innocence and Ignorance

The morning was quiet and bright. After breakfast in the local café, we took a little walk up the steep, tree-lined streets. A
lovely little place of green grasses and gold sunlight. Children
came out of their yards to eye us, little boys and girls softly
calling each others' names, whispering and laughing and keeping a discrete distance. A braver boy whistled by on a bicycle,
whirled about and pedaled up the sidewalk behind us to where
a white wooden Lutheran church stood simply but beautifully overlooking a town where children still know each others'
names—but most of the inhabitants have felt compelled to find
work in nearby cities. But alas, must we do that? Isn't there
enough material for a livelihood and a rich life right here in
Wrightstown? Wendell Berry has been right for a long time, but
few have listened when he says, "We need to study and work
together to reduce scale, reduce overhead, reduce industrial dependencies; we need to market and process local products lo-
cally; we need to bring local economies into harmony with local
ecosystems so that we can live and work with pleasure in the
same places indefinitely."

It was a quiet, sunny day, one of those intermediate days when
the very air seems to be waiting for change. The river was running high and fast. In the night it had been tearing great trees
from their banks and floating them downriver: leafy, bobbing
islands that turned slowly in the eddies and passed us without
a sound. A herd of dairy cattle rested their heavy bodies in the
shade of a grove of trees, occasionally batting an ear or swishing
a tail. Redwinged blackbirds hung like black fruit from the tops
of water reeds, trilling loudly in defense of their territories. Tiny
wrens sang amplified music from overhanging limbs of maple,
ash, oak, and cottonwood. Cardinals pierced the air with sharp,

lilting whistles and flashed red through veils of green. Once in a long while a chattering kingfisher, blue and white, dropped from a limb and swung a sweeping arc toward the water and back up to its perch as if sprung from a boomerang bow. We were alone in Paradise.

Paddling quietly, paddling hard, we followed the bends of the flowing river, hugging one bank or another to avoid the current's growing strength, weaving in and out of the half-drowned trees, riding the backflowing eddies that swirled around bends or snags and carried us upcurrent a few yards. Between maneuvers, we talked of various things. Justin was amused that by drying my sleeping bag too near the fire, I had managed to disintegrate a section of its nylon sheathing into crisp little curls, exposing the white stuff inside. I reminded him that he had scorched a hole in one of his wool socks. But after the banter, we fell silent and listened to the current muttering dark things—but we didn't understand the language.

Suddenly I saw Justin pointing to the left bank. Above green grass and weeds: two large ears pointing straight up. I ruddered toward the bank. Closer. The ears turned in unison left, right, but they were facing into the forest not out toward the river. Closer. The canoe slightly bumped a log and the cream-speckled head of a fawn turned quickly through the grass looking for us. We froze in midstroke and let Natty nudge slowly along the log to within a few yards of a child-eyed fawn that now rose awkwardly on its long thin legs. The wet black nose quivered at the complexities of leaves and logs, rippling waters—and us, poised with raised and dripping paddles. It was all ears, all eyes, all legs, all wet black nose.

It stood there for several seconds "in the morn and liquid dew of youth," then turning, stepped delicately back into the low shadows of the high forest, waving a great paddle of a tail.

"Did you get a picture?" asked Justin.

No, I hadn't. In the power of the moment, it had never occurred to me. But then, memories are, for me, better than pictures.

If there was a Little Kaukauna Lock, which we had already passed, there was bound to be a Big Kaukana Lock. In fact, it was a series of locks one right after another stretching for over a mile around lumber mills and through the city of Kaukauna. The river widened first into a lake and then seemed to pass on either side of a big lumber mill: huge smokestacks, great piles of cut logs by the acre, a roar of furnaces and machinery, lumber trucks coming and going, whistles, beeps, smoke, steam, and a most foul stench in the air.

We tried the left side of the wood mill, but were stopped by a twenty-foot dam and a precipitous bank. We tied up, then pulled ourselves up the vertical bank by tree roots and limbs, coming out at the top where a road skirted the plant. We walked up the road to see if there was a way around the dam, but beyond the dam the river broke several ways over rocks and long low dams, torrents of rushing water everywhere.

Marquette says only that the going "becomes very difficult, both on account of the currents and of the sharp rocks which cut the canoes and the feet of those who are obliged to drag them, especially when the water is low." For us the water was high and the rocks were buried in a loud turmoil of broken and confused waters. Even the noises of the nearby lumber mill were subdued beneath the roar of these cataracts. We could see no possible way of dragging our canoe through that.

We climbed back down the bank, took our places, and swung back the way we had come, racing down past the lumber plant on the back of the running river until we had turned the corner around the plant and found our way back upriver on the other side. There we discovered a small cold stream. We paddled up it, portaged around a drainage pipe, then paddled on upstream until Natty began scraping rocks. Then we put on sandals to protect our feet and climbed into the clear water. Justin pulled, and I pushed our way along the running stream that ran through a rough forest of trees and brush and broken limbs. We stumbled over sharp rocks, pressed through cobwebs, ducked under overhanging limbs, lunged and shoved and pulled with all our might to force the loaded canoe over a fallen log, fell into icy pools up to our chests, slipped between boulders and over mossy rocks.

At length we came out of the forest near a six-foot dam with the water rushing over it. Two boys were playing in the water. They stood back and watched us unload Natty Bumpo for the long portage; the stream was too shallow to continue canoeing. We carried heavy packs on our backs and as much other stuff as our arms could hold up an asphalt road for about 400 yards, then dropped our packs beside some bushes and returned for more gear. After two more trips, I picked up the canoe and carried it the quarter mile to our first pile of equipment while Justin brought up the last of our stuff and dropped it on the grass with a sigh.

"This is going to be a rough portage," I said looking at the roadway sloping up and into trees.

"How far do we have to carry all this?" he asked.

"Maybe a mile."

"If that's one of your estimates, Dad, we'll be carrying all this crap all day long."

"Maybe a mile-and-a-half," I said.

"Back and forth, back and forth," he said. "We're making four trips each to get everything moved. We'll be walking for miles and miles."

It was a discouraging thought.

Just then, a man drove up in a pickup and asked if we needed a ride. My conscience was gone, washed away somewhere in that cold stream. Wet and bruised and panting, my sandal broken by the rocky stream, facing another mile or more of uphill portaging, I immediately said yes. So much for romantic commitments.

We loaded everything into Mr. Vanderhagen's pickup (Justin was pleased) and rode up the rather steep hill on a piece of twentieth-century machinery. And what a pleasure it was. Wretched portages for Joliet and Marquette, humming wheels for us.

Vanderhagen was the father of one of the boys we had seen at the six-foot dam. The boy had reported us to his father, and the man had come on over to lend a hand. More hospitality along the Fox River. He assumed I would want to go as much of the way as possible under our own power (fond idealist!), so he let us off near the Kaukauna Guard Lock, a lock made, I was told, to prevent the migration of fish-killing lamprey eels.

We thanked him, reloaded everything and shoved off again. From there to Lake Winnebago, we would be passing through a continuous series of towns and cities: Kaukauna, Little Chute, Kimberly, Appleton, Menasha, and Neenah—about sixteen linear miles of city paddling.

We made our way under bridges, and along a park where the river broke to our left over two dams. Heavy cables joined large floating balls warning boaters away from the surging waters. Pulling hard through the current, we were making little progress, so we cut for the left bank hoping for quieter water. As we stroked toward a line of apartments, we could see smooth water flowing rapidly over the dam and hear the eruption below as the river dropped six or eight feet and exploded into heaving waters. The current pulled us sideways toward the cables, drew us toward the dam like a sorcerer conjuring. But we were inexperienced and feared not. Having overcome the winds of Naubinway, the mighty waves of Seul Choix and Big Bay De Noc, how could a smooth current sweep us away? In simple ignorance, we waved our fawn-tail paddles through a river that was running dark and strong beneath us like a pack of hunting wolves.

Reaching the far shore, the current did not relax. We fought our way upriver. The air was warm and humid, the surface a swirl of daylight. Back patios and sliding-glass doors of the long row of apartments crept slowly by. Through doors and windows, we could see comfortable tables and chairs, microwaves, cabinets, stereos, deep couches, lamps, televisions. I felt the time warp: a three-hundred-year-old passage beside the mown lawns, barbeque grills, and lawn chairs of the comfortable world.

As we forced our way beyond the dams, we found slower water where the river spread or curled back on itself, or rounded a fallen log, but always the faster water would catch us again. I began longing to walk, to move over a stable surface that doesn't slide back with every step.

"How you doing, Justin?" I called.

"This is hard. Try to get in those eddies, Dad."

"I'm trying. There's just not enough of them."

A large snapping turtle sunning on a log watched us move by at a turtle's pace. Tiny ducklings paddled frantically away, their mother quacking out warnings.

We reached another lock. We hauled everything up a muddy bank, through the soggy, mucky trails of a forest park, over a slippery streamlet, through shoe-sucking mud, into a wet forest, to a sliver of grass at the far end of the lock. There we gave up hope for the day, and set up the tent, slid empty Natty into the water, and tied him to a tree.

A father was there with his eight-year-old daughter trying out her new fishing pole. He said they used to catch all kinds of fish here in his youth, but few fish remained. He showed his little girl how to bait the hook with a nightcrawler, how to punch the button on the reel, hold it, and let it go at just the right moment; bobber and worm flip-flopped out into the still water near the lock. We went back three or four more times for the rest of our gear. As we dropped the last of it near the tent, the young girl caught a five-or-six-inch smallmouth bass and was enormously pleased. So was her father. So were Justin and I. Much joy in a small fish.

They left us alone with the evening. Worn out and muddy, we stripped and waded into cold water, washed out our hair and soaked the mud away. A swarm of black tadpoles wriggled away over shallow rocks. Justin swam for a few minutes in the still, cold water, but I climbed up the bank. Somewhere boys were popping firecrackers and calling to each other through the twilight forest. It was Midsummer Night's Eve, the night Puck and Oberon and his fairies haunted the forest with their games. Mosquitoes floated out of the mist and began their attacks as I unzipped the tent. No fire tonight. No supper, though considering what we faced next, we should have eaten.

Charybdis

The morning was bright and calm. We were moving up a side canal, not the main river, so the current was no problem. But the portages were. We portaged over the Upper and Lower Combined Locks, over the Little Chute Lock and Guard Lock and the day was not yet old.

Once we stopped to have a close look at one of the spillways. We left Natty Bumpo in the side canal and walked over to the river. The spillway ran straight across, interrupted by concrete abutments. Several feet above our heads, the current ran smoothly, powerfully over a curved mossy surface, then plunged several feet below us like thick sheets of hard glass into thundering madness. Bright spray exploded, chaotic waves leapt and snapped back like a pack of mad wolves then shattered into the forward rush that churned under, swept around, boiled up, and smashed into contrary currents, erupting suddenly from the depths in geysers slapped down by the thundering weight of the charging current. Then it all hurried hysterically away.

"Remember Odysseus's first sighting of Charybdis?" I asked. Justin looked at me and nodded. We had read the tale of the roaring sea that had wrecked his ship and drowned his men. We watched the waters, fascinated. No man or canoe could live through that, we decided.

We came to the Cedars Lock and portaged around it.

The map said three miles to the next lock, a relief from portaging, but we were back in the main river now and the current was giving us trouble. We passed under a high bridge where the current near a pier swirled us half around; the sorcerer was waving a lethal wand. Private docks along shore had huge posts set like tripods on the upcurrent side to protect the walkways from drifting logs.

The river was swift, the sun was high and hot when we struggled past a great white ball of a building near the shore, as if an architect had decided his love for golf balls should find expression in building design. The current here was all but impossible. Justin took the prow rope ashore, stepping from rock to rock, pulling when he could, while I tried to keep the canoe from slamming into the shore-side rocks. It didn't work, and Justin climbed back in.

What we didn't know was that the Army Corp of Engineers had issued warnings that boaters needed to use extreme caution on the Lower Fox River because they were releasing a maximum amount of water out of Lake Winnebago due to recent rains that had caused flooding across large sections of Wisconsin. We cut for the opposite shore, where we used half-submerged tree limbs and fallen logs to break the current. We passed Peabody Park on our right, a pleasant stretch of grass and trees backed by apartment buildings.

Portage again. This was the Lower Appleton Lock. Men were

mowing grass along the lock as we carried our heavy packs up the embankment, along the lock, and down to the water again. The foreman came over and told us we weren't allowed on government property. I nodded and told him we'd move on. We piled everything back into Natty Bumpo again, but the map said our next portage was no more than a half mile away around a sharp bend, so we failed to snap down the spray skirt and failed to stretch the bungi cords over our packs. Midsummer fools.

As soon as we passed the quiet water near the lock, we could see the warning cable and its great floating balls to our right. Not far beyond the cable was another raging spillway. On our left the current poured round a sharp bend and into trees. We paddled fast but made little progress along the rocky shore overgrown with flooded trees. The current was too much for us. We began grabbing limbs and pulling ourselves along. Long-legged spiders whose webs decorated dead limbs would drop into our boat, but we had no time to scoop them out. I paddled while Justin pulled us hand over hand along a leafy limb; when he released it, I grabbed it and he paddled. We thought about getting out and pulling, but the water looked too deep and swift. Neither of us had remembered to put on our life preservers.

Finally, I decided to cut across to the inside of the river bend where the water would be slower. Justin was skeptical. He wasn't sure we could make it across without hitting the warning cable. Then the blind god Ignorance came by to advise me. "If we hit the cable, just grab it and we'll pull ourselves to shore," I said. Justin shrugged, and off we ran, the current sweeping us steadily sideways toward the cable. The spell was strong now, the sorcerer had us in his grasp, and the wolves were coming.

The iron warning cable catches Justin in the waist. He tries to duck under it, but the force of the current tips the canoe into the oncoming current, filling it immediately with water. I tell Justin to jump, hoping the canoe will right itself and we can save it, but my end swings round and I hit the cable. The canoe leans back into the water and I jump to avoid completely capsizing. Cold water engulfs me. I bob to the surface and see Justin holding onto the prow wondering what to do. I swim over with only one thought on my mind: save our canoe. "Grab it and let's swim it to shore," I command as I swim quickly around him, reach for the prow, and begin kicking through the water. He's behind me, holding the gunwale. With our free arms and feet, we begin stroking and kicking hard for shore. But our canoe is heavy with water and leaning into the current. A clothes duffel floats by us. We scissor kick through the water; I realize I still have my canvas shoes and wool socks on my feet, but I have no time to take them off. I glance at the rapidly passing shore; we seem to be making no progress. Then I notice the warning cable that has capsized us. It looks to be fifty yards away and receding, which can only mean that the spillway is near. Rocks and broken slabs of concrete on shore are flowing past, behind them more distant trees and buildings rotate by in slow motion. I let go of the canoe and see the rifle in its case come bobbing by between us, the muzzle end sticking upright in the moving water. It is my son David's rifle, and I want to save it, but there is no time. I look at Justin who has one hand on the gunwale, the other stroking for shore, and for the first time I feel a sudden emotion, not fear, but a great sadness sweeps over me. I realize that he is, perhaps, a minute away from certain death.

"Forget the canoe!" I say. "Let's go for shore!" Immediately I feel his hand on my shoulder as he struggles to go by me; his stroke forces me under. When I kick back up I see him swimming hard for the shore rocks some twenty or thirty yards away. But I can't bear to lose Natty Bumpo and with him the remainder of our trip. Before I leave him, I reach up and jerk loose his yellow prow rope, drape it over my shoulder and begin swimming for shore. Out of the corner of my eye, I see the approaching con-crete abutments of the spillway. I put my face in the water and swim for all I'm worth for the nearest rock, the rope playing out over my shoulder as I kick my water-logged shoes. I turn my head and suck the air. My heart is pounding.

I near a rock and see I am being swept past it. Beyond it the shore sweeps back and away so that I doubt I can reach it before being washed over the spillway. I stroke madly for this single stone of refuge, consciously giving up on the rope, letting it float away. My heart is pumping, my breath comes in gasps. I think Justin has made it to shore, but I've lost sight of him. My fingertips just reach the jagged rock as the current pulls me by. I clutch it with desperate hands, but the river pulls my feet and torso downcurrent, twisting me onto my back and dragging me off the rock; pieces of finger skin rip off on the rock as I'm pulled under. I throw up my head and see a watery shadow of my son on the rocks above me reaching out, "Dad! Dad!" he shouts. I grab for him and he grabs for me. Our hands clasp and he holds on tight as I kick with all my might and pull on his arm until I reach the rocks and struggle ashore.

We both stand up panting hard and turn to see Natty Bumpo, our old friend, listing to leeward, floating sideways, surrounded by a menagerie of floating packs, duffels, paddles, tarp, blue camera case, all moving together in slow motion toward the crashing waters of the spillway. It is a long and desolate look we give our old companion as he slips over the curved surface and disappears. Then we run—over the rocks and along that back-swerve of the bank and down toward the spillway. Justin sprints ahead, I come gasping behind. By the time we pass the spillway dam, Natty is flipping over and over and over and over, caught like a wounded fish in a backwave hydraulic that won't let him go. He has been washed clean, not a single item left in-side. All his packs, his spray skirt, everything gone beneath the thundering waves as he flops over and over and over, unable to break free of the crashing waves. Then we catch sight of one of our stainless steel coffee cups floating down the river. Something else bobs to the surface and we leave the spillway and speed down the shore, panting, hoping to retrieve something.

Justin far outstrips me, dashing ahead, dodging through trees, ducking beneath limbs, then jogging along the stone wall that borders Peabody Park. He sees my maple-wood paddle caught in tree branches near shore, but he has no time to stop, the canoe is the first priority and it seems to have suddenly leapt free of the waves and is drifting downstream, its nose just above the surface.

By the time I pass the trees, I'm gasping for air and slow to a fast walk. The canoe still looks to be in one piece. Justin sees it and shouts. It seems the current might bring it within thirty or forty yards of shore. I see Justin run along the wall, then dive off and swim for the canoe. I walk fast along the bank, panting hard, hoping he isn't swimming too far out for his strength.

He reaches the prow and grabs on. I see him gasping for air. For a minute or two, Justin and Natty Bumpo float together, his head and Natty's nose to nose, floating in slow motion. Then he grabs the rope and swims for shore, but he is too tired to keep hold of the rope; he lets it go and barely makes it into the shallows, panting heavily. I begin running again, passing him and moving on downshore to a little promontory on the other side of a boat ramp. Kicking off my shoes, I jump in, wade out up to my neck, then swim for the passing canoe. I reach the rope Justin managed to stretch out and begin to backpedal toward shore, swimming on my back, occasionally righting myself and reaching for the bottom with exploratory toes; I am exhausted, but must keep swimming. At last my feet discover mud. I swim-walk into waist-deep water and grab hold of the rope; it slowly tightens as the weight of the water-filled canoe begins to swing round. Justin soon joins me, and he and I, four hands on a tight rope, drag Natty Bumpo slowly to shore.

Heaving and pulling, we struggle to get the canoe onto the boat ramp, tipping out water until we have it safely out of reach of the sorcerer's power. Natty Bumpo has survived unbroken. Every thwart and seat is still in place.

But all else is gone. I'm devastated and relieved at the same time: grateful for my son's life, but overwhelmed by the thought that our trip is over. Even the paddles are gone; when we went back to the trees where Justin had seen my maplewood paddle, it had already washed away. How can we search for whatever equipment has managed to escape the pounding waves and sucking currents without paddles? Then Justin catches sight of one of our big Duluth packs floating toward us; it is the lightest of the three: the pack with our sleeping bags—and fortunately, that morning we had strapped Justin's clothes duffel into the pack to save us portaging trips. Then a life preserver comes floating by. Justin grabs it, straps it on, and uses its buoyancy to float out after more supplies. But what will we do without paddles, without our food pack, which had the last of our money, how can we continue without a tent, with no cooking equipment, no wood saw or axe, no camera, no book bag with all my notes, no fishing equipment, no food. With one slick wave, the magician has made it all vanish.

Newspaper Reporters

Some people had come down to shore to watch us retrieving odds and ends: a rope, both coffee mugs—not much coming our way. I told Justin to grab everything possible, and I would search the shore downstream for our paddles. I hurried away down a little path that followed the river along a forested slope. I kept stopping to peer through flooded trees at the passing current. Nothing. I went on, coming out of the forest and making my way through back yards, still hoping. But it was not to be. The only thing I found was a rain jacket caught on a tree limb. I struggled out neck-deep through the cold, fast-flowing water, clutching the rough bark of a long limb that lay in the water and grabbed the jacket. The sleeve was punctured in several places, but it was better than no rain jacket at all.

I was deeply discouraged, mad at myself for my foolishness regarding the warning cable, trying to come up with some plan to retrieve enough gear to continue our journey. The clever Odysseus always found a way, but I was not Odysseus.

By the time I walked back to Peabody Park, Justin had pulled a few more items ashore, most importantly our second big pack, the Rude Mechanicals with the cooking gear, saw, axe, medical kit, and boots. The tent too had floated down, so our little domed home was still with us, though its second skin, the fly, was gone for good. And gone was Natty's spray skirt, and my clothes duffel.

I paced the shore. An attractive woman in shorts and a sleeveless blouse was sitting on the grass watching. She looked up and asked if she could help. "Do you know anyone with a motorboat?" I asked. "We need to get out there and find our paddles." She said no. "Is there a sporting goods store around here?" She didn't know of any. Of course that was pointless, since I had no money.

Justin was pulling wet sleeping bags from the pack, stretching them out to dry. "What about that man we met downriver?" he asked.

I remembered Mr. Fritsch the cabinet maker, but by the time he could arrive, any gear that didn't catch in a tree would be washing over the next spillway, and then the next, and next.

The woman stood up. "What about the newspaper?" she aked. "Maybe they could help out somehow."

A good idea. I said I'd talk to a newspaper man if they'd help get us restarted on this trip. I had avoided publicity, but now we needed help. She said she'd give them a ring; she lived in the apartments next to the park. Her name was Mary. She deserves a good deal of credit for whatever else we accomplished on our trip; without her, the trip would have ended ingloriously in Peabody Park. After making the call, she brought us back a drink of cold water, wondering if there was anything else she could do.

Within a half hour, a reporter from the Appleton *Post-Crescent* and a photographer drove up. While the young woman with the camera smiled beneath her mechanical eye and snapped pictures, Steve Wideman the reporter asked a couple questions. I told him I'd be glad to fill him in, but right now I needed to find any equipment we could. He was not what I expected from a reporter. No rapid-fire questions. No rush to acquire a story. A heavy-set man with a quiet voice and a gentle way, he immediately offered to drive me around to the spillway to have a look around. Just then Justin spotted my book bag floating down the river. Wideman would later write: "For more than a half-mile the blue canvas backpack managed to stay afloat Thursday in the Fox River, despite raging currents and a cargo of water-soaked books, navigational maps and notebooks. The backpack seemed determined to reach its owner." And reach me it did. Justin splashed out into the current and brought it back.

I was pleased. I opened up the plastic liner. The books were wet, but they were all there: a Bible, the *Odyssey,* Greene's novel, *Huckleberry Finn,* Cliff Jacobson's canoe book, but most importantly, the maps. They needed drying, but I thought we could save them.

Wideman drove me up to the spillway. Nothing. Then he

drove me several miles downriver to the next spillway. Again nothing. I asked about sporting goods stores, though I told him I had no money. He offered to drive me out to a sporting goods store in a mall on the outskirts of town, and wondered if he could talk the management of the store into helping us out. "They do quite a bit of business with our paper," he said. It sounded good to me. Luckily he was spared this difficult negotiation when I discovered a credit card in my soaked billfold.

As we drove several miles to the mall, Wideman punched on a little tape recorder and began asking his questions. We fell into conversation. He had been a baker once, but had decided he wanted to go into journalism. Though he had six kids, he, like me, had gone back to college. He had earned his degree and was now a working reporter. I liked this man a lot.

At the store I bought two long green paddles, a couple pairs of slacks for me, socks, two 3/4 inch foam sleeping mattresses, a life preserver, and a nylon tarp to replace our lost tent fly.

On our way back to Peabody Park, Wideman stopped in at the newspaper office so I could call home. When I reached my wife, she was worried sick. Two hours before, she had received a call from the Appleton police reporting that a camera had been found floating down the river with her phone number on the case. I told her we were fine and we had every intention of pressing on.

At the newspaper office, Wideman introduced me to our next benefactor, the night editor Bernie Peterson, who, when told of our accident, immediately offered help. (Where do they find newspaper men like these?) He said the forecast was rain, wouldn't we like to spend the night at his place? We could throw everything in the dryer, take a bath, have a good night's sleep, and be ready to go the next day. An offer I could not refuse.

By the time Wideman, Peterson, and I had returned to the park, Justin had managed to retrieve our last big pack, the Duluth foodpack had somehow survived the spillway turbulence and come floating down, far out in the river, barely an inch above the surface. All those cans of soup, those oranges, bagels, peanut butter, jam, and our money, must have been churning around and around in the spillway turbulence for almost two hours before it finally kicked free and came floating downriver with just its eyebrows above water. Justin didn't think he had the energy to swim out a hundred yards and drag it back, even with his life preserver on, so he hurried along the bank hoping the current would bring it closer. But it stayed out there.

Then a guy on a jet ski came buzzing up the river—the only jet ski we'd seen all day. Justin started shouting and dancing and pointing at the pack. The guy got the message. He tried to pull the water-logged pack onto the back of the jet ski, but it almost capsized him. He tried again and again, finally managing to prop the end of it on the back of his little boat. He held the pack with one hand and steered his jet ski with the other, slowly chugging into shore. Even a river demon is not beyond redemptive uses.

All three tough Duluth packs had survived, our plastic liners had let in a little water, but our equipment was saved. Justin had also found one paddle. We loaded everything in Bernie Peterson's little Ford Escort and tied Natty Bumpo on top, then drove through the tree-shaded streets of Appleton to his home, a white house in a quiet neighborhood.

He showed us to our rooms, a room for Justin, a room for me: old-fashioned beds of dark wood, thick mattresses, simple covers; clean oak floors; a black-and-white picture of his parents on the lamp stand; he gave us shirts and socks, knowing we could never return them; he took us into his carpeted living room and showed us how to use the television; he recommended his deep hot tub with its water jets, took us into the basement and helped us load soggy clothes and sleeping bags into his dryer, gave us directions to a nearby hamburger place, then hurried back to work, leaving the house to us.

America, America. Who would have thought such hospitality and trust still possible? After our losses, it was a young woman and a couple of newspaper men who handed us hope.

Twilight had settled into the town as Justin and I walked up the shadowy sidewalks toward the hamburger place. I grabbed a handful of maple leaves and ripped them off the limb. I picked up a piece of bark and rubbed its texture. I slapped Justin's shoulder as we walked side-by-side. I felt the hard sidewalk meeting my feet with reliable solidity. On my newspaper route at home I have a redbud tree whose bark I lay a hand on every night as I walk by it. It is to me a testimony of simple reality, which on an atomic level may be strange and complex, subject to the vagaries of quantum mechanics, but for me, that curved limb, its rough bark in winter, its pink-red buds in spring, its heavy, leafy thickness in summer, is a steady reminder of solid "thereness," and the pleasure of contact between my hereness and its thereness. Justin, beneath my hand. Here. Now. Not lost over the slippery road of an unforgiving river, but still here, now, with me.

A teenaged boy had died that afternoon, lost in the maw of the nearby Wolf River. Another boy (also named Justin) had drowned swimming in a rock quarry the day before; Steve Wideman had covered that story too. My foolishness had handed my own Justin into the river's power, but somehow it had been his hand that clasped tight to mine and pulled me from its current. He had told the reporter, "I just did what needed to be done."

We returned to Peterson's house and took turns bathing in his hot tub. Fed, clean, and safe, we turned on the television and there was Paul Newman as Rocky Graziano in the movie *Somebody Up There Likes Me.*

Athene Or Proteus?

I don't know what time Bernie Peterson came home from working the night shift, but he was up before we were. He took us
out for breakfast at Mary's Family Restaurant and fed us eggs
and sausage, pancakes and orange juice. He was himself a man
who enjoyed adventures. Steve Wideman had told me he had
committed himself to visiting by bicycle the hometowns of his
entire night staff. He had already accomplished most of those
trips, traveling up and down Wisconsin's country roads and
bike trails rain or shine. In a culture increasingly cut off from
the natural world by speeding machines, this is a welcome remedy: to move by muscle power over old country roads.

He spoke of his love for these towns along the Fox River:
they have the feel of small towns, but certain advantages—being all strung together—of the larger city. Unemployment is low.
Educational opportunities are good.

He talked of strangers. Wisconsin, he said, had welcomed
immigrant populations for over a hundred years. They had built
their communities across the state: Norwegians, Icelanders,
Poles, Germans, many others, and now the Hmong people from
Laos. Each in turn had taken up the responsibilities of being
Americans: Wisconsin-Americans.

After breakfast, we loaded up our gear in his car. But before leaving for the river, I told Bernie I'd forgotten to buy Justin a hat; with his sensitive skin, he needed one. Mr. Peterson
obliged, driving us to an Army surplus store downtown. When
I walked up to the door, a sign said the owner would be back
soon. Soon? We waited a half hour, standing under an overhang
in the rain, feeling our imposition on Peterson's time. At last the
man returned and we made our purchases: a hat for Justin, a
rain jacket too, and flexible poles and long shoestrings to rig up
a fly for the tent.

Peterson drove us six miles above Peabody Park and let us off above the Menasha Lock. We were skipping the dangerous Appleton Locks where, we found out later, the 1973 group of canoers, who were making the three-hundred-year-anniversary voyage commemorating Joliet and Marquette's voyage, were caught in similar currents. One of their canoes almost washed over an Appleton spillway, saved only by a rope thrown over a railroad trestle.

Wideman was there to see us off. We waved good-bye to our good hosts and shoved away. The rain returned, soaking through our rain jackets, wilting our hat brims over our ears. Roughened by rain and darkened by low-running clouds, the river lost its reflective polish. Natty Bumpo's spray skirt was gone, so the rain soon gave us an inch of water in the bottom of the canoe, and we had forgotten to buy sponges. As we fought the current around tethered sail boats and protruding docks, we saw St. Michael the Archangel watching us from a nearby yard, painted eyes on the river, plaster wings half-folded.

Three rain-washed miles of bucking the strong current brought us to the choppy waters of Lake Winnebago, Wisconsin's largest inland lake: thirty miles long and five-to-ten-miles wide, but rather shallow and given to capsizing small boats in sudden winds. We planned to follow the west shore about fifteen miles to the city of Oshkosh, then take the Upper Fox River through Lake Butte Des Morts and on up the Fox until we reached the canal that was supposed to connect the Upper Fox to the Wisconsin River. This was an old passage the Indians had been making since the ice age. The first Interstate.

But our immediate goal was a little island that our limp, wet map told us was some ten miles away. The rain passed downriver. A general haze eased in after the rain, fading the shores that circled vaguely away. A steady breeze in our faces chopped up the waves and kept us rocking and working the paddles.

We stopped in the town of Neenah, bought sponges at a hardware store, and noticed our pictures and story all over the front page of the *Post-Crescent*: "WILD RIDE: Father and son fight for their lives in roaring Fox River." We stopped a few minutes to watch the terrific currents pouring over the dam. People had gathered to watch the spectacle.

It was a day of elastic distances and strange gods. For an hour or two a heavy haze condensed our world into a rough circle of broken waves. A barren, rocky isle with a single leafless tree appeared out of the mist. White seagulls perched on its branches to one side, black cormorants on the other side of the same tree. Both tree and allegorical birds soon faded into fog.

By the middle of the afternoon the wind had weakened and the haze drifted away, spreading the horizon over faraway hills that rolled away south beyond the lake and beneath occasional collections of spent thunderclouds.

Justin was cloud reading. Pointing to a long line of yellow-white clouds along the southern horizon, he said, "That's Dad taking it easy while I do all the paddling." I could see the semblance of a man lying on his back, a Rip Van Winkle beard flowing over a massive stomach. "Slander," said I. Justin laughed and remarked on how my stomach was growing.

Within a few strokes of death the day before, and here he was making jokes. What strange beings we are. But what can you do? Go on muscling over the choppy waves that keep slapping you around, and laugh when you can. It was good to feel the muscles at work, to feel the breath coming and going, to watch the distances contracting and spreading away; it was good to be laughing with the young man before me whose life was still before him.

Three hours later we discovered that the island we had hoped to camp on was posted with no trespassing signs. Though Joliet and Marquette never had to deal with No Trespassing signs, the Indian tribes of their day were constantly claiming and counter-claiming territory. The great Sioux federation was pushing eastwards, driving the Hurons back into Lake Michigan. The Iroquois federation was raiding westwards, shoving tribes like the Mascoutens (the modern Potawatomies) before them.

After years and years of emigration, resettlement, and further emigration, the Mascoutens finally took a stand somewhere in this area. In time, their old enemies the Iroquois found their fortified village and laid siege. But the Mascoutens had stored up supplies of corn, squash, and smoked meat. As winter came on, it was the Iroquois who went hungry. At length, the Mascoutens offered to settle a treaty with their enemies; they invited the Iroquois warriors to a feast of boiled corn to seal the agreement. Armed Iroquois gathered to the great cooking pots set up in the forest outside the village stockade and filled themselves on the good corn—which had been poisoned.

As the poison began its work, the Mascoutens, or the Fire Nation, as they were called, ran out of their fortifications and ran down the gut-wracked Iroquois, spearing and hatcheting and knifing. Some elements of the Mascoutens still live in the area; the Iroquois never returned to the scene of their gastronomic defeat.

Disgruntled by the No Trespassing signs, we angled back toward the mainland. But the shore was fully housed, streets and cars and homes appearing everywhere through the trees. No camping place there. As we neared land, we came upon a beautiful girl with golden hair keeping watch over two younger boys who were playing among the rocks and pebbles. "It's Athene herself," I told Justin as we approached, "here to guide us to a proper campground."

"No it's not," responded my contrary son, "It's old Proteus come to trick us."

"Proteus!" I laughed. "That old grey-bearded sea god. Look at her! She's gorgeous!"

He was looking all right, but he refused, as usual, to give in. "Proteus is a shape-shifter, remember?"

"But Justin, look at her; she's a Greek goddess for sure. Even Proteus couldn't make himself so beautiful. Let's ask her for a place to camp."

We paddled close and called out to her. She cast a look of radiance upon us, listened for a moment, then pointed far away at a distant water tower. "Over there!" she called. "There's a park over by that water tower."

"You see?" I said. "Athene."

"Proteus," said Justin, still glancing back for another look at her.

An hour or two later, we were moving toward a dock beneath the water tower. Boys were shooting baskets at a nearby school building. Seven or eight men sat on two docks fishing. They sat silent, unsmiling, watching our approach. We paddled in, maneuvering to avoid their fishing bobbers in the water. As we coasted near the dock, a grey-haired Indian in a lawn chair said severely, "You can't come in here."

"What?"

"You can't come in here."

"We're just looking for a place to camp."

"You can't camp here."

"Why not?"

"This is a prison."

"A prison."

"That's right. A reform school. You've got to move on out."

I watched the eyes of two of the grim watchers; they took a long, yearning look at our canoe as we pulled away. One of them pointed down the coast. "You can camp over there, on the other side of those trees," he called. No one else moved. The grey-hair stared out to sea.

I decided we'd move farther down the coast than the man had suggested.

Justin was laughing. "Proteus! You see? It was old Proteus after all! She said a park under the water tower. Some park!"

Asylum Park, actually. We found it later on the soggy map.

Late that afternoon, we paddled through swimming geese into a bay enclosed by the Oshkosh City Park, a large expanse of green grass and trees with shelter houses. A small train hooted its way over narrow tracks. Men and women and children were visiting the small zoo, or paddle-boating on a little lake, or lining up before tiny concession stands. I doubted they would allow us to set up our tent, so we waited till after dark and pitched between a tree and the backside of a shelter house, rigging the black, nylon tarp as a makeshift fly. Black was good, melting us into the shadows.

Oshkosh

Saturday came in with a northwest breeze running through clear sunlight and over the wet books and maps that we had laid out along the dock. But, as Hilaire Belloc put it, "the chief anxiety of a civilised man was spreading over me like the shadow of a cloud over a field of corn in summer": lack of money. We were on our last twenty and we weren't halfway through our journey. So I left Justin to watch our goods and walked into town to find a bank. The bank's main lobby was closed, so I took my place in a line of cars (two-legged anachronism that I was) and eventually found myself standing beside a drive-up stall. I used my credit card to order three-hundred borrowed bucks. A man must eat.

I found a hardware store along the old brick highrises of the aging downtown area and bought metal snap hooks for the new tent fly. When I returned to the park, a fullscale union picnic was rocking to taped music over loudspeakers in the shelter house next to our tent. An emcee held a microphone to his cigar and announced, "First off, I want to make clear this is a UNION party, not Rockwell's. This is Rockwell International Number Two-Nine-One. Rockwell Corporation's got nothing to do with this." A hundred men and women were milling about, or setting up tables, or ladling out pork and beans, mounds of cole slaw, and potato salad onto paper plates, or lining up next to the smoking grills to pick up hot dogs and hamburgers, or standing in the longer line near a beer truck.

The emcee introduced a local politician. "Now you all know we got to get them Republicans out of office; they're no friends to working people. And you all know this fellow here. He's going to do just that and wants to have a few words with you." He handed over the microphone, but most people seemed more intent on the beer and hot dogs. He was a congenial fellow, offering us words of stunning banality. The beans were better.

I settled down on the grass to thread two thumbs I'd cut off onto the black nylon tarp we'd bought to replace our tent fly— leather thumbs actually, cut from a pair of gloves. These leather thumbs, I hoped, would hold the flexible rod I'd bought at the Army Surplus in Appleton. By the time I was done, a middle-aged lady and her husband had walked over and handed Justin and me two paper plates filled with beans, slaw, and hamburgers. Midwest hospitality.

That night we walked into town and ate at a Country Kitchen. The old regulars sat alone or in pairs or threes, lingering long over coffee and cigarettes. They were the poor who still lived in apartments or houses in this old section of town. An elderly woman with thin, stringy hair and watery eyes stared out at passing headlights; a man with open sores across his scalp sipped coffee and mumbled to himself. Two heavy women sat trading words with a younger man whose hollow eyes and long stubbled jaw haunted the table.

I found the restroom where I attempted to wash my eye glasses. While wiping them dry with a paper towel, a nosepad dropped off my glasses and fell to the floor. I began searching the tile floor when a man walked over to the urinal, made his peace with nature, and stepped over to the sink. He was tall, with a shock of grey-black hair combed straight back. He knew I wasn't one of the regulars.

"Where you from?" he asked.

"Kansas," I said, my eyes scanning the floor.

"Kansas?" He shoved his glasses up a very short nose with his middle finger. "Ain't that somewheres up in Canada?"

"No, it's down south." I stooped over searching the square-inch tiles and the net of grout channels between. I needed that nosepad. How could I wear my glasses without it?

"Ka-a-anzuz. Is that a country or something?" He shuffled a broken-down brownleather shoe back and forth across the tiles, as if vacuuming for my nosepad. "Ka-AN-zuz. I heered of it. It's a city, ain't it? A city."

"No, it's a state. South of Nebraska." I was beginning to feel the desperation of broken glasses. They had survived winds and waves, even the plunge into the "raging" Fox River, but now to lose the nosepad in an Oshkosh men's room.

"Naw, it's a CITY. I heered of it."

"Well, there is a city, Kansas City, but it's also a state, south of Nebraska."

"Nebrasky," he was staring up at ceiling tiles. "I think I been there before. All them faces corved up the side of that there mountain."

"I think that's South Dakota."

"Ain't Nebrasky?"

"No, I . . . Here it is!" I picked it up and bid my geographer good-bye..

After waiting out irregular rains, we left Oshkosh. Heavy, erratic waves kept us dancing along the shore until we turned up the Fox and passed into Lake Butte Des Morts (Hill of the Dead) with wind and wave behind us. Then it was a long haul along hills bordered with houses where the living piece out their days with television while through their picture windows the lake sparkles and blows and changes through blues, greens, greys, indigos, and into black.

A man is strapped to a big colorful kite and is being pulled along by a motorboat a hundred feet above the lake. He is floating high up in the blue air, attached to the boat by a long, curving rope. As we struggle up the lake, he floats away above the weaving motorboat, attached to his life by that single cord. The Greeks pictured Fate as three old women: one spun out the cord of life; one measured it; one clipped it off. His cord was still attached; so, apparently, was ours.

Rush Houses

We searched through inlets choked with masses of floating reeds, the "wild oats" of Marquette's journal, trying to find the mouth of the elusive Fox. But every inlet we paddled up, every possible river mouth, eventually snapped shut with toothy reeds. Acres of head-high reeds everywhere, floating in dense mats along shore and out across the shallow lake. The afternoon wore away. We circled back out on the lake and headed for a line of trees that extended far out into the water. Beneath the line of trees was a gravel road, on either side of the road, lakewater and more reeds. We climbed out of the canoe and walked the road until we spotted a small red buoy beyond the reeds on the far side of the road. At last. But how did those French canoes find their way into the right opening?

We uprooted reeds, broke off some limbs of bushes and trees, and laid them across the gravel road. Then we pulled and shoved loaded Natty Bumpo up onto our reedy blanket, pushed him over the covered gravel, and into the water on the other side. Such genius.

The river channel meandered slowly back into Wisconsin, passing through miles of wild rice. Wherever the ground rose a little, trees hung their foliage over the water. The river here was wide and the current slow, so our progress was correspondingly good, an easy-going passage through smooth, green water—a long way from the wide-open Great Lakes; and still a long way from the "Mes-sipi."

Next day, the river was high, flooding through bank-side silver maples into long-grassed pastures. Our new paddles, long T-handled paddles with gaudy gold shafts and green plastic paddles, were not as efficient as those we had lost. We christened these new walking sticks Fe-Fi and Fo-Fum, but climbing this giant green beanstalk of a river was slow going.

The world was green. We passed Hoger's Bayou, a channel that lost itself in two-to-three miles of marsh and reeds. It's a good thing we had a map or we'd easily have slipped into the wrong channel and lost our way. This green, beanstalk river sprouts a thousand twisting branches guarded at intervals by solitary, spear-headed blue herons that stand on fallen logs or ankle-deep in jade water cocking a bright eye at our slow progress. If we came close, they flapped laboriously away, shrieking their hatred. We passed stagnant backwaters where brown waters went black beneath thousands of silver maples. Unseen ducks clucked to unseen ducklings from behind masses of reeds. An eagle lifted heavily from a tall dead tree and flapped away. Once we glimpsed a fawn plunging and splashing away through water and reeds, and a red-tailed hawk beat her way out of thick foliage from which a squirrel peered out to scold her passage and ours.

Mile after mile. Grey, cool skies. Glad to be out in the wide world; glad to be fairytaling up the magic river with my son. A woodchuck scrambled along a stone wall, a palomino pony swished its tail, sleepy-eyed in summer's sunlight.

We passed under a bridge and spotted a ramshackle house that served as a bar to the little hodgepodge of houses called Eureka. The sign over the bar read, Happy Jack's; young Jack must have settled down here after the giant's money ran out.

We tied up to an electrical pole and walked over to the bar. Inside, three or four people were talking with the woman who ran the place. She stepped behind the counter to take our order, then returned to her friends. Justin spotted a pool table in the back room. I'm a lousy pool player, but that day Justin was worse. After two defeats and the end of his Coke, he agreed to go, under protest—declaring with absolute confidence that he would destroy me the next time we played. I have competitive sons.

Fourteen miles upriver brought us to the little town of Berlin, the former fur and leather capital of Wisconsin. This was the approximate location of Joliet and Marquette's last stop among known friends; there was a mission here among the Maskouten Indians. Three tribes were gathered there at the time: Miamis, Maskoutens, and Kikabous. The tribes had pinned their reed huts on the heights above the river. These houses made of rushes, says Marquette, "are no great shelter against the wind, still less against the rain when it falls in torrents. The advantage of this kind of cabins is that they can roll them up, and carry them easily where they like in hunting-time." They are, of course, all gone now, vanished in the winds and rains, as all the present homes of wood and brick and stone will someday vanish too: "Soon shall oblivion's deepening veil/ Hide all the peopled hills you see."

Marquette was pleased to find a tall cross planted in the midst of the village "adorned with several white skins, red belts, bows and arrows, which the good people had offered to the Great Manitou (such is the name they give to God) to thank him for having had pity on them during the winter, giving them plenty of game when they were in greatest dread of famine."

Joliet called the chiefs together. He told them that he was sent by the French governor to discover new countries, and that he needed two guides to take them forward. He gave them presents and awaited their response. The chiefs responded "very civilly" and presented the Frenchmen with a reed mat to serve as a bed on their voyage, and provided two Miamis as guides, for though the French knew the direction of a river "emptying into the Missisipi," they had been told that "the way is so cut up by marshes and little lakes, that it is easy to go astray, especially as the river leading to it is so covered with wild oats, that you can hardly discover the channel." Yes indeed.

Justin and I had no guide but our maps, and I was concerned we could easily mistake a side-channel in the flooded marshes for the river channel. As we left Berlin the next morning, I tried to keep track of the river bends: U-bend to the right, stay out of channel straight ahead, ease left a half mile avoiding channels on right and left, curve right, keep to left channel. But I found it impossible to gauge how far we had traveled, and once lost, the map was largely useless. We tried following the current, keeping within the path of the slow-moving water, but as the river spread out on either hand into wide marshes, the current slowed and disappeared. We were in a broad lake of wild rice with intertwining channels and groves of silver maple trees that stood on little mossy islands or in flooded acres of quiet water.

The White River Marsh covers well over thirty square miles, more during flood time. The White River (more creek than river) snakes slowly into it from the northwest and the Puchyan River from the southeast, but we could not distinguish what was river and what was standing water. We would paddle up a likely opening that eventually filled in with reeds, and then return, hoping to find the original channel. False leads beckoned into still, wide pools that in turn led into alternative channels that looped and slithered through impenetrable walls of wild rice, then squeezed tight. We would back out and coil through another anaconda channel. At one point I took a compass reading on the highest hill I could find to the south of us, thinking it might be the Mount Tom on my topographical map, but it seemed we were farther west than I thought we should be—or that wasn't Mount Tom; it looked no more than a slight hill. We were lost.

It wasn't a desperate lostness; we had a tent and we had food. Still, I wanted out of this labyrinth before dark. Long, muddy, tree-covered ridges raised their spines above the surface, then sank again, only to hump up again a hundred yards away. But these, ribbed with hard tree roots and skinned over with wet moss as if the giant serpent of Indian legend had coiled, twisted, and died here long ago, were no place for a tent,.

Hours later, circling back out of another maze of channels, we spotted a man in a steel jonboat pulling a wire mesh fish trap up from beneath flooded trees. We slipped toward him through leafy shadows. The place was dark and still, the maples rising high over our heads. He was concentrating on his work and didn't notice us. We were just yards away when I said, brightly enough, "Hello!"

He jolted upright. The fish trap plopped back into the water, its chain rattling away along the metal gunwale of the boat. He stared at us as if he were seeing the ghosts of Joliet and Marquette.

"We can't seem to find our way up the Fox River."

He looked at us for a few seconds more, then pointed out the other side of the grove of flooded trees.

I nodded and we maneuvered away, back into sunlight, where a wide sheet of green-brown water passed into vast fields of wild rice, but to our right, the open channel took a leisurely bend around and through another line of water-wading trees. It looked no different than the channels we had been exploring all afternoon, but we did notice the slightest ripple of slow brown water around a fallen tree. Where there is current, there is river. We paddled on.

Old habits die hard. Here I was, lost in a world of slow time, a place that measures time by the imperceptible passage of seasons, not by minutes and seconds, yet I was anxious to get beyond these quiet marshes, find a camping spot, and chart the number of miles we had paddled that day. I felt the pressure to move on, to make progress, to make up for lost time. Lost time? This was *found* time. Time salvaged from the rush and crash of Carworld. Why did I feel this need to press on? "Impatience," to quote my philosopher John Graves again, "is a city kind of emotion, harmonious with 'drive' and acid-chewed jumping stomachs, and I presume we need it," he says, "if we are to hold our own on the jousting ground this contemporary world most often is. But it goes poorly on a river."

Part of my problem was the goal I had fixed for our journey; I wanted to reach the Mississippi and spend at least a few days Huckleberry Finning it down the big water. Time-conditioned goals often deprive me of present pleasures. The Now gets pushed rapidly behind as I plot my distance from the projected goal. If I do reach that goal, another one has already intruded into my thinking so that I keep following a line of receding hopes.

Better to just look and listen and smell: "Lakes windless with profound sun-shafted water" or "Slow creeks which bear fleck-ed light through depths of trees." An idle poet understands that ". . . he alone is summer's who relents/ In his poor enterprisings; who can sense,/ In alleys petal-blown, the wealth of chance;/ Or can, supine in a deep meadow, pass/ Warm hours beneath a moving sky's expanse. . . ." says poet Timothy Steele. When my goals have long since evaporated, this marsh, that carried Joliet and Marquette over three-hundred years ago, will still be its water-soaked, insect-rich, fish-loved, and duck-happy self. At least I hope so.

We moved our vagrant prow up the channel, swanning slow-ly up the river, feeling the sleepy sunlight, occasionally passing the canteen back and forth to drink warm water. Blue dragon-flies ever-awake would flit over from a half-submerged log, stop dead in the air as if momentum had no part in their definition of physics, then flash away again. Turtles, baking in their shells, re-luctantly tipped to one side and slid into coolness. Our paddles kept dipping through liquid brown sunlight.

Miles of riverbending marshes brought us up against a steep, tree-covered hill. The current picked up considerable speed as it rushed through the narrower channel between the root-held hill and high ground on the opposite side; we were out of the marsh. Seeing a small patch of thin grass at the base of the hill to pitch our tent, we came ashore, unloaded our gear, and pulled Natty Bumpo out of the current and onto the bank.

We hadn't eaten a campfire-cooked meal since that wind-singing night a week-and-a-half ago when we lay in the sand be-side our fire watching distant fireworks blossom across the dark waters of Green Bay. Justin got the fire going. It was a good

place, the dark current purling by just beside us. I wished we
still had our fishing poles, but the Fox had swallowed them.

Thick smoke from our fire drifted up through the foliage of
the thickets and oaks that climbed the steep hill beside us. I was
concerned our smoke would bring irate farmers upon us, so I
sent Justin up the slope to scout around. He came back telling
of an abandoned farm just over the hill.

After eating, we climbed the hill. Near the crest, we ducked
out from overhanging limbs and stood up in knee-high grass. A
weathered barn stood before us, charcoal-brown wooden slats
built over a first level of rough limestone. We walked inside. Old
stalls where cattle had wintered for many a year.

We climbed a ladder to the second floor. A bundle of old
magazines on the floor: *Better Homes and Gardens*, farming
magazines, catalogues. Odds and ends of farm machinery rusting in dusty hay. Justin climbed on up into the loft and found an
old wooden lapstraked rowboat thick with dust, its long paddles
lying beside it like the useless arms of a dead man. Milk cans,
dented, rusted, waist-high, lined one wall, a rope dangled from
a high pulley. Justin gripped the rough braid and put his weight
on it; the loft doors began to open to the wide fields. It was, for
city-bred Justin, an opening onto another world.

Down below, I pushed open double doors and looked eastward over long acres of tall grasses that fell away toward a distant line of trees. Beyond a stand of pine trees, a doe bounded
away through the sprinkled ochre of ripened grass seeds.

Across the yard to my left, an abandoned farm house. The
lap siding had weathered to a pale grey, but the windows were
unbroken, reflecting the dusky fields. The house rested there, im-
material in the late afternoon's frail light, the soul of a house.

I have been haunted by that lost little farm. All the evidence
of long life and hard work were about the place. A long stand
of pines had been planted in careful rows, thick-trunked and

tall. Walking over to the back porch of the house, I found a straw hat hung from a hook as if the farmer's wife had just come in from harvesting sweet peas. How many generations had invested their lives on that lovely place, passed the land on to their children, and then again to theirs?

Justin joined me and we walked up to a little graveyard on a nearby hilltop where we found gravestones dating some 200 years of occupation. From that hilltop graveyard, we looked out over rolling green hills on every hand. Sheltered among distant trees we could still see scattered barns and silos. But the long rope in the loft below us hangs useless, the doors have swung shut. Four family farms a day fail in Wisconsin alone. At this rate, all the small family farms in Wisconsin will be gone within twenty years. Is that what we want? "Productivity, profitability, efficiency, limitless growth, limitless wealth, limitless power, limitless mechanization and automation can enrich and empower the few (for a while), but they will sooner or later ruin us all." So, the old, unheeded prophet from Kentucky.

And what does America lose in the loss of a small farm? It is the cutting of a long friendship between family and land, the heart-stopping loss of hard work and love once combined, of man, land, and animal joined and interdependent, together having made these fields lovely. The word *culture* comes from the Latin word for cultivation. When we lose our intimate relationship with cultivated land, culture grows brassy and hard; we urbanize our souls. Just 100 years ago almost 90 percent of Americans made their prime income from the land. And now an entire culture is vanishing. Corporate farms, mega-farms, agri-businesses buy up the old way of life and turn the land into a production line worked by salaried employees. As late as 1970, the average American dairy farm had 19 cows—a modest income for a single family. Now the average dairy has 88 cows. A North Dakota cheese factory is recruiting farmers who will need 900 cows apiece.

David Ehrenfeld, professor at Rutgers, lists some of the costs of dairy-farm industrialization: increased debt-to-asset ratio that sends control of dairy farming to distant banks and drives the smaller farmers out, "worse environmental impact, more labor strikes, decreased personal knowledge of individual animals, and, finally, greater centralized control and more nonresident owners, with a consequent breakdown in 'economic vitality and social cohesion in rural communities.'" The use of growth hormones increases milk production, but also increases feed costs and mastitis in the cows. And then, something else: small farm cows eat "red maples and alders, phragmites, reed canary grass, purple loosestrife, and similar invasives that otherwise choke our wetland vegetation . . . . Thus if you want to find the tiny bog turtle, the fen buck moth, the showy lady's slipper orchid, or the spreading globeflower—all of them rare and endangered—you will have to go to a small dairy farm." The big, industrialized farms that feed their cattle "high-protein food supplements in temperature-controlled buildings, do not serve the smaller farms' unexpected function of maintaining the flora and fauna of wetlands."

But so goes the run of current affairs, and with the rapid decline of the small farm, the current seems to be picking up speed: "Ill fares the land, to hast'ning ills a prey,/ Where wealth accumulates, and men decay."

Worm Life

Next morning we duck-footed on up the river to the little town of Princeton. We ate breakfast at a cafe, listening to a man at an adjacent table talk about landing a steady job in insurance. After food, we left his world of insured securities, what Daniel Boorstin calls "the cozy satisfactions of predictable, statistical benefits," and took to the river again.

Two miles upstream, we looked at our map and decided to portage one-and-a-half miles over the neck of a long oxbow in the Fox River. This would save us eight miles of upriver paddling. We were tired of fighting the current with our arms. Walking sounded inviting, especially since a road cut straight across the oxbow.

We unloaded everything, consolidated as many odds and ends in the big Duluth packs as we could, and climbed the thirty-foot embankment to the blacktop. First, the heaviest packs: Rude Mechanicals and the Food Pack carried a half mile along an undulating road bordered by sandy fields of foot-high corn on the left, thick pasture and an occasional home on the right. A purple bloom was on the clover beneath the barbed wire fences. Bumble bees, seeming too heavy for their wings, rose and fell among the flowers. Above, a hawk rode a thermal into a cool sky. Crows called from a distant tree while four or five of their clan paced about through the corn looking for insects. They will find few. We have so insecticided and herbicided the soils that the natural inhabitants both farmer-helpful and farmer-hurtful are gone. A farm boy recently told me that he used to grab a handful of soil and sort through a multiplicity of tiny bugs, mites, millipedes, worms, grubs, beetles, larvae, all writhing in a single handful. Now, he said, he can take up handful after handful from any of his neighbors' fields and finds nothing but dirt.

A half mile of leaning, shoulder-weighted trudging and we dumped our packs in the tall grass at the side of the road, then returned for the Sleeping Sack, or Nap Sack, with its blankets and sleeping bags, and picked up paddles, book bag, and the rest. It was a lot of work. On the third trip we lifted the canoe onto our heads. We had now metamorphosed Natty Bumpo from a web-footed, two-legged water bird into a long-beaked, four-footed terrestrial, something like a wingless griffin, but with none of its magical powers.

Off we lumbered up the road, our cut-off bleach bottles we used for bailing swinging on strings from the thwarts. Cars whizzed by from time to time, all eyes within turning upon us as they passed. When we reached our packs, we kept going for another half mile to the place the blacktop turned suddenly left. A gravel road moseyed on down toward the river, so we deposited our amphibian and returned for the packs. On our way back, Justin heard something run into the tall grass. He gave chase, yelping like a young coyote, tearing a zigzag through the grass as some furry little beast rippled the grass ahead of him. At one point he dived and touched fur, but the animal vanished, as if the mere touch of a human hand was enough to vaporize it.

We finally dropped Natty Bumpo back in the river and were glad to be working our arms again. The day was going, so we paddled into the flooded yard of the Pineview Resort: a tavern surrounded by a dozen small cabins that had been built a long time ago as vacation cabins for working-class people from Chicago and Milwaukee. Inside the tavern we met a blonde giant named Tim tending bar. While we ate hamburgers and fries, he showed us photographs of acres of reeds that, during the recent flooding, had broken away from the main mass across the river and floated into his boat dock, wrenching the dock sideways, and then had drifted on down the river and into several back yards where they stay. "They've got some additional property now," he said with a grin.

Rivers are a chancy thing.

Big Tim was good to us. He let us pitch our tent near his tavern and let us use his shower house free. After the showers, Justin was hot to beat me in pool—Tim's tavern had a pool table. He beat me two games out of three. We walked outside and Justin spotted a basketball lying next to Tim's garage. He wanted to play me in basketball. A teenage boy's energy bears no relation to the amount of work he has done in a day. Ask him to mow the lawn when he's been lazing on the couch all afternoon, and he will be too tired to move. Let him spot a basketball, and he wants to go one-on-one after staggering under ninety-pound packs all afternoon.

"Come on, Dad! Just one game."

I consented to a game of Horse, spelling out the name of this brother beast of burden with several ungainly shots.

"Just one more game, Dad. Please?"

"I'm too tired."

"We'll play Pig. Just a little Pig. That won't take long."

We played Pig. Justin was on a roll; my role was losing. He bounced the ball between his legs, fired in fade-away jumpers, drove for a back-handed layup, huffing and puffing to blow my house down. I was a pig.

I offered my usual excuses and became a pig for the second time. Justin had the Circe touch. "One more time," he said. "Just one more." One more pig appeared with my name on it. Enough. Three little pigs are enough for one old boar to take responsibility for. I returned to my house of nylon to wallow in defeat.

I pulled out our dried-out, crackling roll of maps and found myself wondering about that eight-mile oxbow we had by-passed by portaging. What had we missed by taking the land route? The flat blue worm that serves as a river on the map hugged a high bank for two miles and then took an abrupt turn back into the marshes, but a decoy channel continued straight ahead along the highland for another mile then curved like the head of a cormorant back into the marsh where it disappeared. I will never take that trip, neither the wrong turn nor the right; I will not live within that cormorant's head. And I was sorry I could not travel both channels and be one traveler. And what about Green Lake there on the map to the east? The deepest lake in the region. And the old railroad grade cutting straight through Snake Creek Swamp? What a walk that might be. So many marshes unexplored. Our own path was a disappearing wake, a single ripple through this world so broad and deep but even now smoothing into forgetfulness. I wanted to see it, not just once but through the seasons, to take it in as if I were consciously diffused within the map, lingering in a thousand places, gazing at a thousand horizons, perceiving each flash of light within the complex whole, each ray differentiated by color and form but shining each with each as in a window of stained glass to reveal the meaningful whole, to listen to the sounding world in such a way that each note has its moment and every note flows together symphonically.

But we do not have the mind nor perspective to contain the whole, so I will do the best I can, chafing, perhaps, at the limits of our tunnel vision, each one confined in his minor corridor, though just now my tunnel looks wide and expansive as I, sitting outside my tent, glance from horizon to horizon and out into the evening air. I am not wholly limited to the linear logic of time or to a single succession of thoughts.

"Look you, this brave o'erhanging firmament, this majestical roof fretted with golden fire"—and look you past those amber-lighted windows of the fading cabins there to the wide marsh now darkening and winking with distant fireflies and see an old man and his wife in a rowboat, creaking slowly into the purpling waters for a night of fishing, their single lantern swinging on a rod between them; and listen to Justin, still thumping the ball on concrete and clanging shots off the basketball rim in the sinking light, and hear the rhythmic crickets scraping out their night tunes, and frogs yiping and yelping and rum-bub-bumbling, and tinny radio music dancing out of one of the cabins, and a crack of wooden balls through the open screen door of the nearby tavern followed by a laugh, and the fried hamburger cigarette air lifting smoky from that screen door, and the sound of a car hushing past on the hillside gravel road above us, and memory already weaving into the present a mysterious day long ago: I am sailing with my father on a volcanic lake high in the mountains of Ethiopia. Completely encircling us are the low, broken ridges and hills of the volcano's rim, covered in shrubbery and the occasional grove of eucalyptus trees. The lake is deep, very deep. My friends say it goes down forever. No one has ever found the bottom. Above is the high blue sky where tiny single-engine planes dive and swerve and cut their engines; they are the miniscule planes of Ethiopia's paltry air force practicing maneuvers which will not save the country in time of need. And beyond the tiny insect machines is a distant sky I as a child have wandered wondering through into infinity, a sky that must just go on and on and on. Around my father and me there is a sound, a quiet whispering all around as the small sailboat effortlessly severs the surface of the deep waters. I am six or seven, somewhere near the age when consciousness drops away into the unconsciousness of early youth. My father is at the rudder, the wind in my face is the wind in his hair and I can think of nothing but the great depths below me and the high sky above me and my father there at the rudder so that the dread of depth and height is somehow transformed into a manageable risk, transfigured from fear into excitement, and excitement for a child is a pure delight. We are carried as if in a dream—this and much more all at once is passing through me, time past and time present not lined up letter after letter and line by line in this worm squiggle writing, but coming simultaneously over and through me like music.

Books, Business, And Peacocks

For over an hour we had been trying to negotiate our way through another field of wild rice. Joliet, Marquette, the Beaver, the Mole, and the rest of that little band, knew the risks of places like this. Three decades before, in the summer of 1642, the Jesuit priest Isaac Jogues and four Frenchmen had joined some thirty-five Hurons for a journey to resupply an outlying mission. Early one morning they stopped to examine footprints on shore. Some said they belonged to the enemy Iroquois; some maintained they belonged to a friendly party. A Christian chief named Eustace Ahatsistari, known for his courage and feats of arms, ended the argument by saying, "Brothers! Be they the bravest foe, for such I judge them by their trail, they are not more than three canoes, and we number enough not to dread such a handful of the enemy." It was a fatal mistake. About a mile upriver, the Huron canoes were avoiding the rapid current in the center of the river by skirting reedbeds that lined the shore when musket shots exploded from the reeds. Musket balls smacked through birchbark, but only one Huron was hit, shot through the hand. Four Iroquois canoes shot out from the reeds paddling straight for them. In a panic, most of the Hurons leaped into the water and splashed for shore while about fourteen Indians and Frenchmen stayed to fight. It was a hopeless battle. Eight more Iroquois canoes swept out into the current from the opposite side of the river and made for them. Seeing the battle lost, most of the remaining fighters jumped into the river and made for the forest. Isaac Jogues leaped into the reeds and ducked down. But a Frenchman and several Hurons were quickly captured. Seeing his companions taken, Jogues decided he must not leave them. It was a decision that would cost Jogues incredible hardship and pain.

One of the Frenchmen, a young man named William Couture

made good his escape into the forest, but then, looking about him and not seeing Jogues, he too decided to share the fate of the captives. He turned and began retracing his steps just as five Iroquois warriors burst into view. As Couture was still carrying his musket, one of the Iroquois pointed his own musket at Couture's breast and pulled the trigger; the gun snapped but misfired and Couture in his excitement fired his own weapon, dropping the man dead at his feet. The four others grabbed Couture, disarmed him, and dragged him back to the other prisoners where in their anger they ripped off his clothes, tore out his fingernails with their teeth, and stabbed his right hand through with a sword. When Jogues saw his friend's mistreatment, he rushed through the standing warriors to throw his arms around him. The Iroquois stood still, seemingly stunned by this display, but then, says Jogues, "as if recollecting themselves, and gathering all their rage, they fell upon me, and with their fists, thongs and clubs beat me till I fell senseless. Two of them then dragged me back to where I had been before; and scarcely had I begun to breathe, when some others, attacking me, tore out, by biting, almost all of my nails, and crunched my two fore-fingers with their teeth." The same was done to the other captured Frenchman, Rene Goupil.

Three Hurons were killed during the battle; one, an eighty-year-old man, refused to go with his captors. "What!" he exclaimed. "Shall I, a grey-haired old man, go to a strange and foreign land? Never! Here I will die." And there he died. A man slammed a tomahawk into his head and left him lie. Twenty-two prisoners were taken, including the three Frenchmen and the chief, Eustace Ahasistari (who, like Couture and Jogues, returned out of a sense of solidarity with the captives). Thus a priest, a layman, and an Indian turned themselves in to share the brutal fate of other captives. These were, without doubt, acts of high courage and compassion, but, as Jogues admits, they were decisions that caused their friends much grief, for they were all forced to witness the sufferings and sometimes the deaths of their companions, a mental anguish that did nothing to alleviate their companions' sufferings.

The war party gathered up their captives, loaded them with the goods from the canoes and set off for home. Jogues, stripped of his black robe, burned badly in the sun; black flies and mosquitoes took their turns on his peeling skin. Near the end of their long journey, the whole party ran out of food and no one ate anything but heated water the last two or three days back to the Iroquois villages where the prisoners were forced to run the gauntlet at each new village, then tortured, killed, or made slaves.

Thirteen months later, after a long and miserable winter, Jogues managed to escape with the help of the New England Dutch. But Ahasistari, Goupil, and many of the Hurons were killed.

Joliet, Marquette, and the other men knew the story well, as they knew of many other Frenchmen and Indians who had been captured and tortured by hostile tribes in recent years. If I, passing such reedbanks, could not forget the stories I had read, how much more must these men, paddling into the unknown to face unknown tribes, have feared for their lives in places like this.

We crossed Lake Puckaway and soon were snaking through rice fields again. At our approach, great blue herons would lean forward, slowly unfold their wings, and flap away up the river, croaking their annoyance. They looked like old men: tall, gaunt, grim-eyed, with untidy hair, lanky necks, undernourished bodies, and long, knobbly-kneed legs with bad skin; old cranky men sunning themselves in shorts. They moved laboriously on the wing, but let that vigilant eye spot a kicking frog or a silver-flashing fingerling and zap! like a blue spark the spear strikes. In two months of lake and river travel we saw hundreds of herons standing patient vigil; only once did we see one strike; it did not miss.

The river stank. Mats of tiny green platelets had settled into the crooks of half-submerged driftwood or into backwaters or up against partly-flooded docks. They may have been algae spores floating down from Buffalo Lake, but I never found out for sure. They were rotting and reeking terribly. A teen-aged girl stood on a dock to sweep the wet, stinking carpet away and into the current. She stopped her sweeping for a long look at Justin as we paddled by. Justin smiled and nodded. She looked down quickly and went back to tidying up the river.

A dry snow of cottonwood seeds drifted out of high trees and settled lightly across the current. The sun burned down. We dipped our hats in the water and poured water over our heads. The current moved lazily between grassy sand ridges dredged up years ago to keep the channel navigable. A big snapping turtle poked about through submerged grasses near shore and several mallards tried to outswim us, then flew away into the seed-snowing heat.

By six in the afternoon, we had reached the dam that holds ten-mile-long, quarter-to-half-mile wide Buffalo Lake; it makes a long, C-shaped bend and on the map looks more like a widening of the river than a lake. The water poured over the dam and ran rough for a hundred yards. We decided not to portage this late in the day. Instead we took an alternative channel, the Montello River, that wound up through the little town of Montello toward a city park.

We ducked under a low bridge and paddled our way along the narrow channel past houses, by a grove of trees, and on, winding around back yards where dogs barked and into the back alleys of the downtown area. The old brick buildings piled up along the bank were shelved with little balconies, a footbridge crossed the stream above us; it looked like an old Italian town. We pulled Natty Bumpo out of the water near a trash dumpster and decided to camp next to it. We couldn't go on; a high dam blocked the narrow passage ahead.

We left Natty Bumpo, walked over the footbridge, around the corner, and onto the sunburnt main street. There we found an antique store that sold ice cream: a double benefit for us, for we bought strawberry cones from a lovely, dark-eyed clerk and found two cheap paperbacks with yellowing pages for fifty cents each: *Zorba the Greek* for me and Owen Wister's wonderful tale of the old west, *The Virginian*, for Justin. Justin had read Zane Grey and Louis L'Amour, but I had always wanted him to read Wister's romance of frontier Wyoming as Wister himself had seen it as a young man. I had already introduced Justin's two older brothers to the Virginian, whose cleverness and courage were an American match for Odysseus. I was glad Justin wanted to read the book.

I looked at the 1969 paper cover of my new acquisition. Zorba was there on the cover, fingers clicking the air above his head, Greek-dancing in a red shirt. I opened the cover and read a blurb: "He is Sinbad crossed with Sancho Panza." All right. I don't mind being introduced.

Licking our strawberry cones, we turned the corner of the brick apartment house across the stream from our canoe and passed two Mexican men drinking Old Style beer and talking in Spanish. A dark-haired boy was fishing from the footbridge, but down below, next to the dumpster, we saw five or six children picking over the contents of our canoe.

We walked across the footbridge and down. The children smiled and backed away. We slid Natty Bumpo back into the water and slipped back down the current and around a bend.

At one point we found two unfenced yards on either side of a roadway. I was hoping someone would let us camp overnight. I left Justin with the canoe and walked up to the road. Left or right? I flipped a coin and it sent me left, but on second thought I chose the house on the right. I knocked on the door. No answer. Knocked again. No answer. So the coin was right. I crossed the street and asked a woman who was weeding flowers next to a tall, white, woodframe house if we could camp overnight in her back yard. Just then a short, balding man in a white t-shirt that stretched over a hefty stomach stepped out of a truck in the yard. The woman looked at him. He looked at me for a moment, then said, "Sure."

I followed him back into the partially flooded yard and he introduced me to Bobo, a goose who had recently become surrogate mother to a family of ducklings. The mother duck still attended her young, but Bobo was in charge of the back yard and that stretch of the river. My host called over his big black Newfoundland dog. "Had her shipped as a puppy," he said. "Cost me $125." My host was a merchant trader; he measured in dollars. "She's a good-natured dog. Once Bobo the Goose bit her on the ear and the dog never even snapped back. Good natured dog; she won't give you no trouble. But the goose you got to watch." The merchant glanced at the goose. "Once had a little bitty boy visiting us and old Bobo charged him and bit him on his privates."

A goose to give Mother Goose a bad name.

I returned in a few minutes with Justin and we set up the tent keeping a wary eye on the perverted goose.

The merchant, his wife, and a teenaged grandson, wanted to show us around. We drove west in their white van along Buffalo Lake. He told us the story of a deer hunt he had taken with a crossbow.

On a frozen day he was perched in a tree stand, a little contraption of boards nailed up in a tree, waiting for a deer. As he told me the story, I could see him there, his breath frosty on a bitter Wisconsin morning. A buck approaches. He sees its grey flank moving through a tangle of brush and overhanging limbs. His breath stops. The buck stops, its breath coming like snow in the grey brush. Then it steps. Stops. The merchant leans out for the shot, sighting along the short arrow and taut crossbow, finger on the trigger, measuring his breath, anticipating the step . . . step . . . into the opening below. CRACK! The whole tree trunk breaks and he crashes into the snow below. The snapped tree trunk slams across his shin breaking the bone. Stunned, he looks up at the leg torn in half at the shin; the broken tree limb lies across his broken limb; the lower leg is attached to the upper by a little skin and blue veins; hot blood steams and cools in the snow around him as he shouts with all his remaining strength for his friends.

He almost died. It took his friends three hours to carry him out of the freezing woods and to a hospital. He showed us the scar on his leg. He was a man of many scars. He pulled up his t-shirt and traced with his finger a white line across his sagging chest: six by-passes; his finger followed another white groove over his heavy stomach: appendix. He had retired from the navy. During the Korean War, he had been an underwater demolitions man. He and a buddy had scuba dived up a Korean river and attached mines to a ship. Their orders were to swim away even if the other guy didn't show up for the rendezvous, but the young merchant couldn't leave his friend. He swam back and found him hurt. He grabbed his friend and they both swam for their lives, but the mines exploded, blasting them over and over through the dark water. A piece of shrapnel slammed into the merchant's ear. Another piece ripped into his side, but both men escaped. The French explorers were not the only ones to exhibit courageous solidarity in tough times.

We drove back into town. The merchant pointed out the store he was remodeling. He had owned five bars in Milwaukee years ago and then three in Montello and other surrounding towns. Now the new store would sell anything and everything: dolls, brass elephants, glass-faced cabinets, televisions, t-shirts, pants, tables and chairs, air conditioners—all stuff he picked up by driving around the country to auctions, close-outs, bankruptcies, and wholesalers. A true son of the merchant Joliet. Later, in his home, he showed us some dolls; his eyes rolled toward the doll. "How much do you think they're worth?" I didn't know. "Come on, how much do you think?" I didn't know. "Just guess!" I did. Too low. He beamed. They turned out to be a part of an expensive set. He had gotten them cheap and was selling high.

They drove us out through town along Highway 23 to White Lake, a resort where his seventeen-year-old daughter worked in the restaurant. He and his wife were proud of her; she was a hard worker, and responsible.

Night had fallen. As we drove under pine trees and parked along a wooden fence, we heard the crackle of fireworks; we were just a week away from the Fourth of July. Then, from the surrounding trees, came loud, desperate cries. I glanced out the car window and grabbed the door handle.

"Peacocks," said the merchant.

"Peacocks?"

Yes indeed. And the birds hated fireworks.

We walked down to the lake where their daughter joined us, a pretty, heavy-breasted girl in a swimsuit of blue. Justin pulled off his t-shirt and waded into the dark lake with the girl and the teenaged grandson while the merchant, his wife, and I sat on a wooden walkway, swatted mosquitoes, and talked politics. It was a presidential election year and the candidates were out and about stirring up a cauldron of apathy across the country. Though the paper headlines dutifully reported the latest, in the cafes I had heard not one mention of politics.

But the merchant was a frustrated entrepreneur: "I feel like all I do is pay and pay and pay and pay. I should go to heaven because I'm in hell now." He went on about tax burdens for a while. Then he said, "I don't vote for the party; I vote for the man. Clinton's been in there for four years and ain't done nothin' but give money away to foreign aid and let a million slant-eyes in here when we ain't got enough good jobs ourselves. Clinton's helping the rich. Those rich people hire them refugees for minimum wage and leave the rest of us without a job." The merchant didn't strike me as a man lacking in employment. And I thought of the Mexican family we'd seen earlier. God knows they work hard enough for their meager wages.

Thirty or forty yards out in the lake, Justin climbed up the ladder of a diving platform, his wet body catching the light from shoreside houses, climbed past the dark tree line of the far shore and onto the high platform where he stood up among the stars. And what would Justin be? Merchant? Trader? Politician? Missionary? His grandfather, my father, had wanted to be a doctor. He had been a good student and a hard worker. He'd bought a Model A Ford and driven a country paper route while paying his own way through college. But then he had met my mother and given over all his plans in order to work in a most inhospitable region of the world. The famous British general Gordon of Khartoum said of the Sudan, "the climate is such that only a man who is finished with life and longs for death will go there; such men are not common." The first British explorer to walk from the Cape of South Africa to Cairo, Egypt, said of the region where my parents lived, "For God-forsaken, dry-sucked, fly-blown wilderness, commend me to the upper Nile; a desolation of desolations; an infernal region, a howling waste of weeds, mosquitoes, flies, and fever. I have passed through it and now have no fear of the hereafter." Within seven years of the establishment of the first Catholic mission in the southern Sudan, twenty-two priests died of disease. There my parents settled, planning to spend the rest of their lives, and there my father came within a few breaths of dying of malaria and eventually contracted a viral infection that gave him bleeding ulcers that almost killed him.

The choices he made led to the risk of early death. But then, life is always lethal.

I saw Justin lean forward on the platform and dive into star-lit waters.

The merchant was talking money: "Four-hundred dollars a week for one of these cabins," he said, shoving his double chin at cabin lights that winked from the trees like a diamond neck-lace all around the lake. I slapped another mosquito.

People off to our left were unfolding lawn chairs in the sand. Someone lit a fuse and began rocketing off explosives from a nearby dock. Rapid-fire whistles screamed into the night and gave a flat snap among the stars. Peacocks wailed.

That evening the merchant and his wife insisted we sleep in-doors. "It's damn humid out here. Thick, just thick. Come on in and we'll let you sleep on a real bed."

We sat on their living room couch munching popcorn, sip-ping Pepsis, and watching *The Guns of Navarone* on the televi-sion. After a while, Justin followed the grandson and daughter upstairs to play Monopoly, but I stayed to watch the commando unit lay dynamite charges on the massive artillery pieces on the cliffs of Navarone as the merchant, the old demolitions man, criticized the way the German officer handled dynamite. "You can't do that with dynamite; you'll blow yourself to hell."

After midnight, they showed me to a room upstairs, even lending us their only electric fans, as the night was hot. I switched off the bedside light. A soft bed beneath me, clean sheets, a quiet fan blowing the warm, dark air over me. I lay wakeful, listening to the sounds of an unfamiliar house: voices across the hall where the three teenagers were still playing Monopoly. A refrigerator door closed downstairs. I lay alone, listening out the window to the flowing of the river.

My wife lies in our bed alone. I am out running my newspaper route. She awakes in a panic. She glances at the clock: 4:10 a.m. She knows I am in trouble. She does not know what to do. She is certain I am in trouble. But she does not know my 30-mile paper route; how can she find me in the darkness? She lies down, staring at the ceiling of our bedroom, her heart pounding, prayers rising in her heart. She lies awake in the darkness till a grey light begins rising in the east.

About seven that morning, the sun is up. I step into our bedroom. She sits up and asks me directly, "What happened to you last night?"

"Someone shot at me."

"Who shot at you?"

"I don't know. Five or six shots from behind a house. I heard the bullets ricocheting off the street around my car."

In the morning, the merchant's wife heated up a plateful of little sausage-and-biscuit sandwiches she had taken from a cardboard package. "They're cheap but they're good, aren't they?" asked the merchant.

Justin and I nodded as we ate. He insisted we eat more. We ate. The wife poured us coffee.

"Guess how much they cost." He held up a little sausage biscuit between his finger and thumb.

I had no idea.

"Come on. How much?"

I looked at Justin. He smiled and shrugged. But they were good. Even a cheap sausage biscuit can be the fuel of friendship.

The merchant was going on about how people take advantage of him, wanting to borrow his truck or trying to get him to help them out with work around their places, but never offering to pay him for his services. He was tired of being taken advantage of. But after breakfast, when I pulled out my billfold and offered him payment for all their services, he arched grey eyebrows and gave me a disgusted flip of the hand. "Keep it. I ain't takin' no money from you."

Middle Earth

Green algae textured the long blue surfaces of Buffalo Lake. We stayed to the center channel that was relatively clear of the stuff. When we tried cutting nearer shore, we ended up plowing through shag carpets of algae and through flat mats of those stinking platelets, losing all momentum.

The sun grew small, hard, and white as it moved over us in its race west, the sky tortoise outrunning our bigfooted river rabbit. The wind was hot. On our left, we watched bright orange paddle-wheeled machines churning slowly through the green mats cutting algae a few feet below the surface. They cut parallel swaths through the waves like Kansas combines in the heat of the June wheat harvest.

Some time after noon, we took our overheated bodies ashore at Packwaukee, a small town on the north shore, and walked into the air conditioning of the Sportsman's Cafe. We slumped into chairs at a side table and took a look around. Stuffed birds and animals decorated the walls; on a counter a stuffed weasel was preparing to dine on stuffed rabbit. We ordered the all-you-can-eat perch and plenty of iced tea.

As we waited on our order, I read my paper placemat: Presidents of the United States, forty-two faces looking up through little framed black-and-whites. It was a little disconcerting to notice that my lifetime took in the entire bottom row, ten presidents, almost one quarter of the lot. How could I be that old? Another thing worth noticing: not a single president of this two-centuries-old republic is smiling before Richard Nixon. Thirty-six faces of solemn purpose. But starting with Nixon, well, *apres moi le deluge*; they are all grinning terribly as if everyone of them has now caught the joke.

This is a democracy. I expect they wouldn't be smiling if we didn't expect them to be smiling. Has our image of this country's highest office so changed that we now insist that our leaders put on a happy face? We seem to have traded in that older expectation of a man of tough dignity for an I'm okay, you're Ok, everything's Ok kind of agreeable guy. Can you imagine Abraham Lincoln with a wide-happy smile? George Washington flashing his false teeth? Teddy Roosevelt was known for his exuberant smile, but his official photographs and his sculpted face on Mount Rushmore maintain a serious purpose. Soon the spin-doctors will be sending the sculptors back up Mount Rushmore to chisel in the incisors and bicuspids: four presidents grinning through granite.

An hour later we walked out into the wilting heat. The temperature was climbing through the nineties. With stomachs stuffed with perch and potatoes, lemon pie and tea, we decided to delay our journey and find a place to read our books, *Zorba* for me, *The Virginian* for Justin. We found our way along hot sidewalks to the library, an old brick school building with high ceilings and old wooden doors. We walked down a dim, hot hallway and opened a door. Air conditioning. I breathed deeply and found my way to a table. Justin slid into a wooden chair beside me and struck up a relationship with the cowboy from Virginia.

I opened the yellowed pages of my cheap paperback and

found myself in a Greek seaport before dawn. It's cold and black outside. A great wind is blowing, smashing the waves into steel-hulled ships. Rain pours down outside this little café; a couple of men in heavy overcoats gurgle their hookahs, others stare stolidly out the steamy windows. Someone asks what happened to Captain Lemoni, then looks out angrily at the sea and growls, "God damn you for a destroyer of homes!"

I am cold. I pull my overcoat around me and shuffle my feet. "The world's a life sentence," murmurs someone else. "Yes, a life sentence. Be damned to it." I am sipping a hot glass of sage and fighting fatigue. Outside in the darkness before dawn, boatmen and carters are beginning to cry out, ships' sirens howl through the pouring rain. The cafe door swings open, the sound of the crashing sea pours in as a thickset sailor stalks over to a table, his long moustaches drooping with water. Voices erupt around me, "Welcome Captain Lemoni! Welcome!" He sits down heavily, austere and taciturn, and with a deep voice starts talking about the water spirits who climbed up his masts during the storm: "they are soft and sticky. When you take lots of them, your hands catch fire." He says that when he stroked his moustache the strange fires illumined his face, "and so, in the dark, I gleamed like a devil." Meanwhile my thoughts are swinging between the dirty weather outside, the stench of men's bodies, the scent of brewed sage, wet wool, and rum, and hard memories . . .

I looked up into summer sunlight shining gold across the wooden floor, up at the old wooden shelves, the horizontal lines of vertical books. I listened to the quiet hum of the air conditioner. Justin was still beside me reading. A barefoot girl of about nine, about my Snoofer's age, with a lovely golden braid, squirmed on a bench as she paged through a book. A boy of about twelve in black leather suspenders and a blue shirt was walking about. Suddenly he announced loudly in toddler's language, "I walk here today!" He looked around the small, high-ceilinged room and smiled. It was clear he had either a speech or a mental impairment of some kind. The librarian, a young woman with dark hair, smiled and nodded at him.

The old building sitting out another summer's heat felt like an older version of Middle America. In medieval times, they called this bit of soil, water, air, and fire caught between Heaven and Hell the Middle Earth. The American Middle West at the end of the twentieth century is, I suppose, as much a part of this Middle Earth as Owen Wister's Wyoming, or Nikos Kazant-zaki's Greece, or Graham Greene's central Africa, or Homer's Mediterranean (another word for middle earth). And since I have reached middle age, I might be excused for trying to find my way backwards and forwards through this maze of channels false and true.

It is midsummer now, the middle of the year, and we, my middle son and I, are in the middle of Wisconsin, about halfway through our journey, time traveling as it were, from the primitive northern wilderness—in some places not much changed from the days of Joliet and Marquette, now into a region of dairy farms and small towns—in some ways not much changed from nineteenth century America, a landscape integrated between those who work the land and those who support them: "Landscape plotted and pieced—fold, fallow, and plough;/ And all trades, their gear and tackle and trim." But we were heading out toward the Mississippi where commerce and industrialization will rush us toward the twenty-first century. The question of course, both personally and as a society, is—Are we moving forward or backward?

"Justin," I say. He looks up from the austere skies of Wyoming. "We've got maybe twenty miles to go to Portage, Wisconsin, just twenty more miles upriver, then we cross to the Wisconsin River and its all downstream from there." We'd talked about this many times. "Let's paddle all night if we have to and reach Portage tonight," I say. "We'll celebrate tomorrow with a steak dinner."

This was not the voice of reason, but Justin was as anxious as I was to reach Portage. It was another major milestone, a midpoint on our journey. We would be leaving our uphill fight with the waters that flow to the Atlantic and would be joining the waters that flow south to the Gulf. For Joliet and Marquette, it meant leaving their two Indian guides and passing from the scarcely known to the totally unknown. For us it would mean leaving the slow-flowing American past and being carried into fast-paced modernity. Why was I in such a hurry?

We walked away from the library and into the blowing heat. The sun shone down with a terrible grin.

By midafternoon we had passed under an ugly iron railroad bridge and reached the end of Buffalo Lake. We wandered about for a time through openings in the marsh looking for the river, found it, and once again began working out those marsh puzzles, trying to avoid the looping channels that soak away into miles of high reeds. Gentle hills on either hand came down to the marshes for a drink; the river's current was in no hurry and in time the staring sun began to glance away to the west and relax his concentration on this end of middle earth. The steady winds, released from the constant pressure of the sun's will, sighed and wandered aimlessly about, then died away as the sun declined.

We were moving more or less in a southeasterly direction, sometimes skirting the red soil of the hills where small stands of stiff pines grew up among elegant elms and graceful willows, sometimes looping back into the marshes where the sand ridges thrown up by the old river dredgers were covered with leafy bushes and trees. We startled a deer. Several sandhill cranes with impossibly long necks stretched out before and as long legs stretched out behind flew low over the acres of wild rice. Fish began popping the quiet surface for insects or shooting away from our approach, drawing quick, panicked lines along the smooth surface. The world was silent, and so were we, dipping our paddles through the deepening blues of the main channel and the blackening, watery greens near shore.

As we followed a long U-turn through the marsh, our eyes fell upon a leafy limb swimming toward us. The V-ripple around a stationary branch would naturally expand toward us, carried our way by the current, but the V-ripple here was inverted; the limb was swimming our way, faster than the lazy current. We kept paddling and the limb angled out to meet us. Then we saw the wet, furry head of the beaver, its teeth clamped around the branch, oblivious to our presence. We stopped paddling. The beaver kept coming. Three feet from our prow, it concluded we were an unusual addition to the flora and fauna of the area and plunged straight down with a quick percusive burst of water. Justin turned to me and smiled. He could have reached out and touched it with his paddle.

We moved quietly, the channel turning liquid black and cobalt blue beneath us. A few wisps of high clouds flushed a rosy pink, and the sky behind us glowed orange and russet with straight shafts of white light shooting across the sky like a child's painting of a sunset. In the lush green of shoreline grasses far ahead, two deer grazed. The tops of spreading oak trees behind them went gold in the sun's last rays.

It is Eden, and we are the first man and his son, awake with calm astonishment.

The reed beds release the long day's heat, the soft brown of the two deer are still cropping the waterside shadows, lifting a head now and again and turning their ears to wonder into the evening air, and we are moving quietly so as not to disturb a leaf, and the water drops fall jeweled from our paddles into the whorled necklace of our little wake, and the night is already rising out of the reed beds with a smell of marsh and water to lie along the lower banks, but the sky is still wet with many colors. And now, movement from the deer—bounding, stopping, wide-eared to peer toward us up the channel, then walking, stopping, jogging over the bank and away, and a silver, three-quarters moon above the oaks gathering gold from the coming night, and the air clear and wide and open and warm, and my own son dipping the waters before me in the now-familiar stroke of many weeks, and both of us here together, alive and awake, and moving around another bend. A raccoon is puttering about under oak trees, moving quickly through cattle-cropped grasses from stump to log to bush, a regular rhythmic motion, sniffing like a trailing hound at everything, reading the day's messages, sometimes running into a black coat beneath the oaks, then running out into reddish fur and striped tail in the afterglow of day, never seeing us, making his way along a barbed wire fence and eventually up and over a rise. And then a coarse squawk from behind a nearby sand ridge. Not a heron squawk. Something like but not the same. A long-necked bird is stalking tall along the sand ridge, a grotesque apparition: all legs and neck and beak. We slip into shore and climb out for a look. The sandhill crane paces over the ridge and on through tufts of grass inspecting for insects. He does not concern himself with us. We decide we want to see him fly, so we raise our voices like soldiers and charge down the side of the sand ridge. But rather than fly, he, seeming almost as tall as we are, flaps his wings, squawks loud, and charges us. We stop. He stops. It's a wild west showdown between that hard-eyed, spear-headed native and us. He is proud. He has no fear of featherless men. Justin shouts and flaps his arms. The armed bird squawks an incredibly loud and grating squawk and stands his ground. We charge again. He turns with a strained dignity and jogs away, but refuses to dignify our efforts by flying. Another crane appears out of the shadows and strides along with the first like two stick-legged beings from a surreal dream. We stop and so do they. We stand and stare; they begin pacing along through the tufts of grass looking again for insects, frogs—important things—ignoring us. We return to the canoe wondering at the temerity of birds.

The sky turns a luminescent grey; the moon, rich gold, follows us above the black tree line on our left. And now the mosquitoes come, singing past our ears, drawing measures of blood from our necks and shoulders. We paddle and slap and slap and paddle. There's a line of trailer houses to our right with lighted windows and barking dogs. We slide up to a deserted dock and climb out to spray on the insect repellent. I spray Justin; he sprays me.

And then it's back to the waters, following an irregular sky up the river between the trees, floating the image of that sky between black trees that send their reflections straight into the calm waters on either side with no evident break between solid tree and watery image; we must stay to the sky-reflecting part of the river so as not to collide with sunken trees or floating logs. Through river moonlight a muskrat swims, waterwalking its reflection, trailing a long grass stem, carrying the slight gleam of its double wake into the fluid shadows.

Passing close to a sand ridge, a deer snorts and rushes away. Far away a farmyard dog is still barking at our passage, but the river is silent, dark, and lonely, though the moon has called out a crowd of stars for company.

After a while, Justin needs to urinate. "So stand up and let loose," I say. He says he will if I will. I stand up, but the craft wobbles under my feet and the current immediately begins to drift us sideways. I have images of falling into the water while pissing. It's a humiliation I tell Justin I can do without, for I know he'll repeat the story. He laughs loudly and tells me to go ahead, but I have visions of him rocking the boat at precisely the wrong moment. I choose to take us ashore.

Then it's on the water again, laughing at ridiculous thoughts, talking, singing our way up the river night, our voices unnaturally loud between silent shores. How few the songs we've sung together through the busy years:

> Summertime, and the livin' is easy,
> Fish are jumpin,' and the cotton is high;
> Your daddy's rich . . .

We bellow our way up the river this silent summer's night . . . two working fools who care not who hears us. We're strutting to the music, up a silver road, star-syncopated sky above. For a time I don't recognize the stars, but rising above the tree line behind us is Lyra and just below, Cygnus the Swan.

After an hour or so, we run out of songs and jokes and easy talk. The quiet closes in. The work of paddling upcurrent takes its toll and a growing anxiety keeps me watching the river closely for obstructions or the ripple of shallow waters. It's no time to be caught by an outgrabbing snag or a waiting rock.

Hours pass. The moon has lost its way, wandering aimlessly, sometimes lifting clear of the leftbank trees, sometimes dropping behind us, sometimes racing ahead like a hunting hound, its movement caused by the winding of the river. Trees lean toward our passing. Moonlit hills open out to our left and marshes close in on our right. Two horses, one dark brown, one a pale grey, stand on a spit of gravel and lift their dripping muzzles to watch us pass. An owl hoots from a nearby tree. Justin picks up his flashlight and flicks it on catching its big eyes that glow like red coals. "Look at that!" he whispers. "Weird."

Sometimes we envision a farmhouse through the trees or the lights of a pickup truck pass away on a country road. Once we hear disembodied voices ahead of us on the river. A brief red glow appears and disappears in the middle of the water and I angle our canoe to avoid it: three men in a boat smoking and fishing.

Later, we catch the brief silhouette of a deer against the stars on a high bank. Moonlight still sleeps along low rolling hills where crooked oaks and squat junipers stand black against pale grasses. We drift beneath tall black cottonwoods whose leaves hold communion with the stars. The old solid world has lost its voice and we are floating a dream.

It is almost midnight and my flashlight casts a bright moon upon our map. We had passed under a little bridge a mile or two back. I locate that bridge on the map. I see that we have at least five miles to go to reach the Portage Canal that links the Fox River to the Wisconsin River. The canal itself looks to be another two miles long. We can make it tonight, I think, but then I notice that there's a lock on the river a mile or two ahead. Another damned lock! Trying to avoid a dam and portage around another lock in the dark is too much. I tell Justin the news, and he's ready to make camp.

But now to find some high ground in these marshes. We paddle on for a few minutes, passing a lightless farm house on our left. On our right, a black bank rises out of the reeds, and I steer for it. Something moves in the darkness up ahead. I tell Justin to grab the flashlight and see what we're heading into. He clicks it on and there, twenty feet ahead, a dozen green globes, about the size of large marbles, hang in the air glowing strangely. Some are half globes, others are round and swing back and forth. We lift our paddles and stare. We are drifting straight into them. There's movement, a rough grunt. Several florescent globes sway away; others seem fixed. We coast toward them. Then the black faces of several calves materialize around the green globes.

"Cows!" Justin exclaims with some relief.

Yes, calves, six or seven of them, their large eyes glowing green in the flashlight. They stand still as we paddle straight for them, then, as we touch shore, they break away and thunder over the rise. We hear them splashing through water and then thumping up another bank.

We pull the canoe up the bank and quickly unload the tent. We can see the calves in the moonlight watching us from a marshy pasture fifty yards away, but by the time we stretch out inside our tent on our sleeping bags, the curious calves have returned. They sniff and snort around the tent, stamping away mosquitoes, swishing their tails, cropping grass.

Portage

Early morning found us back on the river, not wanting to explain to a local farmer why we were keeping his calves company. The river was shallow now; once we had to maneuver through a tree that had fallen completely across the narrowing channel. Along one stretch of river we found two dead deer lying in the water. Deer have become a pest for the farmers. Either these two were shot or they had eaten herbicides or pesticides. A farmer in Kansas once told me that if a cow walked into a field that had been sprayed in the last hour with a certain chemical it would drop dead.

It was nearly noon when we made the final portage from the Fox River into the Portage Canal that connected the Fox with the Wisconsin River. Joliet and Marquette left the Fox on June 14, 1673. Carrying their canoes into the unknown, they counted their steps: twenty-seven hundred paces from the Fox to the

Wisconsin. We had the benefit of a two-mile canal, though it is no longer in use.

In 1838 the Portage Canal Company, hoping to provide a reliable passage between the Mississippi and Lake Michigan, began digging. They spent $10,000 (which was a bundle of cash in those days) and gave up. In June, 1849, Secretary of War Poinsett convinced the U.S. Congress that they needed a route for military communication and transportation. They dug some more—and gave up; there were conflicts between the State and the contractor, and the men with the picks and shovels were not being paid.

In March, 1851, someone described the partially finished canal: "The banks of the canal are crumbling before the thaw in many places and falling into the stream. The great part of the planking is afloat. Repairs were made and the water let in." In May of that year, the steamer, the *John Mitchell*, tried to pass from the Fox River through the Portage Canal to the Wisconsin River. Unfortunately, another steamer, the *Enterprise*, coming from the Wisconsin River had the same idea. Neither captain would yield, so neither went through. Foiled again.

Two months later the Board of Public Works tried strengthening the banks with posts and boards to prevent quicksand from pouring in and filling up the bed. At the end of August, they let in the water again. Next morning they found all those boards that they had so painstakingly fastened to the sides of the canal had pulled out of the banks and were floating on either side of the canal: two miles of floating plank roads. You could walk the canal, but you couldn't boat it. Disgusted, they gave up again.

Then one year later the Wisconsin River decided to do a little excavating of its own and demonstrate the classic approach to channel formation: the river broke into the canal and tore a channel through the south bank some fifty yards wide and ten feet deep. Take that.

But these Wisconsin folk were not quitters; they would meander along that rotting double-plank roadway and muse about the possibilities, which is to say they mused about money. A new company was formed, the Fox and Wisconsin Improvement Company. They began work again, but the Money Muse is not a reliable friend; this company too sank into bankruptcy.

Still, the canal had its uses. In 1854 the city fathers felt it necessary to pass an ordinance forbidding nude bathing in the canal.

Finally, in 1856, during high water, a small steamer named the *Aquila*, coming from Pittsburg, Pennsylvania, by way of the Ohio River, and up the Mississippi, and then on up the Wisconsin, managed to squeeze through the canal and make its way down the Fox to Green Bay. But little was done to refurbish the canal until the Army Corps of Engineers took over. In 1874, eighteen years after the *Aquila*, the Corps began digging and completed its work within two years. On June 30, 1876 (120 years minus one day before the passage of the *Natty Bumpo*), commercial use of the canal began with the passing of the *Boscobel*, a big, shabby tugboat with 600 horsepower engines.

Unfortunately, they soon discovered that the faster, deeper-draft steamboats could not navigate the Wisconsin River to reach the canal. The Corps of Engineers tried building wing dams on the Wisconsin, but they rapidly silted over, thus defeating navigation along the Wisconsin by 1886. Sometimes willpower and money just aren't enough.

Still, smaller craft and recreational boats continued to use the canal until 1951 when the locks along the upper Fox were bulldozed and the Wisconsin River lock was welded shut.

And thus, after a half century of disuse, came the intrepid Natty Bumpo and his venerable crew to ply old passages and revive the past. William Faulkner once wrote, "The past is not dead; it is not even past." This is true, though occasionally the past needs a little mouth-to-mouth resuscitation to get the old boy wheezing again. Looking at the canal on this hot, still day in June, one could be tempted to doubt its resurrection likely. It was a long straight shaft of water 70 feet wide, filled with water weeds yellowing in the hot sun: a long trough of hot vegetable soup. On either side, silver maples were melting in the heat, but the summer sun was high and the shade they cast was reserved for the dried grass and green weeds on shore, not for us. We paddled through the glare, through viscous weeds and floating scum and past a long row of rotting posts.

We began passing houses. We sweated our way between rows of back yards fenced with chain link. The water grew shallower, seeping through mud flats where brown frogs leaped away over mud-sunk beer bottles, past deflated balls, a broken Big Wheel.

No breeze. Very little water in the canal. We "poled" over shallow places by shoving our paddles into the muck. At length we came to a culvert that passed under a street. We jerked our heavy packs out of the canoe. The long, shadowed tunnel was strung with dusty spider webs and dotted with hanging spiders. Justin, the brave soul, rode in the prow, defending himself with two paddles crossed in front of his face while I gave the canoe a hard shove. He glided away, his shouts at the clinging webs and scurrying spiders echoing through the tunnel. Toward the end of the culvert he lost momentum and had to paddle his way out into sunlight while spiders swung into the empty canoe and scurried up his paddle. He pulled the webs from his sweating face and chest and slaughtered the stowaways without mercy.

We repacked the canoe and set off again. But the water was more shallow than ever and the sun was blazing hot. I was panting now, my heart thumping, sweat dripping onto my glasses. We paddled and poled along a muddy rivulet past long redgold brick buildings, to another long culvert. This time Justin was in no mood to pursue his spider collection, so we carried everything, including the canoe, over the street and down to the other side where we sat down exhausted. Along this section of the canal someone had installed walkways on either side, but the canal wasn't much to look at.

We reloaded the canoe and soon found ourselves poling like snow skiers with two paddles apiece through a few inches of trickling water. Then we were mud-stuck. When we stepped out to push, we sank up our shins into brown glue—and there we were, an overheated four-footed beast slogging through a mud pit, caught like a dinosaur born out of time.

Later, a Mr. John Anglim, vice-president of a volunteer group called The Portage Canal Society (this town will simply not give up on this canal) told us that the recent floods had shoved aside the large pipe that channels water from the Wisconsin River into the canal. That was the reason we had such a hard-going, mud-slogging time of it.

At last we reached that welded iron lock that blocked our passage to the long-hoped-for current of the Wisconsin River. The rusted gates rose high above us. There was nothing for it but to unload everything and climb, gasping, up a steep bank next to a brick apartment house. A long mowed yard ran to a point between the canal and the Wisconsin River; I thought we could probably put up our tent at the pointed end of that arrowhead of a yard behind a blue spruce tree and be almost out of sight of the apartment building. But first we walked over for a look at the Wisconsin River, the next leg of our journey.

I had long imagined this place. Pulitzer-prize-winning author Zona Gale lived most of her life in this little river-bordered, marsh-soaked town. She became the first woman newspaper reporter in Milwaukee and perhaps in the nation. Later she worked for the *Evening World* in New York City, covering everything from Wall Street fraud to tenement life in the New York slums. But she missed her little hometown where she had grown up. She left New York's promise of pleasure and fame and returned to Portage. There she wrote about the obscure destinies of her friends and neighbors in short stories, novels, and a drama, *Miss Lulu Bett,* which won her the Pulitzer Prize for 1920-1921. So fame found her even in this frontier backwater.

I had read her description of the view from her own house which overlooks the Wisconsin River:

> On one bank of a river it should lie—the town that one means when one says "small town." Homes should border the bank, small lawns, sloping to lilacs and willows. The current would be lazy and preoccupied, with leisure for eddies, and daily it would bear old dried trees, dislodged from the up-stream rocks before the first energy of the water had dissolved into meditation. On the opposite shore would be a feathery second growth of maples and hickory trees, looking as if they must shelter white temples, but really only covering the Bridge farm chicken coops. Beyond would be hills, neatly buttonhole-stitched against the flat horizon, usually gray, sometimes violet, and on occasion ripe pink and yellow, like a cut peach.

And there it was. No peaches today, just a white-hot sun and heat-frayed hills. And there were the maples and hickories feathering the far shore, and the wide, preoccupied river eddying through sandbars. And there we saw what we had longed to see, a sandy-brown but rather clear and steady current to carry us downstream to the Mississippi. We slapped each other on our sweating backs and smiled. We were pleased with ourselves. We had traveled over 150 miles upriver with much of it in flood; from here on, we would have the current at our backs.

We wandered the streets with nothing in particular to do. In a bookstore, I found a biography of John Muir's boyhood. It turns out that Muir (whose magnificent description of California's High Sierras in the nineteenth century had mesmerized me many years ago) lived as a youth not many miles from Portage near the Fox River, very near our last night's passage. In the spring of 1849, his family had built a log cabin of bur oak "in the sunny woods, overlooking a flowery glacier meadow and a lake rimmed with white water-lilies," as Muir put it. There they had begun the back-breaking work of cutting the trees, stacking the rocks, and pulling the stumps to clear the land for farming. In spite of the work, this area was for Muir a paradise:

> This sudden plash into pure wildness—baptism in Nature's warm heart—how utterly happy it made us! . . . Oh, that glorious Wisconsin wilderness! Everything new and pure in the very prime of the spring when Nature's pulses were beating highest and mysteriously keeping time with our own! Young hearts, young leaves, flowers, animals, the winds and the streams and the sparkling lake, all wildly, gladly rejoicing together!

Young John Muir had been born again as a naturalist. In that bur-oak cabin they first examined the feathers of a wood duck his father had shot in the creek during a snowstorm. "Come, bairns," cried their Scottish father, "and admire the work of God displayed in this bonnie bird. Naebody but God could paint feathers like these. Juist look at the colors, hoo they shine, and hoo fine they overlap and blend thegether like the colors of the rainbow." And John saw. And John believed.

It was to a new house they built later that young John ran one bitter-cold winter day, carrying against his breast a warm, live loon he had captured. The big strong bird must have been stunned or frozen, for it lay quietly in his arms as he panted up to the house and flung open the door. He set it down in front of the kitchen stove. He had an old tortoise-shell tomcat that spent frosty weather beneath that kitchen stove. When the cat set eyes on and smelled that "strange big fishy, black and white, speckledy bird, the like of which he had never before seen, he rushed wildly to the farther corner of the kitchen." But eventually the old Tom's curiosity sent him soft-stepping back toward the quiet bird. The cat crept forward. The bird watched. Slowly, almost imperceptibly, the loon drew back its long pickaxe bill, "and without the slightest fuss or stir held it level and ready just over his tail." The cat reached out a paw and eased forward—in a flash, the bird struck the cat solidly between the eyes. WUCK! yelled the cat as he "bounced straight up in the air like a bucking bronco" then rushed madly across the room and "made frantic efforts to climb up the hard-finished plaster wall . . . and for the first time that cold winter he tried to get out of the house, anyhow, anywhere, out of that loon-infested room."

The temerity of birds.

Justin and I are neck-deep in cool, tea-brown water. The bottom of the Wisconsin River, unlike the muddy Fox, is all sand. The river is wide. Several streams of current weave through the sandbars brown and gold. We've had our steak dinner and are now lazing away a Sunday afternoon in a deep, quiet pool beneath an overhanging elm—our own John Muir "plash" into nature.

For some time now I've been watching a man and woman in swimming suits, picking their way along the sandbars and wading through pools toward us. I'm keeping a wary eye on these two strangers who walk up and step right into "our" swimming hole, still talking to each other. They seem at home with each other and she is lovely. I lay my head back in the water and look at the sky. I've been away from my wife for a month now, with another month to go.

I look over at Justin and raise my head; I mention something about a Mexican restaurant a local man had recommended. The pretty woman glances up and smiles. She asks if we are visitors in these parts. I unload my three-sentence version of our journey upon the couple and they seem as delighted by the whole project as we are.

Soon we are following them up the river toward their home. David is in insurance; Jennie is a mail carrier who walks thirteen miles a day summer and winter. Both had once been in the sandwich business, running a little shop on the West Coast, but eventually, like Zona Gale, had returned to hometown Portage. A good decision. Lovely homes, pleasant parks, a living business center—a fine place to raise children.

I ask about Zona Gale. They live two doors down from her place, which is now cared for by the Women's Civic League, a club Zona Gale had organized. They immediately offer to arrange a tour for us.

"Right now?" I ask.

"Sure," says David. "We know Barbara who takes care of the place. I'll go over and talk to her."

And so it was done.

Soon we were climbing up over stone terraces, past David and Jennie's well-used canoe, up a little footpath into the flowers of their back yard, and on to the back door of their limestone home. They pulled shirts over their swimsuits and we all walked over to Zona Gale's tall white house. Screened porches top and bottom enclosed the back of the house. Barbara Stuetevant, a short, dignified lady with silver hair, impeccably dressed, welcomed us in the back door with a gracious air. The place was in perfect order. I was shirtless, barefoot, powdered with sand, clothed like a savage in damp, faded, green shorts. I followed the elegant Ms Stuetevant around Victorian furniture over clean, carpeted floors, past somber wainscotting, past dark oaken cabinets built into the walls where Zona Gale had kept her books. She turned around and said with a mischievous smile, "You should see my grandchildren when they come to visit—cartwheeling through this library, playing hide-and-seek through the cabinets. If only the Women's Civic League knew!"

"You've brought life back to this house, Barbara," responded Jennie, "It needs life."

We walked upstairs to a room of white carpets and white walls at the back of the house where Zona Gale used to write facing the interior wall so as not to be distracted by a view of the river. It was a clean, well-lighted room of her own.

We stepped onto the screened-in back porch, and there it was again, the sunlit scene Zona Gale had described over sixty years before. We looked out across the river and Jennie said, "It's always changing. Every morning we get up and first thing, we take a look at the river." The patterns in the sand are always shifting, she said, especially on winter nights when the snows swirl over the sands and leave new patterns for the morning light. "Last night," she said, "the river was indigo and red." I turned and looked at the white wall where Zona Gale wrote. I could see why she turned her back on the river, for who could withdraw the mind to study or write when distracted by such a river.

We climbed up some steep, narrow stairs to the attic where Ms Stuetevant showed us the trap door in the roof Miss Gale used to climb through so she could sunbathe on the roof. "Can you imagine a woman in those days sunbathing on the roof!" Ms Stuetevant exclaimed. "She was a bold woman for her times."

That she was—running off to New York City to chase fires and thieves and city hall corruption. It took, perhaps, a different kind of courage to leave all that and return to little Portage and take up the writing of fiction—still unmarried, though from photographs, she was an attractive woman. She took an active part in the little town she loved. She and an entourage of her women friends would invade the all-male city council meetings and make them uncomfortable with well-thought-out plans to improve Portage. The women never forced a showdown, says Virgil Peters of the *Wisconsin News*, but sat silently waiting while "opposition melted away like snowflakes falling on a sun-warmed roof."

We were sitting on high stools next to a counter in David and Jennie's kitchen eating cheese and crackers and sipping a fine white wine made just down the Wisconsin River near Prairie du Sac. There was music in the living room and the smell of grilled chicken and roasting bratwurst. Justin had met their daughter Sadie and her friend Jessica, both about Justin's age. They had left for a swim in the river.

"I went into a six-month depression. I don't know why." Jennie was describing the home in the country several miles out of town they had left to move into this house on the river. "We picked out this house. It's beautiful. We wanted to move. But I guess I knew that place so well, and so much had happened there. We built it, and I knew everything about it. But when the kids started getting jobs in town and we started running them back and forth to all their activities, it made sense to move."

I could see that. It did make sense. But the place you raise your children steals a room in your heart. But then, after all that living, it is the place that remains and our lives that prove transient. It's not strange we would cling to the wood and stones of our children's passage.

We ate well that night, finished another bottle of wine, and talked the evening away. They offered to put us up for the night, and I'm baffled as to why I turned them down—some reluctance to impose on their generosity perhaps, or that desire to rough it all the way. Justin was quite willing to stay in their home; Sadie and Jessica had been good company. But my stubborn soul turned us back, back to a quick dash through a malicious fog of mosquitoes to our small hump of a house and to a slow falling-to-sleep on hard sleeping pads.

Negotiating The Unknown

The first of July. We skimmed along the current making good time. The sky was blue, the air warm, as July air should be; the river itself seemed unchanged from the days of Joliet and Marquette: "very broad, with sandy bottom, forming many shallows, which render navigation difficult. It is full of vine-clad islets." Sometimes those seven men and their two birchbark canoes seemed just ahead, just beyond that tree-covered island, moving through the shadows around that bend.

We had difficulty keeping to the deeper currents. Passing to one side of a tree-covered island, we would find the water slowing to a ripple as it passed over a wide sandbar. We would steer wide of the shallow water and then make a run for the rippling edge. The canoe would sometimes catch and grind as we jammed our paddles into the sand and shoved mightily to scrape us over the crest into dark, deep water. Once we had to walk the canoe through ankle-deep water. I could see why this would be impossible for the old paddle-wheelers.

Toward the middle of the afternoon, the river deepened and widened into a lake; there was a dam somewhere downriver. We were disappointed to lose the current, and disappointed to lose the closeness of either shore. The old monotony of slow movement over long distances settled over us again. Motor boats buzzed by. A jet ski spouting a rooster tail of water rushed us and swerved away. Houses began to dot the shores. The two birchbark canoes ahead faded away into civilized waters.

Justin wanted to return to Portage. He was still thinking of those two young river nymphs he'd accompanied to the swimming hole. I told him river nymphs were dangerous company; they drowned the fools who followed them. He thought he'd take his chances.

By late afternoon, the water had taken on the colors and textures of an impressionist painting: dark textured blues changing into turquoise and grey, to broad, flecked gradations of violet. We were brushing through a Monet, freely revising a frameless Cezanne, smoothing a stroke through a vast, agitated Van Gogh.

As the sun began washing the west in yellow, we began looking for likely camping places. Every plot of land seemed taken by lakeshore homes, but toward evening we found a little grassy half acre surrounded by birches and oaks and thick brush at the foot of a hill.

After making a fire and eating, I forced my way through bushes and began climbing the steep hill behind us. Justin didn't feel like exploring and stayed behind to read his book and dream of river nymphs. As I left the brush and oak trees of the lower slope, the hillside opened into prairie grass and juniper trees: loose, green-black evergreens that spread their lower branches across the grass like a full-length skirt. I walked around the left side of a juniper and stopped dead.

A coyote, not twenty yards away, let out a surprised Hrrrmph! and bounded away into a stand of oaks that bordered a deep ravine. From its feet, four or five pups scattered in all directions. One of them, its ears laid back, raced through sparse grass along the hillside toward the juniper I was standing beside. It scrambled around the other side of the tree and I heard no more.

I stepped back slowly and quietly around the juniper until I came upon it. The little pup stood erect, facing away from me,

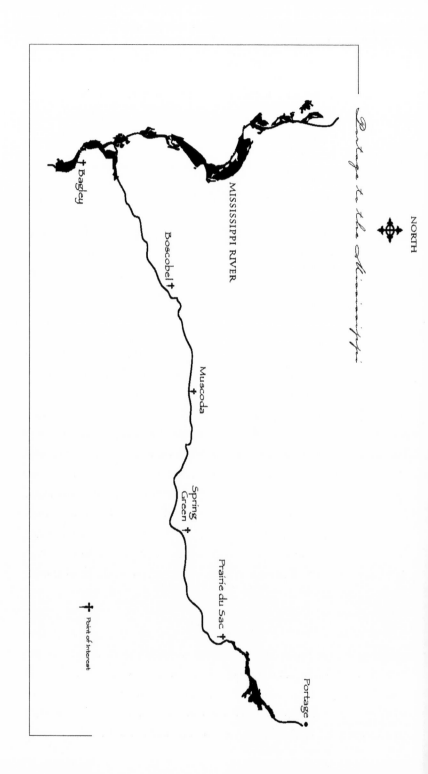

Portage to the Mississippi

NORTH

MISSISSIPPI RIVER

+ Bagley

Boscobel +

Muscoda +

Spring
Green +

Prairie du Sac +

Portage •

+ Point of Interest

looking back the way it had come, its big ears pointed straight up, its grey-brown fur soft, its skinny little tail not four feet from me. The young coyote stood trembling in the shadow of the juniper, yearning toward its vanished mother, waiting for directions. I stood still and watched its quick breathing. I thought of saying hello, but that would have been the briefest of interviews. I waited.

After a few long seconds, the pup trotted hesitantly back into the open grass, head up. I stepped carefully after it. Just then the mother returned, bounding over some brush into the opening and spotted me immediately. Another gruff growl and away she went. This time the little pup knew which way to run and tore off after Mom.

I stood there for several moments smiling at my great good fortune. In all my years of hunting the Kansas hills, I had only seen a live coyote that close once; I had never seen a pup. It is a rare thing to come upon wild animals, though watching television makes us think that it is an expected pleasure in any wilderness setting. As writer Bill McKibben puts it, "After a lifetime of exposure to nature shows and magazine photos, we arrive at the woods conditioned to expect splendor and are surprised when the parking lot does not contain a snarl of animals mating and killing one another. Because the only images we see are close-ups, we've lost much of our sense of the calm and quotidian beauty of the natural world." I was happy to have stumbled onto a close-up.

I returned to camp to tell Justin.

Evening was leaching the color from the blue riverlake as we sat beside the fire and listened for the bubble of boiling coffee. We had lost our grill over the dam on the Fox River, so we propped the filled coffee pot on burning logs. We sat together in the long grass as the flames licked down into coals, watching a world unframed by television screens, living an adventure not plotted by screen writers, a life not ordered by the pages of a book. Tear away the book covers and move into the actual scene and suddenly the vast unknown sits right down beside me and will not go away. We sit on somebody else's land, beside an unfamiliar lake, warming ourselves with wood filched from an unknown man's trees. We are migrants, passing through the lands of strangers with the old giant Mystery as our companion and his brother, Insecurity, sitting nearby.

Marquette and that band of seven men must have felt the power of the unknown much more strongly than us. They had no maps but the one they were drawing. They had only the vaguest descriptions of what lay ahead: somewhere out there a wide, unknown river was flowing south past hostile tribes, man-devouring whirlpools, bellowing river monsters. Before embarking on this leg of their journey, Marquette reached out to lay hold of assistance against this unequal combat with the Unknown: "Let us kneel together in this vast wilderness and commend ourselves to the Mother of God. We will ask her to-day, and every day, to intercede with her Son to protect us and guide us safely through this perilous journey."

He knew that their prayers did not guarantee their safety, for many Jesuit missionaries had lost their lives on such voyages. Father Leonard Garreau was killed by ambushing Iroquois when scarcely out of sight of fortified Montreal. Father Rene Menard carried the baggage around some rapids while his companion was negotiating the rapids in their canoe. When his companion went back to search for him, he found no trace; Menard was never seen again. Father Ribourde, on an expedition with Henri Tonty in the Illinois country, went for a walk in a sunny meadow, breviary in hand, while his companions cooked dinner. He did not return. A marauding band of Kikabous, on the trail of their enemies the Iroquois, found and murdered the old man.

Marquette prayed for safety, but he was seeking something more. He had told the Menominee Indians that he was ready to die, so his prayers were more than a request for safety; they were an appeal for a plot line that fulfills a wider and much more complex story, whether their part in that longer tale was to be tragedy or successful epic.

As our coffee was coming to a boil, the sticks that propped up the pot broke and poured hot coffee into the hissing coals. I grabbed my bandanna and snatched it up from the ashes, but we only saved a half cup apiece and it seemed too late to try again. A small accident.

Two diesel trucks side-by-side are roaring down a hill on Interstate 70 through thunder and night rain. Ahead of them a little red convertible with a white canvas top suddenly slides right, swerves left and smashes head-on into the concrete partition, flips on its side, and skids down the highway. The two huge trucks, side-by-side, slam on their brakes. The driver in the left truck sees the little red car hit the concrete partition again, flip up and crash onto the concrete ridge, catapult back onto the highway, and slam down on its tires—still sliding—coming to a stop facing the center partition, a crumpled relic of a car sitting halfway out in the passing lane. The man in the semi on the right brakes hard. The man in the truck in the passing lane flips on his turn signal, thinking he can miss the smashed car if he squeezes right . . .

> *What might have been is an abstraction*
> *Remaining a perpetual possibility*
> *Only in the world of speculation.*
> *What might have been and what has been*
> *Point to one end, which is always present.*

Nudes, Architects, And River Gourmets

We hugged the shore to avoid the current that swept toward the high dam ahead of us. We were frightened by dams now, and this looked to be five or six times higher than the dams on the lower Fox. We roped the canoe to a boulder and carted our stuff over a ridge and down a steep slope to the bottom of the dam, returned for the canoe, then shoved off again, the water swirling and foaming rapidly away from the base of the dam. We had a current again.

A mile downriver, we shot through a treacherous surge of brown water that angled through the piers of a bridge and turned us half around. David and Jennie in Portage had warned us that canoeists had drowned beneath that bridge, so we were careful to maneuver into the center of the water flow and avoid the churning waters near the piers.

Black-and-white dairy cows watched us from a sandy, brushy bank. Turtles plopped into the water from sun-soaked logs. Steep, wooded hills rose abruptly above flat pastures as we waterwalked the Wisconsin. This was a river for canoeing: current strong, houses few, water darkly clear, banks sandy, hills high and lovely.

A plain blue flag was snapping in the breeze above a little encampment of tents on the south shore. In a remarkably prescient moment, I said to Justin, "It must be a nudist camp; the flag has nothing on." In fact it had no insignia—just a blue flag. We moved around the bend and saw that it was indeed so—I give you the unfabricated truth. Twenty or thirty men lolled about the beach catching the full effects of the sun. Bearded men, men with long mops of tangled hair, clean-cut men, men with white bodies, one man with a muscled burnt red-brown body, paunchy men, gaunt, rib-evident old men, young athletes—with nothing on but sunlight. Some sat on their towels, one lay in another's arms, two walked dangling toward us.

"I don't believe it," said Justin.

We stared.

The two naked men walked purposefully toward us and waded into the water—one was the burnt red-brown muscle man and the other a man of baggier proportions and whiter skin. The latter held a camera and commenced snapping pictures of us as if we were the oddity. They waded up to their waists and watched us.

I was minded of the old joke about nudists: What's so strange about their private parts?

They have none.

In Africa I was used to semi-nakedness. I expect poverty was a key factor for Dinka and Nuer tribesmen; if the choice is between food and clothing in that climate, food wins. Those who could afford it donned western shorts and shirts or Arabic robes. But these men before us were not constrained by poverty; they were evidently well fed. The baggy-stomached fellow kept taking snapshots. As we passed within a few yards, the photographer lowered his camera and asked if we would like a snapshot sent to our home. Say what? Here was a mystery cloaked in a conundrum.

"Where do you live?" he cried as we paddled by.

Justin looked back and gave me a blank stare.

I looked at him.

Then a thought materialized. This taking of our pictures must be a means of defense against those who would harass these men. It wouldn't surprise my Kansas brain if pickup trucks of beer-guzzling farm boys make occasional raids on their camp. Snap our picture and this encampment of the naked and the fed would have evidence of who was tossing the beer bottles or launching the bottle rockets. But we had no wish to singe their skins with Roman candles, or send their tender hides scrambling into the bushes to the staccato beat of Black Cats, or see them leaping like lightning to the thunder of cherry bombs. We paddled on.

We rode the current past wooded hills and around sandy islands dense with green brush and trees. Just after the river made a sharp turn around a steep hill on our left, we saw an odd building above us. A high bridge carried a highway over the river next to a long, low, glassed building that hung out over the cliff. It had a pagoda-like roof toward one end surmounted by a thin steeple.

We tied up our canoe and climbed the steep embankment to the highway bridge. There stood a serrated pole rising out of asymmetrical hexagons as if some artist had tried to catch our eye with originality. Attached to this odd pole was a sign: Frank Lloyd Wright VISITOR'S CENTER. What's this? I had no idea that the famous architect had grown up just across the river in the little town of Spring Green. He had designed this long, low building that looked over the river to his boyhood home. And he had designed and built a home in the hills nearby, as well as long, low buildings beautifully adapted to the landscape that served as a drafting studio and living quarters where fifty apprentices worked the fields, growing their own food while they studied under Wright.

Frank Lloyd Wright had been an original. He rebelled against the ornate Victorian fashions of his day, but did not succumb to the functionalism that has littered our campuses and public squares with assorted shoe-box buildings in different sizes. Inside the visitor's building, whose long wall of windows is cantilevered over the cliff edge, we found a restaurant. We sat down for coffee and a cinnamon roll. Overhead exposed beams supported the long open rooms. Fireplaces of rough-cut limestone created occasional partitions; long panels of polished mahogany swept around the limestone and continued along lower wall sections. There was a kind of functionalism—a straight, jutting terrace of a building with a long row of windows opening a view across the river, but at least it was a simplicity that emphasized the wood and stone; the materials were themselves beautiful. And its long horizontal line and red-orange roof complemented the vertical green pines and rocky hill on which it rests. Wright valued the lay of the land, the perennial beauty of the landscape, and did not presume to conquer it. I scribbled down a quotation:

> "Culture is a way of making that way of life which is a civilization beautiful. . . . Then you have something which will always live, because it is what lives today in all these civilizations that have disappeared. Their way of life is gone, but the beauty created by the artists of that time, their buildings, their sculptures, their paintings, whatever they had that gave beauty to the life they lived—we have it, and it lives for us still."
> —*Frank Lloyd Wright, January 18, 1953*

For that reason, our architects should not have abandoned the ornate for the simplistic. Modernist architects like Le Corbusier and Van der Mies have come upon us like the plague, devising an architecture for the "new world order of the machine," as Bauhaus founder Walter Gropius phrased it. The old stone chislers, the expert woodcarvers, tapestry weavers, needlework stitchers, fresco painters have, it seems, caught the modernist virus and died. In their place the barbarian armies of men in hardhats slam together steel scaffolds from which to hang the concrete slabs that encase us.

Wright wanted to move architectural designs toward the purity, simplicity, and harmony of Japanese art, but there is a great deal of careful detail and decoration in Japanese art. Why should we abandon ornament and decoration for the simplistic? The simple soon becomes plain; the unadorned, bare; the purity of wall and ceiling merely bland. Less is not more, but, as Robert Venturi put it, "Less is a bore."

Walking down the long corridors of lookalike apartments in a standard highrise in Topeka, Kansas, I've seen that the old folks confined there hang ferns in the windows, tape greeting cards to their flat slab doors, hang handmade wreaths according to the season—anything to escape the soulless repetition of cinder block, sheetrock, and steel door. Why should our children live out their lives in cream-colored boxes? Why can't we take back the multi-glassed windows, the gilded domes, the ornamental fireplaces? Give us again intricate arabesques, Celtic linework, Corinthian flourishes, carved oak and chiseled stone, cut tesserae, and wall paintings to amaze us. To be human is to decorate.

After coffee, we stepped out and walked over toward the Wright home on a nearby hill. The place had burned down twice, and Wright nearly exhausted his resources rebuilding it, for a home near one's hometown is worth rebuilding. He turned it into a workshop, farm, and studio for his apprentices. The boxhead bureaucracies of the state of Wisconsin eventually declared the grounds ineligible for tax exemption as an educational institution and Wright closed the school and moved out.

Perhaps it is evidence of Wright's influence on all those apprentices that his beautiful home up there on the tree-covered hill does not appear avant-garde. Jutting terraces, limestone pillars, rows of windows, sloped roofs—from the outside, at least, it could be almost any rich person's home.

We swept on down the river, passing between steep hills on our left, and flat, muddy, heavily forested islands in midstream.

Ruby-red dragonflies flashed out of the shadows and dodged about us. We had seen dragonflies, but these were winged jewels—bright, sunlit rubies flitting here and there. Four independently muscled and controlled wings give them incredible maneuverability. They are good friends to campers and canoers; adults can devour 300 mosquitoes a day. In the days of the dinosaurs, some dragonflies were as big as our hawks, which makes you wonder how large the mosquitoes were.

There are now over 3500 species worldwide: black dragons, blue pirates, green darners (from the suspicion that they could sew up a sleeping person's lips), bog dancers, green damsels, raggedy skimmers, snaketails, spinylegged clubtails, green-eyed skimmers—thousands of jeweled dancers. They even mate in midair, forming a flying circle or heart. They can take off at thirty-five miles an hour, slipping through the air sideways, stopping, hovering, jetting straight up, alighting on our backpacks, waiting with never-folded wings extended, then flashing away like red-hot sparks.

Birds cheeped and trilled from the shadows of tall island trees. Sand dunes on the far bank washed down to the water on sunny shores. Once we saw a bald eagle swing away from a tall cottonwood. Looking up as we passed the place, we saw its huge, ramshackle nest in a fork of the high tree. Eagles add a new addition to their nest every year; this tree had been home for many years. After we passed, the eagle drifted back to its perch and gave us a stern eye.

We stopped for lunch in the little riverside town of Muscoda. Leaving old Natty Bumpo tied to a stump, we walked into town. In a shadowy bar and grill called the Muscoda Inn, a friendly woman served us up huge hamburgers, saucer-sized slabs of ground beef overlapping the edges of large hamburger buns. A man in a bright green t-shirt beside me at the bar asked where we had left our canoe. He looked to be in his fifties, his thin, sharp face burned a leathery brown beneath a green baseball cap, a long nose pointing at the far wall. "Got to watch out for the damned thieves these days," he observed. "Course we have some good cops here." Was this a warning to us?

I bit into my hamburger while the man and his wife ordered their giant hamburgers. "Just got back from the Mississippi with a load of turtles," he said to the opposite wall.

"Turtles? What do you do with them?" I asked.

"Roast 'em."

"We've seen lots of turtles along the river," I said.

"Nah!" He spat out the word. "Those ain't no good to eat. Need the snappin' turtles."

"How many you get?"

He glanced sideways at his wife. "Twenty-five, thirty."

"That's a lot of turtles. You freeze some of them?"

"Nah! Keep 'em in tanks. Let 'em clean themselves out for four or five days."

I bit into my hamburger.

"You'd be surprised what come out of 'em in that tank." A green eye squinted sideways at me. I sipped my beer.

"Duck feathers and all kind of shit. They'll eat a whole duck, ya know."

"Really?"

"Yep. Got thirty snappers a-swimmin' and a-crawlin' all over each other in that tank water for a couple a days, all that brown crap a-floatin' about, starts to smell like the backside of a bull with the trots. Wads of feathers, bones, all kind of stringy crap come a-floatin' up, ya know."

I took another bite of hot ground beef.

"How do you roast them?" I asked.

His narrow eyes moved in his wife's direction. She said, "Brown the meat first, like you would chicken. Then cut it up and put it between layers of onions, carrots, potatoes—just like you do a roast, layer after layer. Then you slow roast it all together. And them drippings make the best gravy for mashed potatoes!"

They both closed their eyes and moaned in unison at the thought.

I laid my hamburger down and took another sip of cold beer.

The thin line of the man's mouth widened for a moment. "You got to watch yer fingers handling 'em, though, don't you?" The eyes slid back to his wife.

She nodded. "Oh yes. Just the other day I told a young man who was helpin' us for the first time that whatever he did, not to git his fingers down in that there water with 'em. When I go to cut up them rascals, I don't want to have to be lookin' for somebody's finger inside of one."

"No ma'am," I said, and took another bite of my hamburger.

The lady behind the bar told us a nearby resident had hitched up a team of mules and taken them across Death Valley to California, following the historic route of the old forty-mule-team wagons. He had been caught by winter, but had finished his journey the next spring. Which just goes to show that if you look under enough rocks, you can find another fool much like yourself.

That evening we camped on a sandbar. Little flakes of papery stuff began floating out of the darkening forest as if someone were burning paper. Soon clouds of these free-floating bits of cream-colored paper filled the air and came to life. As we stripped off our clothes to go swimming, thousands upon thousands of floating moths flickered over us, alighting on our heads, dropping on our backs, crawling up our legs, and swarming about our faces, a shower of living confetti celebrating our arrival. We headed for the water.

The water was cool, the bottom sandy, and few moths followed us into the powerful current that swept by the sandbar. We would slide out neck deep into the current and feel it begin to lift us off our feet and carry us downstream. As I lost control, a little fear would begin to rise in my chest, the brown water carrying me away from the sandbar until the idea of being swept away took hold and I would stretch out and swim rapidly back. We repeated the little game with the strong river as the sun fell behind the tree line and the river ran red-brown, then mauve, and finally into the deep umbers of night. Justin, like all my boys, is a competitor. He wanted to drift farther and fight back harder. I was afraid of the old river. I stood back in still water, shoulder deep, watching him drift away.

Interdependence Day

We pulled our canoe out of the river and into a patch of brush and willows downstream from an iron bridge that ran a two-lane blacktop into Boscobel, Wisconsin. The Fourth of July, midmorning and already hot. We had been running free for forty days and forty nights, and a hard forty it had been. Now at last we were nearing the place where the Wisconsin River pours into the Mississippi River. Time for a celebration.

Justin strapped on sandals over his tanned feet; we stepped over strands of barbed wire, climbed out of the shade and onto the blacktop. The straight road ran for a half mile along a gravel ridge between wide marshes thick with cattails and broadleafed arrowheads. We set an even pace toward town.

Having skipped dinner the night before and having paddled eight miles without breakfast, we were much in need of "belly munitions," as Sancho Panza would say. The "free" life of travel has its requirements. After locating breakfast, we planned to spend the rest of the day strolling around little Boscobel, then catch the evening fireworks display promised on posters in the little towns upriver.

We walked on. Someone had pitched a *Playboy* magazine down the ditch; its airbrushed ladies lay wrinkled in the hot gravel. A gas station and a few roadside homes gradually made their way toward us. No café—but thoughts of eggs and bacon, a pile of salted hashbrowns sprinkled red with Tobasco sauce, three or four pancakes melting butter patties till it drains into the brown syrup—kept our feet moving.

A few blocks into town, we turned left and followed the main street past old storefront windows where posters advertised the Fireman's Parade. Across from the old railroad depot, we found the Vale Inn Cafe, stepped in and sat down near the window.

Six men wearing jeans or bib overalls, were lined up on swivel stools along the counter, each one meditating into his ceramic coffee mug. One of them was talking tractors: "Good traction. It could pull a load, but I'll tell you this. They steered better without that power steering."

His neighbor nodded. "That worm gear on the side."

Just then a young waitress rushed out from behind the counter and chased a heavy-set man out the door. He followed her back in with a sheepish grin, pulling out his billfold from a hip pocket. He had forgotten to pay. "Well, I almost got away," he said.

The six men had all swiveled toward the door smiling. "He likes women chasing after him," said one.

The man laughed.

The place was busy. Elderly couples sat at little tables with red-checkered tablecloths. Six teenagers: three boys, three girls, pushed open the door and walked in. Justin looked up from his coffee—members of his tribe, the teenagers. The six found their way to a larger table and slid into chairs. Two of the boys wore

Nike caps, the other a Nike t-shirt—global conformity in the back hills of Wisconsin. Though they sat as couples, the three girls were talking across the table to each other; the boys read their menus. One of the Nike hats ordered hamburgers and fries, and the other boys followed suit. One hat looked across the table at the other and asked, "So what are you doing today?" The second shook his head. "Nothing *to* do." They looked around the cafe. The first boy shrugged and said, "There's a livestock auction." After a minute, he added, "There's the tractor pull." The second sighed and added, "We could go throw rocks off the bridge." His friend gave a wry smile, "There's plenty rocks."

A grey-haired man in a bright red Miller High Life t-shirt pulled tight across his belly walked in leaning on a cane and eased into a chair next to an older couple. After ordering coffee, he said, "Used to be a man come in here everyday. Would read the Bible for half an hour before ordering breakfast. Drink a couple cups of coffee, but he'd sit right there and read his Bible the half hour before breakfast every morning." He paused for a moment. "Always brought his car into the shop. Used to put upwards of three, four-hundred-thousand mile on each one too." He smiled. The woman at the table added, "Had a nice-looking wife too. Tall. Slim. Pretty hair."

People were gathering outside along the sidewalks for the parade. Justin and I were devouring our little haystacks of hash-browns red with Tobasco, our eggs, our pancakes and syrup, sausages, and sipping at our coffee. Small-town cafes in the Midwest have dependable breakfasts—good prices too: more calories per buck than any other meal.

Newcomers drifted in and stopped to talk.

I looked at Justin. He was pouring syrup on the last of his pancakes. A few bites later he was done. I took a last sip of coffee, paid our bill, and we walked out to join the people crowding the hot sidewalks. Late morning, no shade. An infant dressed in red, white, and blue slept in a stroller; the mother held her white cloth hat over his head.

With the wail of a fire truck siren and a blast of its air horn, the parade begins. The red, white, and blue infant sleeps on.

A handful of blaring trumpets, whining clarinets, explosive snare drums and a thumping bass drum bring on the Boscobel Bulldog Marching Band stepping out in red t-shirts and black shorts.

Policemen cruise by in late-model cars throwing candy. Children scramble into the street, going down on hands and knees for Tootsie Rolls and butterscotches in yellow cellophane.

The VFW, old men in uniform, march by, lift their rifles on command, and fire a staccato volley into the air. A car pulls a flatbed trailer with a group of men spray-painted metallic copper, skin and clothes. They stand like bright statues of the marines who raised the flag over Iwo Jima. "They've won so many prizes for that," remarks a woman beside me.

A yellow, motorized, eight-foot-long fireman's hat weaves along the street leading a parade of six fire trucks—bright yellow, bright red—their sirens whooping, rolling by on tall tires. A little boy in bib overalls is jumping up and down, up and down. The volunteer firemen reach into bags and fling their hands. Candy rattles across the asphalt and onto the sidewalks. Two three-year-olds scramble out, but soon return to their parents with pouting lips; the older kids have scooped up every piece. Another band marches by misstepping to John Phillip Sousa. More fire trucks blaring horns; they must have driven in from towns all over these isolating hills. The men are volunteers; these towns are too small to pay fulltime firemen.

Square dancers go skipping by on a flatbed trailer; it's the Cripple Creek Cloggers. The local Karate Club is kicking and thwacking past on another flatbed. A tiny black train engine putts about the street. Clowns on roller blades throw more candy, aiming at the little ones. A pickup truck comes by pulling a stump grinder. Somebody's passing out yardsticks with advertisements stamped on the back. A little pep band on a trailer is blasting out a tune. The swim team is blowing bubbles. Politicians in dark suit coats stride by shaking hands with spectators and smiling through their sweat. The Dairy Princess waves demurely from a polished convertible. A giant paper mache turkey rolls by advertising somebody's turkey farm. Girls march by holding pro-life banners. The Apple Queen smiles past. The drum and kazoo band comes pounding along, squawking out nasal discords. Men and women in Civil-War-era costumes wave. There's a beer truck. And finally the horses: horse-drawn carts, a daintily stepping midget pony, eight costumed riders on horses bringing up the past.

Justin and I blend into the crowd that is sucked into the wake of the parade. We find our way to the city park. Smoke pours up from canvas tents where sweating men turn the brats and hotdogs and hamburgers on blackened grills. Women pull cold Pepsis and Mountain Dews out of rattling ice chests and slop baked beans onto paper plates. Parents hand over dollar bills and pass hot dogs to waiting children who squirt them, and sometimes themselves, yellow and red with mustard and ketchup then quickly take that first hot bite.

Nearby, in a wooden shelter house, a woman in cowboy boots and tight jeans, backed by electric guitars and drums, is swaying and shouting into a microphone, "I should-a been a cowboy! I should-a been a cowboy!" We walk through the smoke past drifting crowds. A woman with stringy blonde hair sits smoking on the grass beside her sleeping boyfriend. A heavy, balding man strolls by, a mat of greying hair falling down his back to his waist. Children shout and dodge past the legs of strolling adults. A young woman with a fierce face commands a ten-year-old girl, "You go tell Carmen if that's the way she's gonna be, I'll put a fist in her mouth. Now you go tell her." The little girl dances away in a faded dress to pass the threat.

The karate club, all clothed in white, loose uniforms, are doing demonstrations. Lines of white-robed boys and girls, men and women, run smiling toward each other like white-robed angels, then leap and jab and kick the air, and jog back to their places. I am surprised by how many people are participating in this self-defense club. Can there be so much danger of muggings in these small towns that fifty or sixty people need to learn the art of thwacking thy neighbor? I doubt it. The demonstrations are arranged like choreography: shin snapping, kidney bursting, neck chopping are all done in a kind of feinting dance performed to recorded music; it's a nonviolent karate club.

Justin and I walk up the hill, away from the crowds. "How do you like the celebration?" I ask.

He sighs, "Not much to do." Teenage boredom must be a communicable disease.

"We could walk around the town," I say.

"We've already done that. Let's find a movie." Justin's main remedy for boredom.

"But we've already seen the movie that's showing."

"Let's see it again," he says.

"That bored?" I say.

"That bored," he says.

"All right, but let's look at the gravestones in this graveyard up here first."

"Well that sounds exciting," he says, but he follows me into the graveyard planted about with tombstones and pine trees. Old limestone headstones mark the dying of Civil War sons. In the 1860s, Boscobel must have been a newly built town on the frontier, yet the young men left their farms and families and took the trains to Chancellorsville and Chattanooga, to Cold Harbor and Gettysburg, to Spotsylvania and Cedar Mountain, returning dead to this cedar-shaded hill. Was it duty? Was it faith in emancipation? Or was it that yearning to escape the life of livestock auctions and rock throwing off the bridge that sent them so far from home?

We happen upon the gravestone of John A. Nicholson, the founder of the Gideons, those Bible-passing groups of old men who used to stand about schools in my youth and hand out green New Testaments to embarrassed junior-high boys and girls. A sign says that Nicholson had been a traveling salesman who had started distributing free Bibles to help other traveling salesmen far from home. After six weeks, I'm missing home, wife, and children.

Justin and I wander back toward the drums and guitars of the country-western band. The white sun has passed its zenith. A little girl with red hair and dirty toenails leans against a post of the shelter house and watches the woman in blue jeans swaying and singing. The little redhead is about as old as my own little Julia. Julia, my Snoofer, is a firestorm of a girl with a tinder temper and the soul of a poet. She's been scribbling poems since she was six, better poems than I have ever written. This year, absent Justin and me, she and the rest of the family will do what we do every year: walk over to little Washburn University, a few blocks from home, and join thousands upon thousands scattered across the grass for the fireworks display.

Last year a magnificent thunderstorm blew up during the show. As flashing, rumbling thunderheads loomed into the starry sky, the attendants scrambled to let off as many fireworks as possible to beat the storm. Thunder competed with explosions. One rocket misfired and swooped into bystanders sending them screaming. Nobody hurt. Arcs of glittering gold streaked out across the stars. Cannon blasts pounded through our chests, leaving ragged puffs of smoke drifting before the storm. Suddenly, a cold wind swept down over the crowd. People began to stand up. We could smell rain through the gunpowder. Then, with a furious rush, the rain ran over us—icy cold, washing across the shouting crowds. Fathers grabbed up lawn chairs and blankets, mothers reached for the hands of confused children, everyone started to run, fathers yelling, daughters screaming, children laughing. Mothers shouted to keep their kids close. It was like being caught in war.

We were all soaked in seconds, a great mass of refugees running through the storm, faces streaming with cold water, wading cold-ankle-deep through the parking lots. My teenage daughter Johanna, splashing along beside me shouted, "This is the BEST! The BEST!" And it was.

There is always a price to be paid for freedom, and the price is paid in peacetime as well as in war. I'd been seeing this all day: in the sweat of men and women working the grills, in the smiles of firemen waving from trucks, in the hands of a man advertising his business by passing out yardsticks, in the story of the man reading his Bible at a café table, in the handshake of a woman running for office. A Polish poet put it this way: "You pay for freedom with all your being, therefore call this your freedom, that paying for it continually you possess yourself anew."

I accompanied Justin to our second viewing of *Mission Impossible*. It wasn't my choice of activity, but a young man's thirst for excitement needs some attention and we had several hours to kill before the fireworks display. It's a price parents pay for free time.

I didn't want to escape this place and time, here, with him. When would we ever see it again? I'm not against the occasional entertainment, but for Justin, as with much of his generation, movies, television, video games, even books seem to be a kind of antithesis to real life, an exit from the colors and sounds, the smells, the very feel of this earth, and a substitute for real relationships. Granted, the crowds of strangers, a hillside meadow of old gravestones, and the smoke drifting above the cook tents into late-afternoon sunlight may not compete with the anxious plot line and concentrated mayhem of a Hollywood blockbuster, but if we never learn to be at peace with ourselves and gaze upon this "world unfathomably fair," aren't we misfits, self-exiled into phantom worlds of someone else's imagination?

About ten that evening in the deepening night, the first explosion blasts the night sky over Boscobel. A thousand voices rise across the starlit field beneath the dark, crowding hills. A child begins to cry. A mother near us takes off her red tartan blanket and wraps it around her daughter's shoulders. The night is chill. Three more quick concussions pound the night and the show is on. Thousands of fellow citizens lie about us on blankets or lean against trees or sit huddled in shadowy groups peering up as exploding lights flash across their faces.

"Paul! Paul! Sit down!" A little boy has been climbing all over his mother for the last half hour. She lies face up, wrapped in a blanket, enduring. The little boy is wide awake and will not be still. Grandma, who sits close by takes him on her lap. He struggles to get up. "Do you need a spank?" asks grandma. "No," says Paul.

Rocket after rocket streaks into the black sky and rips the night into bright colors. As many as five rockets are in the air at once, wavering high into the stars and exploding in rapid succession. As if one, the crowd roars as a spectacular golden sphere bursts into being, rapidly expands and suddenly snaps away into blue confetti; silver salvos streak upward, bend, and fall into crackling showers. Green lights shatter. Red flowers burst into bloom. The crowd murmurs.

Near the end of the show, an explosion sends little parachutes drifting over the crowd. Each parachute carries a sparkling, smoking, bit of fire. Most of them fizzle out and the parachutes are lost in the night. But one comes drifting over our tree still bravely spitting fire. It floats over Paul and his mother and grandmother, over Justin and me, over many, many others. It seems to have gone out, then it snaps back to life, trailing grey smoke, floating, fading away, still flickering toward the graveyard on the hill.

As the crowds rise to leave, Justin pulls me to my feet and we head back out of town. It's almost midnight. We stop at a late-night grocery and buy doughnuts, then take the gravel-ridge road toward the river, eating doughnuts as we walk. A stream of headlights washes past us into a current of red taillights, heading out of town.

After a while the traffic thins. The night grows quiet. Still walking. There is a constant price for freedom. You learn that canoeing. Nothing's easy and you find you need each other every stroke of the way. We are walking over wide marshes. Justin has his hand on my shoulder. Near and far, on every side, thousands upon thousands of fireflies are winking through the cattails and swamp reeds, their soft-sudden glowings reappearing in the standing waters of the marsh. Rising and falling, turning and drifting, silently signalling each other through the night, they soar among the steady stars and stray around and over us. We walk among them like gods through a galaxy—with ten thousand stars for the choosing.

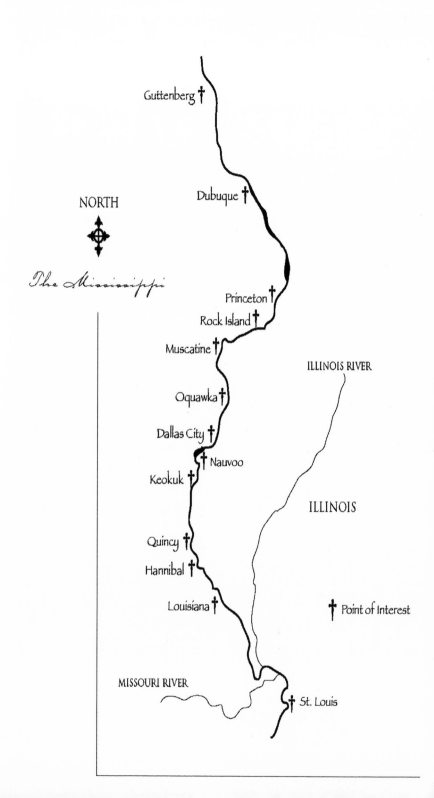

PART FOUR

LOCKED AND DAMMED

And all is seared with trade; bleared, smeared with toil;
And wears man's smudge and shares man's smell: the soil
  Is bare now, nor can foot feel, being shod.
                              —*Gerard Manley Hopkins*

Mississippi

It was full summer. Everywhere the sun increased its power. Swinging near a bank, we reached up for ripe mulberries hung white, red, and purple on overhanging branches. Cattle stood chewing and staring, hoof-deep in hot mud. Flies buzzed up from wet dung and swerved out over the water. The river ran brown and yellow and green around muddy islands of tall trees where shaded birds sang through the heat. High above the forested hills, a bald eagle turned slowly against a pale sky. A warm southwest breeze was blowing in our faces, sending choppy little waves against us as we dipped our hats in the river and poured cool water over our heads and over our shirts. Strange freedom.

I had run out of maps. Back in Kansas, I had decided not to go to the expense of buying maps of the last leg of the Wisconsin River nor of the Mississippi, thinking we couldn't get lost on such big rivers. Another mistake. But one advantage to not having maps was that our sense of anticipation increased. Like the explorers of 1673, we knew the "Big Water," the "Mesipi," was out there, but we were uncertain when we would reach it.

Sometime in midafternoon we approached a high bridge of concrete and iron. Where there's a highway, there must be gas stations, and we were thirsting for a cold drink. We tied up to a tree and clambered up a steep, weedy bank, stepping over a snarl of wild grapevines and through a waist-high patch of stinging nettles. I lifted my arms over my head to avoid the toothy leaves, but Justin, not recognizing the weed, caught some nettles on his wrist. He shook his hand and rubbed hard; the painful white rash would hurt and itch for fifteen or twenty minutes: sharp memories of my boyhood.

Just above us, near the gravel of the railroad embankment, we came upon a opossum hanging dead in a mulberry tree. Part of the hairy skin had ripped away from the skull and flies buzzed about its grinning snout. It hung there like a signal, having been bounced off the track and into the tree by a speeding train. We were leaving the quiet of free-flowing currents, small towns, and dairy farms, and sweeping suddenly into the present industrial age of mechanized transport, big cities, riverside factories and loading facilities, of reconstructed rivers used as multi-laned highways for commerce and leisure. "Two drifters, out to see the world," would find Moon River a muddy, knockabout place.

Late that afternoon we passed under an ugly railroad bridge and turned to see four red engines of the Chicago Northwestern Railroad charge over the river dragging a long line of blackened oil cars. The tall hills on either hand shouted back the roar and rhythmic rumble, and even on the water, we could feel the heavy vibrations shaking through us. A little muskrat, its fur sleek in the afternoon sun, nosed quietly along the bank near some fallen trees.

High hills roughly crowned with limestone outcroppings pushed the river into a relatively narrow channel. Vultures drifted out from behind a hill on our left, then dropped down to skim the steep hillsides, then rose effortlessly to wheel over the hill again. We drank warm water from our canteen and kept paddling. Soon the hills to right and left receded, giving way to flat muddy islands, a confusion of driftwood, brush, trees, and weeds. We could see a high ridge of dark green forest straight ahead. Below that ridge, now cast in late-afternoon shadows, we caught a glimpse of a wide band of water.

After 600 miles, we had reached the great river!

On the seventeenth of June, 1673, Joliet and his men entered the river with, as Marquette wrote, "a joy I can not express." He described the scene as they turned downriver: "On the right is a considerable chain of very high mountains, and on the left fine lands; it is in many places studded with islands. On sounding, we have found ten fathoms (about 60 feet) of water. Its breadth is very unequal: it is sometimes three quarters of a league (over two miles), and sometimes narrows in to three arpents (220 yards)." They saw no sign of men: "We see nothing but deer and moose, bustards and wingless swans, for they shed their plumes in this country. From time to time we meet with monstrous fish, one of which struck so violently against our canoe, that I took it for a large tree about to knock us to pieces." This was probably a Mississippi catfish. Mark Twain, two centuries later, said he himself had seen one that measured over six feet in length and weighed two hundred fifty pounds. The men spotted a swimming mountain lion, and a strange fish with a long flat bone that protruded a foot and a half from the snout, ending in a flat circle as wide as the hand: "In leaping out of the water the weight of this often throws it back."

They saw buffalo for the first time and stopped to shoot one. Marquette is the first European to describe these animals in de-

tail. "They are very fierce," he says, "and not a year passes without their killing some Indian. When attacked, they take a man
with their horns, if they can, lift him up, and then dash him on
the ground, trample him, and kill him. When you fire at them
from a distance with gun or bow, you must throw yourself on
the ground as soon as you fire, and hide in the grass; for, if they
perceive the one who fired, they rush on him and attack him."
Marquette counted one herd of four hundred. But of man they
saw nothing for nine long days and some three hundred miles.

It was different for us. As soon as we turned down the river
we were met by fleets of motor boats, boats of every variety:
flat speed boats with huge engines skipping downriver with a
raucous roar, tall cabin cruisers droning steadily upriver, nasty
little one-person jet skis zig-zagging everywhere, pontoon boats
full of people grumbling slowly along the brown current. There
were hundreds of them on the river on this Friday afternoon,
motoring back and forth, churning up the water, raising steep
wakes to knock us about.

Still, it was a fine thing, after so many weeks of persistence,
to have achieved our entry into the Mighty Muddy. Mark Twain
was tremendously proud of this river. He boasted, "It is not a
commonplace river, but on the contrary is in all ways remark-
able. Considering the Missouri as its main branch, it is the longest river in the world—four thousand three hundred miles. It
seems safe to say it is also the crookedest river in the world,
since in one part of its journey it uses up one thousand three
hundred miles to cover the same ground that the crow would fly
over in six hundred and seventy-five. It discharges three times
as much water as the St. Lawrence, twenty-five times as much
as the Rhine, and three hundred and thirty-eight times as much
as the Thames. No other river has so vast a drainage-basin; it
draws its water-supply from twenty-eight states and territories;
from Delaware on the Atlantic seaboard, and from all the coun-

try between that and Idaho on the Pacific slope—a spread of forty-five degrees in longitude. The Mississippi receives and carries to the Gulf water from fifty-four subordinate rivers that are navigable by steamboats, and from some hundreds that are navigable by flats and keels. The area of its drainage-basin is as great as the combined areas of England, Wales, Scotland, Ireland, France, Spain, Portugal, Germany, Austria, Italy, and Turkey; and almost all this wide region is fertile; the Mississippi valley, proper, is exceptionally so."

Already in Twain's time, bigger seemed better to Americans.

Several miles downriver we saw long square buildings on shore and I noted that there must be a town there. We began crawling toward it, sloshed back and forth by running wakes. A girl in a bikini flipped off her skis near us. Sharp waves broken by successive troughs slammed against our canoe, slopping water over the gunwales; we rocked madly back and forth to keep our little craft beneath us. After a while, we happened to glance downriver and noticed that those long low buildings on shore had moved a considerable distance upriver toward us. We stared. We saw that they were in fact a river barge heading straight for us, and much nearer than we had supposed: a five-thousand-horse-power tugboat shoving a quarter-mile length of barges upcurrent: fifteen long barges, steel-cabled in sets of three. If a little jet ski could send a foot-high wake against us, what would this river monster do to us? I shouted. Justin shouted. We leaned into our paddles and waterhobbled through the breaking waves toward the back side of a small island to escape the barge's wake. We listened to the deep thunder of the engines as the long, mechanical monster passed us by.

But surprisingly, the passing barge gave off very little wake. Though it was heavily loaded and could carry 22,500 tons of goods, it somehow managed to swallow its own wake. Evidently the flat prows of the lead barges channel the water beneath, rather than sending out a wake on either side. (Later we met an older man who told us that years ago the barges had pointed prows and would regularly swamp smaller craft with their wakes.) The tug's powerful propellers did churn up a whole series of rolling water hills directly behind it. The water would boil up into a turbulent mound, then sink down, then rise up again—a whole series of diminishing hills trailing after the moving tug. Days later, we would learn to ride them.

And then we noticed an astonishing thing. On the side of the tug's white pilot house was an insignia: a circle with what looked like a black-hatted Jesuit paddling a canoe. The name of the tug was the *Marquette*.

What are the chances of that?

Storybook Life

Five miles downriver, I'd had enough of six lanes of boat traffic. I decided to take a quiet backwater through the miles of sloughs and lakes that meander through the tree-covered islands and make a green and brown mosaic of the upper Mississippi.

As we passed into the slough, the world grew still. Tall trees rose out of waist-high grasses on either side. A small raccoon peered out from under some brush, sniffed the air, and disappeared. The current slowed. The channel narrowed and began to snake through the trees. We passed another channel that wound away to our right and another that branched off to the left. The farther we paddled, the narrower our passageway. I was trying to determine which channel to take by following the strongest current, but after a while the surface grew still and I could not determine which way to go. For all I knew, this maze of winding waterways went on for miles and never returned to the main current. I had no map. It was already late in the afternoon, and I began to worry about having to spend the night in this labyrinth.

We maneuvered around fallen trees and kept watching for some trickling of current through the half-submerged limbs. Occasionally the sun blinked through the leafy canopy, but along these twisting, quiet channels surrounded by forest, the light dissolved into a dry, green mist. The Indians had warned Marquette of monsters that swallow canoes whole. The farther we paddled, the more it felt as if we had inadvertently slipped into the maw of a sleeping river monster and were forcing our way through its complicated entrails. An hour or so later we were twisting our way through its small intestines, and I was afraid these would divide into shallow capillaries too small for our canoe, and the Natty Bumpo and his mighty crew would end up being nothing more than a lost arterial occlusion.

Deep, deep in that slough, we came upon a couple in an aluminum jonboat fishing. Jonah and his wife? They were surprised to see us. "Don't see many folk back here," said the old man, rubbing a hand through his grey hair.

"Where are we?"

"We call this here Big Cat Slough," he said.

"We're lost."

He smiled and pointed to a channel that turned round another wooded island on our right and told us to follow that west. I was grateful. We made the turn around the island, passed into a tributary channel on our left, and eventually wound our way out a narrow opening and around and through several more, keeping the diffused light of the setting sun before us. An hour later, we squirted out a muddy sphincter into the main channel.

Everywhere motorboats ripped the waves. This way, that way, no particular way. We staggered along at our normal pace.

Vacationers on a sand bar told us we could find a campground near the little town of Bagley by taking a channel eastward until we saw a couple flags sticking out of the water. We found the flags hanging on long limber poles near the entrance of a long corridor of water that ran back between lines of trees. A mile and a half of twisting channels brought us to the eastern shore. The sun was about to set across the river, so it was time to find a camping place. And a camping place we had found. It looked like a major rendezvous for the local tribes. All along the shore campfires burned; the smoke drifted heavily across the water and soon immersed us in the sharp smells of burning wood and the salty smoke of firecrackers. The sky went grey with the smoke we were breathing and soon Justin was complaining of dizziness. Among the trees we could make out countless tents and camping trailers. Rockets zipped over the water and boomed; Black Jacks crackled across the ground. People were barbecuing on grills or sitting around large bonfires on folding chairs. The smoke thickened through the still air, drifting through the trees and tents. It was a smog city of campers, an urban zone of tents and trailers and pickups and cars.

What kind of vacationing is this? Leave the great urban metropolis loud with traffic and heavy with smog in order to join the crowds camping here? America, America. Have you no taste for the quiet life?

We beached the canoe and walked to the main office.

"Thirteen dollars," chirped the young man. "We have just two places left."

Thirteen dollars for Smog Haven? And I had thought eight dollars was too much back in that Michigan state park! So, like a penny-pinching fool from some old fairy tale, I told Justin we'd find a sand bar for less. We walked out along congested lanes of camping vehicles. Teens and younger children crowded down the dirt roads in gangs. Some had gathered in a kind of metal hangar to play electronic video games. Others were firing rockets and setting flame to large rolls of firecrackers. Everywhere staccato banging and little rockets snapping orange and green with a flat dead sound and smoke and radios and televisions and the clatter of passing cars and the rattle of diesel trucks lugging oversized trailers and the chatter of people seated around fire rings laughing and drinking and smoking and staring at their feet and catching their breath in the thickening clouds. Unreal city, city swarming with figures adrift in the smoke.

We found our way out of the ghostly city by walking a railroad track into the little town of Bagley where we sat down in an old hotel restaurant and ate fish. It was a great relief. But by the time we walked back along that railroad track and hurried through the barbarian hordes to push off in little Natty Bumpo, the light was gone in the west.

We paddled out through acrid smoke, Justin still complaining of dizziness. A late motorboat, its running lights burning, materialized in the smoke and coasted by us toward a dock as we made for the twisting exit channel.

The light was long gone. We were paddling through long black corridors of trees across a floor of black marble. We'd escaped the smoke, but no moon had risen to light our way. Far above the tree walls on either hand was the faint sparkle of a thin, winding trail of stars. Behind us, beyond the trees, we could still hear the distant thunder and crackle of fireworks. We felt like refugees fleeing a battle zone.

The silence deepened. We could hear nothing but the dip of our paddles and the distant, muffled pop of the fireworks. Then Justin said, "You hear that?" I lifted my paddle and waited. All around us was a fine, high, singing sound. We listened. It seemed to hover everywhere, the faintest of songs. Something in the air. I told Justin to turn on his flashlight. He felt around in the bag at his feet, pulled out the flashlight and clicked it on. The beam of light became a continuous stream of swarming mosquitoes. Wherever he pointed it, the light caught thousands of them and the air sang with their fierce quiet songs. But they left us alone; insect repellent and perhaps the smoke we had absorbed kept them off. It hadn't been so easy for the Joliet expedition; they wrapped themselves in canvas at night and huddled near smoky fires.

In time, the long corridor opened to left and right. To the right, we knew, ran the main channel. But I was afraid to face the great barges at night, and we had had little experience on this vast river and its powerful current. Off to our left we could just make out a low line of black hills against the stars. There I hoped to find solid ground for our tent.

We turned toward the hills and paddled on. We seemed to be moving into an enormous room in a giant's many-chambered mansion. Far away to our left, in a distant pavilion, crowds were still shooting fireworks and partying through the night. But here, in this spacious domed hall, faintly hung with constellation chandeliers, all was quiet.

A black wall of trees on our right drew near. Suddenly something erupted from the water next to us. Both of us jumped. "What was that?" Justin asked.

It took a second for me to realize that it was nothing but a large, frightened fish. "Just a fish," I said.

"Sounded huge," he said.

In the black stillness of the night, the unexpected explosion of water had shaken us; we were stealing through enchanted rooms, startled by beasts that live in the floors.

We dipped our paddles quietly, as if to avoid detection.

Slowly, the black hills rose before us. In the continuing silence, another fish would blast from the surface; we never got used to them. No matter how quietly we paddled or how much we tried to prepare ourselves for the next one, they always caught us by surprise. Once, a far off train howled and rumbled along beneath the hills, moving fast; we saw its bright eye pass away to the north and wondered if we would find room to camp this side of the tracks.

Then our paddles hit mud. Justin clicked on his flashlight and we saw acres of grey reedbeds ahead of us. We moved away to avoid them, but the mud eased up through the water toward our boat; we were paddling in less than two feet of water. The hills still looked to be a half-mile away and we had no idea if a channel reached shore or if we were running into a vast marsh. Reluctantly, we turned around and headed back toward the main channel, following that line of trees.

It was late. We were growing weary. I was nervous. Repeated checks with the flashlight had found no sandbars. Then the trees closed in upon us on either side and our paddles began sinking into mud again. Fish burst from the surface and rippled away through the floor. Somewhere an owl began hooting, and another responded. We turned back again and made our way around a peninsula of mud and trees, then headed toward the main channel, peering hard through starlight.

I was afraid. Why had I left the obvious safety of the Bagley campground to wander this great river at night? Why should I risk my own son's life for thirteen dollars? When would an underwater snag tip us into a strong current? or a passing barge or racing motor boat run us down? I had made a bad decision. But the Bagley campground was a long way off now.

Occasionally Justin clicked the flashlight on and scoured the bank: nothing but mosquitoes, mud, thick grass, and a tangle of trees. No place to pitch a tent. I looked at my watch. Midnight.

We passed along another wall of silent trees, and another, then a barely visible snag reached toward us as the current suddenly caught us; the long, dead fingers of the old witch clutched at our canoe. We jerked our paddles through the water to escape, missing those broken fingers by inches. We pulled away into a suddenly strong current. And then we spotted a campfire maybe a quarter mile across and up the channel. We angled for the light, pulling hard against the run of the current. As we approached the flames, we could see two makeshift tents draped over poles on a sandy island. There was loud talk and laughter and we could see half-naked figures silhouetted in the red light. More barbarians.

I called out, "We're kind of lost out here. Is there a place there to put up a tent?"

The loud talk stopped. We kept paddling to stay even with the island. Then a man's voice called out, "Hell yes! Come on in! Come right on in!"

I had my doubts. What now?

We set up our tent in the sand about twenty yards from the other tents. The laughter and talk began again, punctuated occasionally by loud, rumbling belches. Three young men and two women, a blonde in a red bikini and a dark-haired girl in a blue one-piece, were standing or sitting around the fire. Beer cans littered the sand. A man walked out of the firelight toward us. "Want a beer?" he asked. But my fatherly instincts counseled caution. I wasn't sure what we had gotten into, so I told him we were exhausted and needed to turn in, which was true enough.

"O come on! Just a beer, buddy!" the man said.

"We've been on the river all day. Need some sleep."

He nodded, belched, and returned to the fire.

For a long time, we could hear them guffawing, shouting, burping, and giggling. Beer cans popped and fizzed. Justin unzipped our window flap and watched them through the screen for a time, but eventually rolled over and closed his eyes.

I had been asleep for some time when I was jerked awake by a thunderous explosion. I looked out the netting to see blue lights flickering down toward the water. Fireworks. Another one wavered up into the dark and burst into fiery arcs. I clicked on the flashlight and looked at my watch. 3:00 a. m. There was a crowd around the campfire now. A pontoon boat full of savages had pulled up and were igniting rockets. Justin rolled over on his elbows and stared.

More explosions, more shouts, more beer all around. I looked at Justin and he looked at me. I shrugged and grinned. "Not much sleep tonight," I said. He smiled and peered out at them.

After a time, the Pontoon People left. I was about to go back to sleep when a blinding light shot through the tent then flashed away. I looked out and saw a single headlight far down the river.

"Comin' barge," I heard a man say.

The light flashed back across our island, blasting our tent with light.

One of the men said, "You ought to give those guys on the barge somethin' to look at."

"Yeah," said another. "They cain't do nothin'. They're stuck on that barge."

"What do you want us to do," asked the blonde in the red bikini, "flash 'em?"

"Hell yes, why not?"

She laughed and looked at the girl in the one piece blue. "Yeah! Let's flash the barge dudes!" The girl in blue giggled.

"Come on!" said the red bikini. She splashed out into the river. The searchlight blazed across our camp, then darted away toward the opposite bank. The two girls were up to their waists in the water, unsnapping their tops.

"Hey barge dudes!" shouted the red bikini. She waved.

We could hear the great engines thrumming closer.

"Barge dudes!"

The dark hulk of drumming machinery churned nearer.

"Barge dudes! Over here!" They splashed and leaped.

But for some reason the searchlight remained fixed on the mud and shrubs on the opposite shore. The sound of the engines rose to a steady roar. The girls leaped and shouted, but the puritanical beam never strayed. I looked at Justin and shrugged again. He shook his head and kept watching.

The barge roared on by, the beat of its engines drowning out the futile shouts of the drunken water nymphs.

Slowly the sounds of the river Cyclops grumbled away. Even if he was uninterested in the cavorting nymphs, we were. It all set my blood to humming, me in my wife-missing kind of loneliness, and I could only imagine what it did for the tight curiosity of my hormone-hopping, as yet unattempted, sixteen-year-old.

Firelight glimmered across the waves. The red bikini shouted, "Hey let's frolic!" and splashed her friend. They romped and splashed and cavorted through the dark waters. The red bikini yelped, "I'm a savage! I'm a cannibal!" On shore, one of the men grabbed his crotch and shouted, "Hey! Take a look at this!" But, as if some faint mist of modesty or disgust still floated in their beer-fumed minds, the girls just turned away, still splashing and screeching and laughing.

Eventually the men returned to the fire and opened more beers. One of them said, "I cain't believe you'd let yer old lady strip in front of them barge dudes."

"Shit, they kin look, but they cain't touch. That's where I draw the line."

The girls eventually walked up out of the black water with their suits back in place, and the night wore on with beery talk.

I flopped over on my back and stared into the dark dome of our little night. It had been a long, troublesome day. Good trouble. Everybody has trouble; some just don't have the right kind. It was as if I had been reading Justin a bedtime story years ago in the comfort of our home and we had suddenly slipped through the walls and into the hard adventure.

I heard Justin roll over. In time he was breathing regularly.

The Wooden Flute

We drank coffee at 6:30 in the morning, folded up our tent, and bid the savages adieu. They were already out of bed frying meat in a pan. We were loading the canoe when the girl in blue crept out of a tent with a roll of toilet paper and headed for the trees. The man with the frying pan called her back and handed her a small shovel. "Hell, we're not a bunch of barbarians!" he said. "Cover it up."

We stayed in the main channel. The day was hot. A warm haze lay like damp cotton over the wide river. On every sandy shore: a clutter of tents, styrofoam coolers, stray shoes, beer cans. smoking grills. Cabin cruisers were parked along the shores like cars on a main street. Tanned men sat talking on lawn chairs. Women stretched their legs to the sun and read books. Children and dogs splashed in the water. Fourth of July weekend on the Mississippi.

A couple hours downriver we came to Guttenburg and our first Mississippi dam and lock. I had no idea if canoes were permitted to pass through these locks made for barges, but when I saw a motor boat drifting outside the lock, I steered toward it and asked. The young couple told us to go into the lock with them. We heard an electronic bell, then the heavy gates swung slowly open. The motorboat putted into the lock, and we stroked after. It was the same system as on the Fox River, only much longer and wider: 600 feet in length, 110 feet wide. Built in the 1930s during the Great Depression, the locks and dams on the upper Mississippi were intended to provide a reliable nine-foot channel for barge traffic. Thousands of underwater wing dams made of stones and branches were built all along the river to direct the current and keep the channel from silting up. Twenty-six cross-river dams with locks stair-stepped the river from near Minneapolis, Minnesota all the way to Alton, Illinois. It was a massive reconstruction of one of the world's largest rivers.

Since World War II, barge traffic has become a major means of transporting goods in the region. But the channeling of the river has, of course, damaged fish and other wildlife by cutting off or swamping large areas of wetlands. The 1993 floods raised concerns about this channelization of the river. Where wetlands and floodplains used to absorb floods, the diking system directs excess water downstream where it can do incredible damage. Once, fearing that New Orleans would flood, merchants motored up the river under cover of night and dynamited holes in the dikes flooding whole towns and drowning a number of people; the side effects of progress can be lethal.

Work has now begun to depopulate floodplains and make them available again for fish and other wildlife, but farmers and businessmen are understandably dead set against losing their livelihoods and are fighting the environmentalists every step of the way. Another problem of this damming up of the old river, at least for canoers, is that it reshapes the running river into a series of long lakes, which aren't nearly as interesting to slow walkers like us. It all seems a metaphor for the modern age. Take the vascular system of a nation, which the rivers surely are, and dam them up and dike them—a recipe for heart attack.

Of course, to treat a river as nothing more than an industrial conduit is to invite its own obsolescence: even more industrialized methods will do the job more efficiently and will rise to replace the rivers. And they have. Railroads, branching out of Chicago bypassed river traffic and now interstate trucking is giving the railroads a run for their money. All of this circumvents the river towns. And now the towns and smaller cities along the Mississippi that depended on river travel and river traffic are dying. There are other reasons, but all more or less related to our constant push toward bigger and faster: farm families vanish because of greater mechanization and the costs of chemical farming that create huge farms and run the small farmers bankrupt; lumbering and commercial fishing fall victim to overexploitation and pollution, barge traffic is dwindling or moving to the big cities. The side effects of progress will kill you.

Six miles downriver, I ruddered toward the east bank and guided us into a large concrete cylinder on the bank. It was a storm drain and a quiet parking place for a canoe. We climbed out of the town drain, and walked into Cassville for ice cream. I called home to let my wife know we had made it to the Mississippi. She told me that several days before, she had heard a radio report that a boy named Justin (once again) had drowned while swimming near Bagley. No premonition of trouble this time, but the report had been enough to make her rush home and search the newspaper until she found an article that identified the lost boy; it wasn't her son.

A long eighteen miles of wide shores, passing barges and motorboats brought us to the romantically named Mud Lake Campground a few miles above Dubuque, Iowa. We paid our five bucks and set up our tent near other tents. Saturday evening; weekends breed tent towns.

Darkness seeped down out of the hills and soaked slowly into the river. A nearby train shook the hills for a long time. Sitting next to our fire watching the coals burn down, I heard someone playing what sounded like a flute. I walked over to the river. A dark-haired woman was sitting on the dock in the evening light. Her fingers, ringed in silver and set with red and turquoise stones, were lifting and tapping the holes of a wooden flute decorated with feathers. A teenage boy sat near her, fishing from the dock.

"You got to just feel with the instrument," she said looking up. "After a while the instrument plays you. But if you let the ego interfere, you lose it." She tapped a finger on her forehead as if playing her mind. "If I'm thinking: How am I playing? or What does he think of it? or How do I breathe or hold my tongue? I lose it. It doesn't come out right. You've just got to lose yourself in the sound."

A mile and a half across the dark river, I could feel the fevered shudder of a passing train.

"This recorder's my friend." The wooden flute returned to her lips and the notes wavered out across the water.

The boy on the dock was tall, thinner than Justin, but about the same age. He looked over and said, "Mom can play the harmonica too. She taught herself how to play the recorder and the harmonica."

"Breathing," said the woman. "You've just got to breathe in and out. The harmonica's a natural instrument. But if you start watching yourself, you lose it."

Halfway across the water, the red and green lights of a late motor boat hurried downriver toward Dubuque.

The woman was thin. Her face looked tired in the faint light. She sat cross-legged on the dock and smiled at her boy. She put her lips to the recorder and the weary notes rippled away across the moving water.

I wondered where the boy's father was. I wondered what this woman and this boy had been through over the last fifteen, sixteen years to draw such lines on her face.

I turned and looked back at our tent. A flashlight was burning inside where Justin lay reading his book. Forty-three days together and still going strong. Scarcely an argument in that month and a half. Perhaps it was not having his brothers and sisters underfoot to annoy him (which makes for explosive times back home), perhaps it was the adventure of daily discoveries, or the freedom of being on the water—whatever it was, in spite of the endless work of paddling, the boredom of slow hours, the flies, mosquitoes, sun and wind, cold and heat, hunger and thirst—in spite of it all, Justin was shouldering his part, seldom complaining. He's as impulsive as the wind, but a good companion.

The woman played on and the old, wrinkled river ran on. I nodded to the boy and his mother and walked away along the shore. The wooden flute sent its single trail of notes after me, and it wasn't hard to imagine an Indian encampment here two-hundred years, three-hundred, five-hundred, a thousand, ten-thousand years ago. And I wondered about the dark-haired men who played their sacred flutes across these waters. A romantic thought? Yes. But the ancient songs would have been sad and tired too; times were often brutal. Joliet's men would cook their evening meal over a small fire, then move on down the river to sleep a few miles away from the telltale campfire. They slept in their canoes, leaving one man always on watch. Indians were killing each other up and down the river (one tribe they would meet said they were at war with nine other tribes just then). Torture, even cannibalism, were commonly practiced on enemy captives, and slavery was an accepted practice.

When I returned to the campfire, Justin had left his book and was pouring himself coffee. He picked up my cup, poured it, and handed it up to me. I sat down on the grass beside the fire, watching the flames run red fissures along the wood.

"So how you feeling about the trip so far?" I asked.

He shrugged. "I guess I'm doing okay."

"Not bored sick yet?"

"It gets plenty boring. I'm ready to be done."

"Still a ways to go," I said.

"How much farther?"

"I don't know, but we need to reach St. Louis by July 25. That's where we'll quit. We'll need to make good time to get there."

"What's the date today?"

"Let's see, two days after the Fourth. It's the sixth."

Justin looked down at the fire. "Still a long ways to go."

"True. At least we're not going as far as Joliet and Marquette. They went another 600 miles in the same two months we're taking, made it past St. Louis to the Arkansas River before they turned back. There's no catching them."

"So we'll be getting out at St. Louis?"

I nodded. "That's all the time we've got."

"I remember this spaghetti place in St. Louis near the river where we ate when I was on that school field trip," said Justin. "It was really great food."

"You're not getting tired of my cooking are you?"

He looked up at me. "You mean pouring soup and a can of corn into a pot every night is cooking?"

"If we make it to St. Louis, we'll find that spaghetti place," I said.

Justin found a volleyball game in camp. I sipped coffee beside the fire and thought of the future. At home, Justin was always rushing off with his friends: playing volleyball, basketball, going to movies. Soon he would have his driver's license. We put that off this summer to take this trip, but there'll be no holding him back next summer. The car is the ultimate escape pod, a glassed-in cubicle bouncing with music and rushing to the impulse of the driver. It worried me and worried his mother more. But how do you resist an entire culture addicted to speed? How do you instill the quiet virtues of observation and contemplation in a jumpy teen? I had thought this trip would help, but now I wasn't sure it would.

River Scribble

Fierce northwest wind coming in behind us. Big erratic waves. Bright skies. Passed through another lock. Rusty brown steel barges steel-cabled along the banks. Passed beneath an iron bridge being repainted—plastic sheeting flapping from the iron girders. Industrial warehouses along the bank. A shore-side casino brightly painted with sagging walkways. A train rumbles over a black-oily iron-truss bridge. Car traffic shoreside. City on left and right. Dubuque Tank Terminal Company—unloads molasses, salt, fertilizer, fish solubles; loads lard, grease, and tallow. Pasco Marketing Inc.—transfers and stores petroleum products, 12 steel tanks: 14,154,000 gallons capacity. Inland Molasses Corp.—5 steel tanks, 3,850,000 gal. capacity. U. S. Coast Guard? What's the Coast Guard doing here? Maintains fixed and floating aids to Mississippi River navigation for river miles 483 to 873. Molo Sand and Gravel. The Pillsbury Co.—grain loading and unloading. Swift Chemical Co.—transfers bulk fertilizer from barges. Koch Industries—asphalt and light oil. Conti Carriers—crane 75 tons, loads 200 ton/hr.

Blowing trees and faded hills rose into a strong wind. Justin slid his two paddles into the sleeves of his rain jacket and hoisted a sail. For three hours we ran before a gusty wind with my paddle as the rudder. Justin's arms began to strain and tire, but like some persevering saint at prayer, he kept them raised in an invocation to Speed. We were skimming along, making good time, but in time, the river bent around some bluffs and we lost the wind.

Often Justin had asked to take the stern position in the canoe. A father wants to be in charge, so I had been quite content being the steersman, but at last I told him he could have a try. A barge was just rumbling by, going upriver, and

I could see another one approaching, but I pulled ashore and we traded places. Justin got settled in the back, then pushed off. We immediately turned a wave-rocked clockwise circle in the water. I told him to switch sides when we started to turn and tried to explain the J-stroke. We then turned a counterclockwise circle. I looked downriver. The barge was getting closer. "Head for the far shore," I told Justin. "We're out in the middle. We've got to miss that barge." The harder he paddled, the faster we turned. The wind, blowing at an angle downstream, was sending heavy waves with the current which made steering difficult, and the big waves from the barge that had just passed were still rocking us about. Justin kept switching sides, but the erratic waves, the wind and current sent us weaving this way and that, scrawling odd letters in the river. Meanwhile, the barge was nearing. We could hear its engines. "Head for shore!" I shouted.

"I'm trying!"

"Come on! The barge won't turn!"

My paddling up front seemed to do no good. I kept switching sides hoping to keep the prow pointed landward, but nothing seemed to help. One way or another, we looped and swerved and scribbled our way toward shore as the long, heavy barge rumbled slowly past.

Justin lay back and laughed. He was shaking his head. "That's enough," he said. "That's enough. You can steer." We stepped out of the canoe and both sank knee-deep in mud.

We bought a whole roasted chicken and other supplies in Savanna, Illinois. Four miles downriver, we slid into the sandy shore of a little sliver of an island set like a comma in the long river's story. We set up the tent atop a sand dune that was scrambled over with wild grapevines, then walked our tiny fiefdom. In sandy clearings among the matted grapevines, tall, lavender flowers were alive with bumblebees. A few trees held tight to the sand as the strong brown current swirled by.

As we were carrying our sleeping bags up the sand dune, we accidentally uncovered a batch of white, leathery turtle eggs. Snapping turtle eggs, as big as golf balls. We brushed the sand away and found fifteen to twenty eggs buried together and another fifteen or so nearby. I'm not a great friend of snapping turtles. Once, when I was a kid, my friend Mark and I had caught a stringer full of bass and catfish while camping at a small Kansas lake. Next morning we found a stringer full of fish skeletons. The turtles had beaten us to our breakfast. And snappers are such ugly monsters—that glaring eye, the thick muscled neck with those powerful jaws. Once I was walking up a clear little stream in Kansas with my two oldest boys and saw a heavy brown plate skim away into a knee-deep pool and slide into dead leaves. I crept over, carefully reached down through the clear water, grabbed its tail and jerked it up. It was about the size of a large dinner plate and heavy. As I held it up for the boys to see, the reptilian head lunged at me, the jaws snapped and it hissed. I could smell stale fish on its breath. The boys held a stick to its nose and quick as lightning the jaws snapped it in two. They are not a loveable creature , but then neither are we a good portion of the time. Justin and I reburied the eggs in sand and avoided walking up that way again.

We ate the roasted chicken. As the sun went down, we read *The Odyssey*.

After a time, I put the book away and leave the tent. Night has come. Barefoot, I walk the wet, hard-packed sand along shore where we had seen the claw marks of the turtles. There's a light breeze making restless the leaves of the nearby trees and bushes. "And high overhead and all moving about,/ There are thousands of millions of stars." Fireflies slow-blink through the grasses and vines. Across the river on bluffs to the west, the many windows of someone's mansion shine like amber. An owl keeps hooting from a nearby island. And all around me the dark river is moving, unhurried, strong, continuous, its million-year memoir written in sediments and sands, in islands, sloughs, curves and contours, floodplain and a valley; this sandy comma of an islet will soon be lost to the current revision.

I take my pipe, straddle a tree trunk near Natty Bumpo, and strike a match. On the far shore, a train rumbles by under the bluffs and away.

An hour or so later another train hurries past.

The lights in the mansion on the far bluff wink out. The breeze is picking up, washing through the leaves of a silver maple behind me, bleaching the leaves from black to silver to black to silver. Down river, bright Venus descends into the tossing trees of a farther island where an owl is still calling. I smoke and think of the fullness of the present moment.

Bedlam

> And the road on the farther bank is a highway of hell, straight as doom, black in color and screaming with machines . . . shooting from their clots in the vile cities to their still viler clots in the casinos which defile the oily sea. I say oily—yes, oily—the shores of the sea have become great patches of oil, sheeny with changing colours like a dying snake, and grit floats on them.

So wrote Hilaire Belloc of a place he had once loved. We are camped thirty-odd miles down river from the little sandy abbreviation of an island we camped on last night. We have heaved driftwood and a washed-up railroad tie aside to find a patch of dirty sand for our tent. Our little grey dome sits cramped between tree trunks and a tangle of brush and broken logs. The sand is brownly carpeted with crisp, dead mayflies—thousands of them—they crackle underfoot. A couple hundred yards away another infernal tug is growling by, its brown wake plowing ashore, wave after wave slopping into driftwood, dead insects, and sand three feet from our tent. The river here is narrow and swift. Behind us, rising 200 feet into the summer night, a steel grid tower holds a red light that flashes continually; the giant tower's steel arms hold heavy electric cables that droop across the river to its automatic, blinking twin. Across the river, trains hammer their way beneath bluffs that bounce the noise clattering over the river. Their triple air horns blast three times at every road crossing, of which there are many: nine tiers of noise for each crossing. We are camped and cramped into an echo chamber. We can even hear the persistent whine of tires on the opposite highway that parallels the train tracks, and the tut tut . . . tut tut, as steel-belted radials clip over cracks, of which there are many. Just off shore a grey tangle of roots, like the hair of an old hag, rises from the water near a patch of reeds that has been rotting in the summer sun; the hag's stench washes in with the waves.

And now our Spam and beans are bubbling in the little saucepan on the fire and the night has settled over the glittering lights of the little town of Princeton across the river. The tall giant above us keeps winking at his mindless mate across the river.

A stiff southwest wind was chopping up the center current of the river. The wind was against us. We bucked over vicious waves making for the opposite shore where the going looked smoother. Nearing shore, we dodged around weathered docks held up by rusted poles. The rough waves kept up the attack, for they have digested much bigger prey than us. On we went, bobbing, swaying, and bashing through the waves, on the road to chaos with a deadline to meet.

We passed through the Le Claire Lock. After that the cities were upon us again: four cities crushed together: Bettendorf and Davenport, Rock Island and Moline: homes, factories, pertroleum terminals, the endless Alcoa Aluminum plant on our right, sand and gravel loading facilities, terminals for scrap metal, cement, and new steel—the river sweating oil and tar. The barges banging against their cables in the muddy current.

We camped on a sandy beach below Rock Island, Illinios. But before sleeping, we decided to explore. We followed a concrete bicycle trail along the high dike beneath a great highway bridge, then followed a footpath toward the city until street lights showed us our way into numbered streets intersected, unimaginatively, by numbered avenues, so that we came to the corner of Fifteenth and Fourth, turned left and followed our ears toward a sound of drums and electric guitars. Rock Island was rocking tonight.

The streets began to collect people carrying plastic glasses of Budweiser, hot dogs, stiff pink swirls of cotton candy. Children's rides rotated calmly to one side, booths smelled of onions and bratwurst and fries. People walked by eating sweet funnel cakes, powdering their noses and chins with sugar.

A rock band was banging and blaring from a stage set up in the middle of the street, and a crowd of teens were jumping and jerking in front of the stage, following the gyrations, not of the lead singer, but of a tall, lean, goateed, middle-aged man in a red shirt below the stage. The goat beard raised his hands in the air, rocked his hips and stomped and twirled and kicked. The teens raised their hands in the air, rocked their hips, stamped and twirled and kicked. I stared hard at the man. He looked like the lean, red-shirted man on the front of the 1969 paper-back version of *Zorba the Greek* I'd picked up in that little antique store in Wisconsin. The face even fit the description in the book: "furrowed, weather-beaten, like worm-eaten wood." And this Zorba, like the literary one, was the embodiment of passion. Eyes closed, he saw nothing of the laughing teenage girls who imitated his every move. He saw nothing of the shirt-less lead singer who jumped to the beat of the drums and barked into the microphone. This Zorba was riding the music like a bucking mule; bracelets jangled on his wrists, a huge bundle of keys swung from his belt and clashed against his leg. He was in nirvana. One knobbly fist reached down and throttled a two-liter plastic bottle of orange soda. He threw back his head and gulped sweet orange fizz as his hips and bare feet did the rumba, the samba, the shimmy-shimminee, the stomping turkey trot, and his other big hand swooped under and over and in and out, and the laughing girls' hands swooped under and over and in and out.

And then we had a vision: a young woman in long dark hair was swaying in a long dress of midnight blue, a dress flowing like dark water to the machine-gun rhythms, somehow trans-forming the caustic drums, the thunder of the bass guitars, the coyote yowling of the lead guitar, into a subtle easy movement, a supernatural swimming of silky dress and long sweet hair washing this way and that way and this way—she was a river goddess, her face like the moon at midnight, her long figure supple, continuous in a mazy motion, swaying like a current from shore to shore as all about her girls and boys jerked and jumped and bumped like electrically shocked catfish. She was a lady born out of time, weaving her way into this raucous age, tracing mystery through the summer night.

Muscatine

Rain poured down for ten long miles. People swishing along the highways and byways that net the towns to suburbs to cities would think little of ten miles of rain. A minor inconvenience, windshield wipers flicking back and forth, a louder rush of tires heard above the cheery DJ on the radio.

But for us? Within minutes we were soaked. Our leaky rain jackets became a second layer of cold wet skin. Barges faded out of the downpour and throbbed by, long sullen hulks of grey steel. My cloth hat wilted around my head and the rain drizzled down my neck. Every time I lifted my paddle the rain ran down my forearms and gradually washed cold over my chest. My pants were sopped.

"You wet?" I called out to Justin. Stupid question.

"Soaked," came the reply. His "rain jacket" we had bought in Appleton, Wisconsin, was not a rain jacket after all, just a water-penetrable windbreaker.

Our arms kept up a steady pace, the paddles rising and falling, the blue-green, rain-dimmed shores occasionally bleaching into faint concrete grain elevators. Black iron augers angled down, wet conveyor belts sloped up toward silent cranes, cables slanted out toward a blur of docks and scaffolding and waiting barges. On we went, the current conspiring with our steady paddling to pull us down toward our St. Louis deadline.

"There's supposed to be a little town up here called Buffalo," I called through the wash of the falling rain. "We'll stop and eat. Maybe dry off."

"Where is it?"

"Can't be too far." Stubborn optimism.

Justin said nothing; he knew what to think of my optimism.

Time crawls by like a wet slug when you're paddling through rain. The mind stays out ahead of time by yearning for that next stop, for a roof, for hot coffee, and dry clothes. But the eyes stay with the falling rain and textured waters; the ears stay with the steady swash of rain on river and maybe the slow hum of a disappearing barge; the arms feel the pull of the water on the paddle as a slow chill soaks through the chest, and the stiffening legs have been cold for a very long time. Every half hour or so we would take our cut Clorox bottles and bail out the two or three inches sloshing around at our feet. Then we would pick up the paddles and move on.

The Clarke's Landing Cafe was crowded with men in muddy t-shirts and faded jeans. The riverside factories and loading facilities must have emptied a good number of their laborers into this little cafe while the rain fell. We found a tiny table with two chairs, peeled off our soaked jackets and sat down. The place was loud with talk, but not warm enough for Justin and me. We hunched up our shoulders and slid our hands beneath our legs for warmth. Two pretty waitresses were hurrying between tables: one with long dark hair, and the other with an exceedingly long blonde braid that passed down her back, behind her apron string, and dangled and flipped about her knees like the tail of a nervous cat. The blonde braid was quietly passing commands to the dark hair, who was much annoyed by being ordered about. They were a pleasure to watch, their eyes snapping at each other, their mouths flipping into quick smiles as they addressed customers, their bodies leaning and swaying around tables and waiting men.

Beside us a middle-aged man with a drooping handlebar mustache was wolfing down a stew of cut potatoes, chunks of meat and carrots. A younger man with a beaked nose who somehow looked Creole was forking down apple pie. A boy with scraggly, shoulder-length hair and bad skin shook ketchup onto his hashbrowns. Conversations erupted from the corners of their mouths as they kept shoveling in the provender or tipping in the black coffee.

I've worked most of my life with men like these and I feel a kind of kinship with them. They work with rough hands—shoveling grain or cement or coal, operating the augurs and conveyor belts, pounding nails, ratcheting bolts, cabling barges. Their minds run to beer and women, machinery and crude jokes, but they work hard for little enough money.

A man with broken yellow teeth and a stubble beard pushed himself back from the table and said, "I killed the old Buick up there on the side of highway 40 the other day. Battery was dead as a doornail. So I get out and wave down this car. Woman pulls over, but she don't have no jumper cables. So she says, 'Can't you start it if I push you?' I say, 'Naw, it's an automatic transmission. You got to get up to thirty mile an hour to push start an automatic.' But she says she thinks she can handle that. Well, I'm real doubtful, but I'm a ways from nowhere and I'm desperate, so I tell her to pull around behind and I'll get in and put it in gear. She backs on down the road to get behind me while I climb in. Then I look back in my rearview mirror and damn! Here she comes straight at me at thirty mile an hour!"

The table exploded with laughter. The man with the yellow teeth chuckled and reached for his coffee. I looked at Justin. He gave me a wry smile and looked about for a waitress. We were hungry and cold.

People were still walking in out of the rain, taking off their coats and standing along the walls waiting for a table. The blonde waitress poured in our coffee and we clasped our hands around the hot cups to soak in a little heat.

We lingered long, ordering one thing at a time to stretch out our occupancy of the little table. Eggs over easy. After eating them, we thought we'd try hashbrowns. We waited for the busy blonde to return with coffee and take our new order. Out the steamed windows, we could see it was still raining. We followed the hashbrowns with an order of pancakes and syrup. The long-tailed blonde turned away scribbling on her pad, her tail tip flipping. Our t-shirts were beginning to dry around the shoulders. After slowly eating the pancakes, we put in for two orders of bacon. Coffee pots came and went. It was still raining. Our bellies were getting tight beneath our wet t-shirts. We sipped a couple more cups of coffee and ordered chocolate cream pie, eating slowly. We'd been there for hours. More coffee. Whole shifts of workers sat down, ordered, ate, paid, and left. Others filled their places, ate, and left. We were still nibbling and sipping—dainty little bites—and touching the coffee to our lips like socialites.

The rain ceased. We paid and waddled out like two men seven months pregnant. We had little desire to keep paddling, but everything was wet; there was no place on shore to sit down. We leaned over in gastronomic pain and bailed the water from the bottom of the canoe, then shoved off, leaning back to take the pressure off our distended bellies.

Seventeen miles of slow work brought us to Muscatine. We stopped to buy cards to send to the kids at home and walked by two statues in the riverside park: an antlered stag and a bronze Indian with a bolt through his head. At a drugstore in town, we bought the post cards and asked the clerk why the Indian in the park had a bolt through his head. The young man gave us a quizzical look. "Well, I think it has something to do with a mascot," he said.

"A mascot with a bolt through his head?"

"Well, yeah. Something to do with fish I guess."

"Fish?"

"Yeah. The high school mascot. You know. A fish."

"But the Indian. The bolt."

"It's a fish. Muscatine or something."

"A fish."

"Sure."

"But the bolt through the head. I was wondering . . . "

"Yeah. Something with a fish. I don't know much about it. Muscatine. Fish. Something like that." So much for communication.

Herons stood vigil along the banks eyeing the water that smoothed through fallen tree limbs. Out in the current, a hard south wind running upcurrent chopped the river into steep, two-foot waves that kept slapping us back as we pulled forward. We might have avoided the wind if we'd taken the narrow channel that ran along the Illinois side, but we had no map and weren't willing to risk getting lost in a slough. So, as usual, ignorance doubled our workload.

And then another strange sight. On a tall dead tree, we saw a bald eagle with its wings stretched out—held open as if it were posing for the Presidential Seal. A black vulture sat a few feet away in the same tree closely observing the eagle. As we approached, they remained fixed, a tableau, an omen. I wondered if the eagle were wounded. Why did it hold its wings spread out like that? Was it drying its wings after being pulled under by a devious fish? What was the vulture waiting on? As we neared the shore, the eagle leaned forward and flapped heavily up to a nearby cottonwood. All around it, black crows rose from the trees with raucous cries. The vulture followed, again taking a perch a few yards above the eagle. The damaged eagle remained, wings uplifted, while all about it reeled the indignant crows. After a few minutes, the crows settled back into the surrounding trees cawing loudly, occasionally springing into the air again and flapping noisily about the giant cottonwood like reporters spotting a scandal. It was 1996.

Tortoise And Hares, Mayflies And Machines

The next day we played turtle and hares with a fleet of speedboats. It was a sunny Saturday and the locals were out in force. As we plodded down the river, we would hear the high whine of an approaching motorboat, then VROOOOM! it raced by us in showers of spray leaving us to rock sideways in its wakes. Then another would roar by, then another, maybe three or four at a time, all hellbent for somewhere down river. The girls and women who sat sunning themselves in florid bikinis would turn their sunglasses to us for a disdainful second or two as our slow green-shelled, two-footed amphibian paddled on down the river. Fifteen or twenty motorboats must have passed us in that first half hour.

A slow hour later we spotted them again. Two miles ahead of us they sat drifting like a flock of geese in front of Lock Number 17. They were waiting for a barge to go through. A half hour later, we paddled in among the drifting speedboats. The gates opened, and we paddled into the lock without missing a stroke. We heard engines starting up and the swift fleet grumbled into the lock all around us.

Twenty-five river miles later, we came upon a line of houses perched along a high bank. A regional highway map I'd picked up had a black dot beside the word Oquawka. We paddled toward willow trees through flat black water, our canoe slipping away from the falling current across a sheet of still water that lay beneath the arm of a nearby island. Justin lifted his paddle and looked forward. "What's that, Dad?"

I glanced ahead. Something moving over the surface of the water, maybe a quarter mile away. A glittering curtain undulating over the river.

"I don't know."

Ahead, driftwood cluttered a narrow beach beneath a forty-foot-high sand bank. But between our little green canoe and that sandy bluff something was moving, something translucent, shimmering, as if the summer air had come alive. Out over the brown-black water—we could see them now—clouds of large insects rose and twisted, scattering, condensing, lifting and falling, flickering in the afternoon sun. Millions of mayflies, rising on clear wings as if the black water were effervescing bubbles. Then we were among them, moving through a fairy world of flickering, delicate little creatures, their long, thin bodies arched behind them and each one trailing two long tail whiskers called caudal styles.

We came ashore in shallow waters sheeted with their rustling wings. They festooned the willow trees and dangled from the bushes, they danced along fallen logs, and fluttered slowly up tree trunks; thousands already lay dead in the sand. The living dropped onto our hats and shoulders, flickered about our faces, rose in throngs from the sand and shrubbery as we cleared out driftwood to make a space for our tent.

They are insects of the order Ephemeropta, a word taken from the Greek word, *ephemera*, which means "living for only a day." Adult mayflies emerge from the water in late afternoon, fly, mate, lay eggs before dawn, then fall spent to the ground and die: citizens of but a single day.

Someone once said that we humans, peering up at the cosmos, are like mayflies trying to understand the world's weather patterns. Mayflies have a single, sunny afternoon to read the drift of a few clouds, the change in temperature, the passage of sun and wind. What could they infer of the earth's weather patterns from these few particulars? Yet the entire existence of the human race is surely much less in proportion to the lifespan of the cosmos. But how we do try to understand! We buzz about plotting galaxies on our graphs, squinting around nebulae, postulating black holes, measuring radiation, reading the spectrums of stars, calculating speeds, positing theories, predicting, speculating, puzzling over everything from quarks to quasars to quantum mechanics—trying desperately to comprehend this ancient, orderly, but constantly surprising cloud of mysteries.

Peering into night skies, we yearn to know. And we yearn for more than facts. We are metaphysical mayflies. We thirst for significance, ultimate significance—which is to say meaning linked to timelessness, or to put it simply: permanent significance. We would be angels, not mayflies.

What the mayflies lack in longevity, they make up for in numbers. It did little good to slap them away. For every one brushed off, ten more hovered in. We blinked them away, slapped them, stepped on them, spat them out. The only remedy was to set up the tent quickly and leave.

We took our paddles and shoveled out a level place in the gritty sand beneath the willow trees. Big, sandy-colored spiders with dark stripes on their legs scampered out of the sand and ducked under driftwood. We smoothed the lumpy, root-ridged sand as best we could with our paddles and feet, then pulled out our thin-skinned dome, our brief bubble, and staked it down. There wasn't much room, and we hoped the river wouldn't rise. We planned to stay in this little town of Oquawka for a single day.

We scrambled up the sandy cliff and forced our way past tree trunks, through bushes, brambles, fallen limbs, nettles, and poison ivy until we found ourselves in a little clearing. A wooden sign over a shelter house announced the Delabar Youth Camp, dedicated to three men "who cared"—a small, wooden stay against time, a silent appeal for significance. We found a two-lane black top and walked the mile and a half into town.

At an old grocery store turned convenience store, a short, balding man in a white t-shirt let us in to buy sodas even though he was closing up. A teenage girl behind the register took a look at Justin and offered us a ride back to our tent. But the man thought this not quite proper, and intervened, giving us a ride in his rattletrap Chevy. He said the old car was on its last legs and he needed to trade it in, but money was a problem—a difficulty I well understood (we were brothers in harms). For nineteen years, he had been a hog butcher. He had thought his job secure, but the plant had suddenly closed, just before he could claim retirement, and he had been forced to pick up a minimum-wage job while he lived in a basement apartment. For five years now he hadn't received a single raise. A secure job, like a secure life, is surely an oxymoron.

He dropped us off near the mayflies about nightfall. There we discovered that we had left the tent's bottom zipper undone. I remembered the large sand spiders. Spiders make poor sleeping companions. "We better get the flashlights and search the tent," I said. We found nothing.

The morning brought a light rain. I got up on one elbow and looked at Justin. A large sand spider scampered over his sleeping bag and crouched in the corner of the tent. I pulled out a shoe and did my duty. Another one scrambled up inside the mosquito netting. I murdered him. The thought of tossing about all night with those two roommates made my flesh crawl.

We walked away through a fine, misty rain to Stiffy's, a restaurant on the river. There we met Jim and Paula, a couple much excited about a multi-level marketing program that sold fruits and vegetables in powder and capsule form. I was not interested in pursuing that old trader Joliet down this path to business success, but Jim and Paula offered to take us water skiing in their motorboat. Speedboats are no longer my idea of fun, but I saw Justin's eyes light up at the prospect. During breakfast, Jim and Paula's son Noah joined us. He was a handsome young man, blonde, polite, intense—given to many sports: swimming, bungi jumping, scuba diving, snow boarding, living off the land, water skiing, knee-boarding.

After breakfast, which our hosts generously paid for, we took their powerful inboard roaring across the waves, back the way we'd come the day before. Within minutes, we were far up the river. What a strange thing, after so many weeks of slow labor, to laugh at the power of that old, relentless river and go skipping away counter-current. The sun was generous, the sky blue, the wind light—a good day to ski.

Justin had never tried it before, but he was a natural. His first attempt on the skis brought him hesitantly out of the water and, with bent knees and slightly bent back, he came plowing along behind us. Soon he was leaning back and hopping the wakes, powering out to the side, then back and over the wake again. I was amazed at his skill.

It was good to see him enjoying himself after so many hours, and days, and weeks of steady work. Soon Noah offered to show us the kneeboard. He threw it in the water, jumped in, grabbed the towrope, and lay chest down on the board. As the boat picked up speed, he pulled himself to his knees. By pressuring one knee or the other, he could turn. Away he went, skimming across the brown water, cutting back and forth, jumping the boat's wakes, swinging out wide, even turning backwards, and then frontwards, then doing it all in one motion—360-degree turns, one right after another.

After a while, Justin gave it a try. The first three times he attempted getting to his knees, the kneeboard squirted out from under him. The fourth time he made it. Not only did he get to his knees, but he was soon leaping the wakes and even managed two complete turnarounds. He had an incredible sense of balance and a natural feel for the needed angle of the knee board. Wipe out he did, a number of times, but soon he was up again, his young body gleaming in the afternoon sun, the brown water spraying white from the board, a still figure against the rushing water and passing trees: a moment caught from time.

Then it was my turn. I jumped into the river and swam out to the kneeboard, pulled myself on, then grabbed the towrope as Noah pressed the throttle slowly forward. The board bounced along beneath my chest. Slowly I curled my body to get my knees beneath me. The board slipped and I was down. I tried again and again. Our hosts were patient people. On my sixth try, I was up. HAH! Old Man River! See me now! I'm sailing! I'm flying! Let your old gravity-bound current roll on; I'm running you down! Counter-current, counter-culture, Be-bop, Hip-hop, Fly the latest fashion! How happy we will be! Up the lazy river! The boat roared on, the board skipping and skimming along between the wakes that veed out on either side, my hands clenched to the handle that linked me to the charging machine—I was a functioning part of that eight-cylinder engine; I could feel its power in my arms and legs. Freedom! Liberty! I shoved down on my left knee just a little to get the board to turn. It did. I swerved out over the righthand wake, bounced, and kept going, skipping over those hard, bright waves. Freedom!! FREEDOM!!

Pressure the right knee and back across the wake . . . the board has disappeared, and I am still clamped to that machine, hanging tight to the towrope. I launch headfirst, full speed into the river. Old Man River welcomes my return with a smash hit to my face. My neck snaps back hard, my hands pop open, and suddenly I am floating in a brown liquid daze, I can see dark brown water all around me and light glimmering through the surface a foot or two above. I'm coughing, choking. I kick to the surface, having swallowed a good deal of Mississippi bourbon. Good stuff, says Mark Twain's Child of Calamity, there's "nutritiousness in the mud, and a man that drunk Mississippi water could grow corn in his stomach if he wanted to."

I broke the surface coughing and gagging. The boat was full of wide smiles. I shook my head. One ear was clogged with water, but I could hear laughter. It was Justin. Evidently I'd made a rather spectacular dive. They asked me if I wanted to try again, but I remembered Patrick Henry's famous dictum: "Give me Liberty or give me Breath"—something like that. I chose breath and returned to the boat.

One last thing Jim and Paula did for us. They gave us their copy of the Army Corps of Engineers' River Navigation Charts. They are detailed maps. For the last week-and-a-half, we would be able to plot our way around every island, through sloughs, and over wing dams.

Desembodied Heads

We hurried on, making up for lost time. The dam system of the Upper Mississippi stairsteps the river into a series of lakes so that even though we were moving downcurrent, the actual paddling seemed as difficult as our journey on Lake Michigan. The current was no doubt carrying us along; we could see it flowing by the green and red barrels that mark the main channel, but the widening lakes that culminated in the dams spread the water and slowed the current, increasing the tedium of the long days.

Cutting across the river, we saw a capped human head floating on the water. We had been paddling all day, the sun was declining, dying the brown river several hues of rose and mauve as we looked for a place to camp. A mile across the river, we could see a few buildings that marked the little town of Dallas City, Illinois. Between us and the town we spotted a stretch of sandy beach on a tree-covered island. We turned toward the island while keeping a wary eye on the man's head that seemed to be moving slowly upstream.

I said something to Justin. He was watching it too. Canoeing is a slow and methodical means of transport, so we had time to contemplate this apparition. Suddenly it turned abruptly and floated back down the river for fifteen or twenty yards, drifting along as if made for floating. The Mississippi pushed us closer. Suddenly, the head snapped around and faced us, then began proceeding slowly back up the river toward us, the current dividing into slight rivulets just below the chin. There was no breeze, the river was a clear sheet of reddening water, and we could see the head now quite distinctly: a man's face, a set jaw. It was clearly upset.

We cut across its path on our way toward the island as the current swept us closer.

"What do you think?" I asked my son.

He paused a few seconds with paddle dripping, then shook his head and continued paddling.

We were maybe forty yards away from it, but the capped head paid us no heed. It was concentrating, and mad as hell. It about-faced again and floated back toward a dead tree snagged in the current. It was muttering something, maybe cursing. I thought about going over and conversing with it, asking it if it needed a lift (it was at least a hundred yards from shore and no boat in sight), but what do you say to a floating head with an attitude? It had most certainly seen us, but spoke no word to us, nor glanced our way. It was focused.

We turned and paddled away toward the distant island, glancing back from time to time. Still it moved back and forth along the same channel.

When we beached our canoe on the sandy island maybe a half mile away, we looked back. The head was a tiny speck out there, but we could see it was still patrolling steadily back and forth near that snag. Then we spotted a jonboat tied behind that snag a few yards down from where the head was making its rounds. I assume the rest of him was looking for a lost fish trap, a lost trot line, something very important indeed to keep the submerged part of him tip-toeing back and forth like that along some submerged sandbar. The wide old river is wily and unforgiving; it will snarl a line or shift a trap or rip a net.

As I gathered sticks for our fire, Justin searched the beach for shells. He is a collector: shells, pieces of translucent slag from that Civil War blast furnace in Michigan, snagged fishing lures we had cut down along the way. He had rescued the little container holding his rabbit feet from the Fox River after we had capsized.

A sun of clear gold sank toward the tree line on its pillar of bright river gold. Clouds of white and rose and grey formed a kind of wreath around our island with the sun casting up gold rays through and around the airy wreath as if to bid adieu to old Odysseus, for we were nearing the end of our book. I felt a sense of loss that comes with the ending of good things, but also a kind of completion that tempers and fulfills such endings.

The story of Dallas City seems to be ending. Like so very many towns and cities up and down the Mississippi, like so many more towns and cities dotting the Midwest, Dallas City is fading away. Next morning we walked the little town past sunbleached homes and peeling billboards, past an old mural of geese, an eagle, and dove; bricks were going dark with dirt and age, concrete sidewalks cracked and patched with black asphalt. Shops and businesses downtown had a blank, dull, exhausted stare. On the broken sidewalk outside a tv repair shop, gutted televisions lay derelict amidst piles of electronic panels, junked accessories, and wads of wires: the bones and intestines of a dying business.

It's the same up and down the river: a sense of fading into time. People gather in pairs and threes in an occasional café, an art club, even a boxing club, to wile away the time in buildings that once gave energy and purpose to a town. A river town was once the thinking head of a widespread, interactive body of farmers and fishermen. Government offices, banks, groceries, implement dealers, tire stores, repair shops, accountants, legal offices, warehouses, grain elevators, barge companies, lumber companies, fishing enterprises, social clubs for young and old, churches, all converged here. No more. Thousands of small farmers and their attendant businesses were the body that nourished that head, but the body is wasting away and the nourishment of land and river no longer flows to the head. The towns lie there still, but like the creased faces of decrepit, old men, they can scarcely scare up the energy to breathe anymore.

I don't know what the solution is. Towns and cities and whole civilizations have blown away in time. Ours is no different. It's just that we Americans have had reason to pride ourselves as innovators and problem solvers. Why can't we discover solutions to rescue the dying small towns of America? But maybe the real solutions run against our nature. Maybe people don't want to hear that the real answers must come from within and cannot come from without. Perhaps the integrated life of small farms and small towns requires less appetite, more manual labor, less personal independence, more interdependence, less mobility, more stability, less consumption, more investment, less isolation from our neighbors, more forbearance and good will than we're willing to give. When Kathleen Norris and her husband moved from New York City to her parent's ancestral farm in western South Dakota, to live in "what the rest of the world considers a barren waste," she and her husband had to make "a counter-cultural choice" to trade in the cultural experiences and possessions of big city life in order to discover other things you don't see at highway speeds: "We see white-faced calves basking in the spring grass like the lilies of the field. We see a chinook wind in January make rivulets run. We see dust-devils and lots of little things. We are grateful. The so-called emptiness of the Plains is full of such miraculous 'little things.'" She goes on to quote a fourth-century bishop: "Everything that seems empty is full of the angels of God." But to experience the fullness of "empty" places, one needs a commitment to that place, a willingness to slow down and work it out, slow down and walk it out. Transient experimenters run away like loose soil in the sudden storms.

Justin and I walked the streets inquiring after Abraham Lincoln. He gave a speech here in 1858 on his riverboat campaign trip down the Mississippi. We had found a bronze plaque on a stone near the river, but no one in Dallas City seems to recall the nature of the speech, not even the "town historian" knew of any records of the speech; the little town has Alzheimer's and has lost its way in the world.

We came upon an old school building: it was a tall, limestone edifice with arched windows, bronze cupola, pillars: a unique and marvelous old building built with care when younger Dallas City had real aspirations for the education of its youth. Remarkably, the stone of dedication is dated October 31, 1895. Dedicated on Halloween Day, and the building looks like a place Edgar Allen Poe would relish: strange, gothic, striking. It seemed a place in which a child could learn of "cloud-capped tow'rs, the gorgeous palaces,/ The solemn temples, the great globe itself." It is an original, built with care and pride. But off to its left is a later brick addition. Already in 1925 the rush to cheaper, plainer had replaced the care and originality of the old building. The addition is rectangular, a block of tan brick and glass with only a rudimentary gesture toward decoration seen in reddish bricks that line the windows and border the roof. Then to the right of the central 1895 building and its tall Palladian windows is another, even later addition: a block of brick with fewer windows and no attempt at decoration at all. There, one might imagine, students are told to sit at their prefabricated desks and punch calculators and peck at computers so that they'll fit like cogs, or silicon chips, into the computerized factory systems that await them—but will any of those young eyes ever get the chance to gaze out tall, beautiful windows at the sheer poetry of the real world?

Rain came down as we relaxed beneath a shelter on the shoreside deck of the Never Sail Again Lounge; it's a depressing name but appropriate. I stared across the grey river, watching blackbirds swept by the wind into nearby cottonwoods. Justin was using his shoes as a pillow and lay beside me sleeping. Lightning cracked on the far side of the river and the rain came down across its broad, running surface leaving a strange, pocked surface that looked like the skin of a very old man.

Nauvoo

On February 24, 1846 it was twelve below zero. The Mississippi River froze over at Nauvoo. A few days later, Mormon wagons loaded up and trundled out onto the ice, crossing the river to join others who had been rafting over to the Iowa shore for about three weeks. The long migration, first to Omaha, Nebraska, then on across the prairies and mountains to Salt Lake City was on. Twelve thousand Mormons eventually left Nauvoo and its surrounding farmlands for the west, driven out of Illinois by settlers who were enraged by stories of sanctioned adultery and polygamy, by reports of Mormon raids and Mormon killings. The Illinois settlers also feared the establishment of an economically powerful theocracy that was already more populous than the city of Chicago. Historian Wallace Stegner writes that in just five years, the Mormons had "transformed a stretch of high prairie and wooded bluffs, a malarial riverbottom swamp, and a fever-and-ague hamlet called Commerce into the city of Zion, the largest town in Illinois and the show-place of the upper Mississippi, with a population of 20,000."

But by 1846, says Stegner, the once friendly people of Illinois had become hostile, and the whole state, "from high-placed politician to the lowest border ruffian" was demanding that the Mormons go. Joseph Smith, their prophet and leader, and his brother Hyrum, had been murdered by Illinois militia while held in the Carthage jail just a year-and-a-half before. And now night raiders were harassing the outlying Mormon farms and officials were threatening to arrest the Mormon leaders.

So Brigham Young, the new head of the Mormons, decided to move out in the middle of winter. It was a decision that would cost his people dearly: months of frozen camps, rain-slogging trails—horses up to their bellies in mud, no fodder for the animals, sickness, deaths. The wagons that didn't make it over on the ice were loaded on flatboats and floated across the freezing waters. Once a boy spat tobacco juice into the eye of an ox on one of the flatboats. The heavy beast jerked away and plunged overboard breaking out the sideboards, dragging another ox with it and sinking the flatbed: the oxen drowned in the freezing water; a load of food and clothing was lost. It was a tough beginning for a torturous journey. For months the flatbeds kept ferrying new pilgrims across this mile-wide curve of water.

By August, most of those who remained in Nauvoo were sick or old or destitute. But the Illinois mobs wanted them gone. They converged on Nauvoo in the middle of September with about 2000 men and attacked. Perhaps only 100 or 150 of the men inside the city were capable of defending themselves. After three days of rifle fire and artillery bombardment, the Mormons agreed to leave. They were sent over the river without shelter, with little food, and with few means of transport. The militia had orders to shoot any Mormon who stayed behind. Thus the largest city in frontier Illinois was sacked, the sick and poor thrown out to shift for themselves.

We stopped for just a few minutes on the low shore where the wagons must have rolled onto the flatbeds that bitter winter. A Ford van was there. A grey-haired lady sitting inside took a look at our canoe and asked, "You have any furs for trade?"

She told us this year was the 150th anniversary of the long trek west. A wagon train of Mormons would be commemorating the journey by retracing the journey, starting from Omaha, Nebraska and going west.

Afternoon found us on the broad lake that ends in the Keokuk Dam and Lock. I looked toward the distant dam and said, "Look, Justin. Over there, it looks like a Greek temple."

He glanced up and said, "It looks like crap."

"Greek temples don't look like crap," said I.

"It looks like crap."

I paddled on in silence. He had been holding up pretty well. A half hour before he had pointed out a sundog, a red-gold shimmer in the high silver clouds. Later he had asked me how a plane's contrail could cast a shadow on the clouds above it. I spotted the shadow, a dark trail above silver, but I couldn' t explain it. I'd been pleased with his observations.

But now this.

"Justin, it does not look like crap."

"It's crap."

An hour later we paddled up to the Keokuk Lock. The attached power station was colonnaded like a Greek temple—made of concrete. But I didn't pursue the argument. The boy had paddled long and hard over those long Mississippi lakes. While we waited for a barge to go through, we walked up to a nearby restaurant, drank coffee and ate chocolate pie with ice cream.

I wondered if this journey would now, in these last long reaches of the great river, begin to tear at us, if the spirit of adventure that had taken us so far would now in these overheated days of July fray our tempers and begin to wear away the relationship we'd so painstakingly sewn together over all those miles. And what would become of our relationship when we returned home? I would of necessity return to my fast-track life of working two jobs and finishing my education. And what would Justin do? Having endured the long pull of this slow journey, would he spring like an arrow into the self-indulgent life of his runaround friends?

When we returned to the river, the sun had gone down. Sitting in little Natty Bumpo at dusk, we were looking up from the bottom of a long canyon; the lock rose forty feet above us, the black water slipping down the wet walls lower and lower. We could hear the slush and gurgle as water purled out through the sluices. A wounded catfish kept us company in the bottom of the lock, turning its white silken belly to the evening air, wriggling along the surface, then flipping back down out of sight only to bob back to the surface again. I wanted nothing to do with the deep dark world where the catfish lived, and the fish wanted nothing to do with mine. It slapped the dry air with its tail, diving for the black, heavy pressures, the close, blind, bottom embrace, its world of fluid tastes and sounds. I filled my lungs with the air that made me stranger to this disabled fish and waited. In time the tall gates creaked open. We let go the long ropes that held us to the wall and slid away into the open night.

There was a strip of sand beneath tall dark trees on the opposite shore; we cut hard through swift water, landed in sand-silted mud, and set up camp beneath the trees. Huge trees lay uprooted along the bank, the round disks of their tangled roots, higher than our heads, looking like the giant cogs of derelict machines.

*   *   *

Next morning, we passed the Des Moines River, thus leaving Iowa behind. The sun kept dissolving in broken clouds then resolving itself again into bright heat. It was July 17. A TWA jet exploded over the Atlantic that day killing everyone. The news flashed across the world, but not to us. We were weaving through quiet miles of muddy islands, stands of cottonwood where the beavers had stripped away sections of bark. We were watching hawks drift over and away. We were feeling the brown-blue waters swirl and bob and turn and eddy as we rode the back of the ancient, moving giant. On and on we paddled, absorbing the patience of the slow river and the imperceptible glide of the sun. While the media went mad with guesswork about the cause of the midair explosion, we moved on with no news but the old news of another summer's day.

Romancing The River

The miles swam by in a solar haze. The sun danced off the little brown waves and glittered like broken glass. We steered our battered canoe for the shade of high cottonwoods and trailing willows along shore, but the sun was a tyrant, high, powerful, and conceding no shade, and the trees blocked what small refreshment we had found in a southern breeze. The upper Mississippi River in mid-July is an endless coiling of tree-choked islands and twisting sloughs, long channels of mud-brown water and heat.

Somewhere along this section of the river Joliet and Marquette found human footprints. Leaving their two canoes in charge of the five men, cautioning them strictly to beware of a surprise, Joliet and Marquette walked in alone, undertaking, as Marquette wrote, "this rather hazardous discovery for two single men."

They discovered an Indian village four or five miles from the Mississippi and approached it in silence. They heard Indian voices nearby and shouted out to appraise the Indians of their presence. At their cry, the Indians rushed out of their rush-mat wigwams to see the two standing there alone: one in the jacket and trousers of a French merchant, the other in a neck-to-ankle black robe. Soon four old men approached. Two carried tobacco pipes made of polished red stone trimmed with colored feathers. "They marched slowly, lifting their pipes toward the sun, as if offering them to him to smoke, but yet without uttering a single word." The four approached and offered the Frenchmen the pipes, then led them to a woven-rush hut where many Indians had already gathered. Outside the door of this hut, they met another old man standing perfectly naked with his open fingers raised to the sun. The light passed through his fingers and fell across his brown face.

"How beautiful is the sun, O Frenchmen," said the old man in the language of the Illinois which Marquette understood to some degree, "when thou comest to visit us! All our town awaits thee, and thou shalt enter all our cabins in peace." He turned, stooped, and led them into the rush-covered hut where many were already gathered.

The ceremonial pipe passed from hand to hand. There was an exchange of presents, the old sachem giving the Frenchmen a sacred pipe decorated with the feathers of the white eagle which would prove essential later on. He also laid his hands on the head of a young slave boy and gave him to the Frenchmen.

Marquette explained their mission and asked for information about the sea into which the great river flowed, but the sachem petitioned them, on behalf of his whole nation, not to proceed farther because of the dangers they would surely encounter. Marquette replied that he did not fear death, that he esteemed no happiness greater than that of losing his life "for the glory of Him who made all." But this, says Marquette, they did not understand.

A great feast followed. The first course consisted of "sagamity," a cornmeal mush flavored with grease. The master of ceremonies fed three or four spoonfuls of this to Marquette in a wooden spoon "as we would do with a little child," then repeated the same with Joliet. The second course was fish, carefully deboned before them, then placed in their mouths by the master of ceremonies. Then came dog meat, which the Frenchmen refused, then fat pieces of buffalo.

They counted three-hundred rush huts in this village of the Illinois. After spending the night with these Indians, whom Marquette called the Peoria, the whole village followed them back to the canoes. Children laughed and shouted, sometimes sprinting ahead to lie down near the path to watch these two strange ones walk by; dogs yapped and gamboled about, women and old men crowded along the path behind the young men until they all reached the canoes about midafternoon. There the whole village saw them off.

Late in the day, the sun finally melted through the tree line. The heat was terrific, having steadily increased through the long hours of afternoon. We were ready to quit for the day and began looking for a place to camp. In time we found a bare little island sifted over with sand that interrupted the exit of a tiny stream. Sparse grass grew through the sand, thickening a little toward the back of the island. It looked as if Old Man River had raised his balding head from the muddy water. Upon this wrinkled head we decided to camp. When we climbed from the canoe, we sank to our knees in sticky, stinking mud, but managed to clamber onto a log of driftwood and then crawl up it shouldering our backpacks, clawing up the log like two mud turtles. The sand on top of the island was firm, pocked by hoofprints of deer whom the Old Man had called in to trim his hair. As we walked the log back down to get the rest of our equipment, a grey snake slithered away. A lousy place, but what do you do on the river when the sun goes down?

At sunset the wind expired, and the light slowly evaporated. But the heat remained, intense, still, demoralizing, more present than the river, more tangible than the sand and mud. We sat beside our tent and sweated. To take our minds from discomfort, we tried reading *Huckleberry Finn.*

Why does floating down the Mississippi infer some romantic sense of freedom to Americans? This book is surely to blame— Huck and Jim floating into adventure. But the book itself is not a pleasantly romantic tale. It's a story cut with murders, dirt-rag poverty, traveling charlatans, thieves, money-grubbing preachers, abusive fathers, young boys shot dead in the river, slave-hunters, superstitious ruffians, snake bites, dusty, hog-stunk, dog-mangy, scrawny riverside towns. Where's the romance?

The night came on heavy with heat. Justin said he couldn't stand it in the tent, so he smeared on the insect repellent, pulled his sleeping bag from the tent, flopped it onto the sandy grass outside the door, and lay there in the humid darkness waiting for a breeze. Above him, a few stars smoldered into vague existence, heat lightning flickered to the south. The great river was the color of night.

I had no wish to fight heat-crazed mosquitoes, so I crawled inside and opened the back window and doorway flaps, zipping closed the mosquito netting. Still no hint of a breeze. It was so hot the mind could think of nothing else. The heat owned the tent, the mud-sand island, the river. We breathed heavily and lay in our sandy sweat.

Yet somehow, in spite of *Huckleberry Finn* and in spite of the long, tedious miles of the muddy Mississippi itself, the idea, the intuition of romance and freedom still lingers along this river.

Floating away from your troubles, leaving town, abandoning shoreside responsibility, and drifting away under the night stars. It does something for the soul.

Langston Hughes was on a train to Mexico, appointed to work for his father's mining interests, when the train rumbled across the Mississippi at sunset. One look at the river enameled with the setting sun's golden light, and he turned about and caught the next train east to become a poet instead of a manager of mines. There was gold on that river.

What is it, then, about this long, sultry, flow of rotting banks and endless snaking sloughs swarming with mosquitoes by night and flies by day, mile after same-old mile that somehow overcomes the harsh, repetitive realities and draws us down and away?

Maybe it's the movement itself, irresponsible water on the move, so unlike the apparently dependable shore. We have something of both within us: a bit of soil, a lot of water. And we've got movement in us all the time: arterial rivers, vascular tributaries by the thousands. We are fluid folk. You can see it in liquid eyes going happy or bored or bitter. You see it in nervous hands and fidgety feet. You see it in anger rushing up, or lust moving fast and shallow, or love easing down wide, deep, reflective. We live on land and we think of ourselves as having roots there, but we ourselves are rivers on the move, everyone of us, with just enough rock and silt to keep us from running away.

You sit on the bank, but you see the waters teasing away the images of rooted, shoreside existence and rippling them into a confusion of moving lights, taking rock wall and brick warehouse and steel bridge and wooded hill and even your own image, dissolving all into sky and cloud and current. Something in us longs to go the way of the river, to lie down on those silken currents and swing away from the bank and move along mile after mile. There's something there that's wild and strong and asleep in mystery, mystery wide as any river, especially at night.

Huck and Jim felt it right away: "It was kind of solemn, drifting down the big still river, laying on our backs looking up at
the stars, and we didn't ever feel like talking loud, and it warn't
often that we laughed, only a little kind of low chuckle."

The ancients who worshipped rivers were closer to the truth
than we who see them as little more than commercial highways,
places for "leisure activities," sources of irrigation. T. S. Eliot
understood:

> I do not know much about gods; but I think that the river
> Is a strong brown god—sullen, untamed and intractable,
> Patient to some degree, at first recognised as a frontier;
> Useful, untrustworthy, as a conveyor of commerce;
> Then only a problem confronting the builder of bridges.
> The problem once solved, the brown god is almost forgotten
> By the dwellers in cities—ever, however, implacable,
> Keeping his seasons and rages, destroyer, reminder
> Of what men choose to forget. Unhonoured, unpropitiated
> By worshippers of the machine, but waiting, watching and
>   waiting.

Life-giver, killer, solemn god or roiling demon; road to slavery,
roadway to freedom, shouting glory with the morning, soaked
too in the nights of sorrow and loss—just like us. Mud-saturat-
ed river, carrying the excrements and poisons of farmland and
city, yet struck with sunlight distilling pure rainwater, raising
mists like a prayer to float away on improbable clouds to replenish the earth with morning dews and violent thunderstorms
and long night rains—just like us. We are "brutish, uncouth,
impure," says the narrator of *Zorba the Greek*, "composed of
love, the flesh and a cry of distress," yet distilling poems, and
floating ideas, and sanctifying our lives in the long mysteries of
faith.

*   *   *

I woke up in the night, still hot. Justin was shoving his sandy sleeping bag back into the tent.

"It's raining a little out there," he muttered.

There was a flash, and then low thunder.

"Maybe it'll cool things off," I said.

I heard Justin smoothing out the wrinkles of his bag and trying to scrape off some of the sticking sand, then he flopped down exhausted. The rain pattered lightly over our tent as if the sparse clouds were shaking out a little dry salt to annoy us, but the heat remained. The merest breath of a hot, humid breeze eased through the mosquito netting from time to time, stirring the sluggish heat around the tent. We lay in the hot soup and tried to imagine sleeping.

But such is the price of exploration. I would say, such is the price of reality. Poet Czelaw Milosz wrote, "The best cure for illusions is hunger, patience, and obedience." On the river you find that hunger, and thirst into the bargain. On the river you learn patience or you don't travel far. On the river you learn to discipline the will.

I had thought this mixture of romance and discipline would be good for Justin. But now I don't know. He dreams of speed and escape. The symbol of teenage freedom and romance for the last half-century has been the highway, not the river. Jack Kerouac didn't quite know what to make of this big river. He saw it briefly at night and remembered something of its romance: "the river's all rain and roses in a misty pinpoint darkness," but he's moving fast, as always, in a car with young friends, and when they cross the river at Port Allen, the river is "a great black body below a bridge." "What is the Mississippi River?" he asks. "A washed clod in the rainy night, a soft plopping from drooping Missouri banks, a dissolving, a riding of the tide down the eternal waterbed, a contribution to brown foams, a voyaging past endless vales and trees and levees, down along, down along, by Memphis, Greenville, Eudora, Vicksburg, Natchez, Port Allen, and Port Orleans and Port of the Deltas, by Potash, Venice, and the Night's Great Gulf, and out." And in that blur of passing cities, he speeds this slow and mighty river into a modern blacktop highway flashing by the lights of innumerable cities. Kerouac and his friends had no patience for slow rivers. The youth of the last half-century haven't seen rivers as roadways to freedom—they want speed—they want power under the foot. They want the radio bopping and their friends hopping. For Kerouac and his kin, the river at night is nothing more than a passing glimpse of a dark mystery beneath an iron bridge, a boundary marking passage on the long, fast highway of anticipation and excitement: "and zoom went the car and we were off again for California." Patience and obedience have no place in their ethos and their dreams.

Justin and I could have gone hissing along the serpentine highways strapped in an air-conditioned cocoon, catching glimpses of the river from time to time. We've done that often enough. But I wanted to catch the reality of the river in my own two hands. I wanted to swing away from shore into the hard life of free travel at nature's own pace. I wanted to feel and see and smell and hear the mysteries of the night—night, after day, after night, after day, after night. For that you must stop the car and open the door. For that, you must take on the slow disciplines of nature and pay a price in comfort.

Pause a Little, Huck and Jim

Whatever romance you might find on the river, you won't discover it in Hannibal, Missouri. We steered Natty Bumpo up a finger of water between a docked excursion paddle-wheeler and a dusty dike. The high sun glared down. If the night on

Bald Island had basted us in our tent, the day was broiling the leftovers.

We found an air-conditioned lunch among the tourists at Becky Thatcher's cafe where an impatient old man was feeding money into an insatiable cash register, then walked back to our canoe, stopping to buy ice cream cones—sweet strawberry ice cream. Whoever invented ice cream ought to be celebrated as one of the great inventors of the age, and the churches ought to beatify him for bringing a bit of heaven to earth. "Interior perfection," said a great theologian, "is in two parts, knowledge of truth and love of goodness. The first is perfection of the intellect, the second the fullness of all the affections." Strawberry ice cream, fitting into this second category, is therefore a great perfecter of the soul.

The sun poured heat like boiled honey over the river, and we poured river water over our heads again and again, the coolish warm water soaking our hair and our hats and our t-shirts to stave off heat exhaustion for a half hour at a time. We squinted through the blaze of midafternoon at the green bluffs on our right where, they say, is the cave that inspired Mark Twain's idea for Tom Sawyer's cave. The cave, or the thought of it—its coolness of mosses and dripping water, was, if not an inspiration, something of an antidote to the indecent power of that summer sun. Meanwhile, a bright yellow tugboat chugged up the river, not pushing a barge, just drumming upcurrent like a bad headache. Bright yellow, as if a piece of the sun had broken off and fallen smoking into the river. Our hearts beat fast and we panted like dogs. No breeze. Not a cloud. We began promising each other a swim on the other side of the next lock.

After sweating through Lock and Dam 22, we paddled over to a sandy shore to take the swim. A hot, humid stillness forecasted violent weather, and in fact, we could see thunderheads climbing over the wooded hills to the south. We had read the night before of Huck and Jim's first thunderstorm: "with a power of thunder and lightning" and the rain pouring down "in a solid sheet." I thought we should keep an eye on those clouds.

The canoe slid grinding into the sand and I stripped off my t-shirt for the swim. Just then two men walked up, each with a beer can in his hand. The thinner man had on a hat pinned with a political button, and he walked up just like a politician to shake my hand and introduce himself with a wide smile. Indeed he was a politician, the first Republican County Commissioner in the county for decades. His name was Willy Richmond. He and his friend Mike, an old college friend, were joining a couple other men for an annual camping trip on one of the islands.

I introduced Justin and said a word or two about our trip, and soon Willy and Mike were inviting us to join them on the island. I demurred. I didn't want to intrude upon their annual campout, or, more likely, it was just my usual social reticence. Mike pointed out the approaching storm clouds and said we'd have to hole up soon anyway. I glanced at the darkening thunderheads and shrugged. "We'll see," I said. "We might just join you."

After a good swim in the swift brown water below the dam, we bid good-bye to the two men and headed downriver. Towering clouds were flashing and grumbling over forested hills on the Missouri side. Several vultures swept over the river, outriders of the storm, swinging back over the hills, then gliding in tight circles across the river. As we paddled past a mile-long island on the Missouri side, we saw Willy and Mike sputter by in a little jonboat. They waved.

By the time we'd paddled another mile, the clouds were looming high, tall and dark against a pale sky. I saw Mike standing on the beach of a little, forested towhead island waving us over. Just then lightning broke from a nearby cloud and the thunder cracked and rumbled away up an intervening valley. It was time to seek cover.

We shot the canoe onto flat sand and jumped out to pull and push it higher. Then we scrambled to set up the tent and transfer our packs inside. Thunder was barking all around us, the farther hills on the Missouri side were already heavily veiled in rain.

When the storm broke above us, Mike and Justin and I were crouching low beneath Mike's blue tarp. We had the tarp staked down on the back side and held it over our heads to keep it from blowing away in the first gusts that swept across the river. Within minutes the storm hit us full force. We gripped the flapping tarp, peering out across the river as the current vanished into a white wash of driven rain. The tarp wasn't much protection; rain poured and leaped from every fold of the clapping tarp, but it gave us a chance to live within the furious heart of the storm, which is a thing worth doing.

Mike was good company. A handsome, balding man who wore a khaki hat cocked on one side, and sunglasses; he had a quiet sense of humor and didn't seem to mind the chaos all around us. I asked where Willy was.

"Oh, he's in his tent. Willy doesn't drink much beer and we had a few. He's feeling a little queazy," he grinned. "A man's got to keep in practice when it comes to drinking beer."

The rain rushed down through the trees. The wet winds hurled themselves at our island, slapped water in our faces, and tried to jerk the tarp from our fists.

I looked at Justin and asked if we had zipped up the door and window of our tent. He wasn't sure, but volunteered to run back up the island through the trees and check on it. He ducked out and sprinted into the rain. He wasn't gone two minutes when the air was shocked by a brilliant explosion. Lightning had struck our little island in the direction of our tents. I looked at Mike and he looked at me.

The next moment I was running through that solid sheet of rain, ducking into a wind so strong it was like swimming upcurrent. I scrambled past Willy's tent on the right and Mike's on the left to our own thin dome covered with the flapping, black, make-shift fly I had put together on the shore of Lake Winnebago so long ago. Not seeing Justin about, I unzipped the tent and tumbled in. Justin was there, of course, comfortably riding out the storm on his sleeping bag.

He was grinning. "Did you hear THAT?"

"Did I hear it! I thought maybe you'd caught it."

"It was close. Just a few trees up the island."

I heard Mike outside, shouting through the rain to hear if Justin was okay.

I called back that we were fine and he ran for cover.

Ten minutes later the rain was gone. We emerged from our tent into a stunned silence. The only sound was the rising river curling through a fallen tree. The leaves hung limp and dripping. Across the river, wet green hills faded away into smoky blueness. Low clouds, detached from the higher thunderheads, floated like fish through the valleys that ran down to the river. The air was clean and cool, washed free of the day's fevered heat.

We walked back to the downriver side of our soaked little island. Mike was sitting there on a wet stump in his cocked hat, looking like a wise leprechaun. I sat down nearby.

Willy crawled out of his tent and joined us, evidently feeling a little better after bad weather.

We got to talking. Mike asked how my wife liked my going away for two months. I told him she was pretty good about it. He shook his head in disbelief. "My wife would never have allowed that." Mike was divorced. "Beautiful women will steal your heart," he said. "Then later they get the house, the car, and the boat too."

I looked over at Natty Bumpo. The river was rising and his stern was already afloat. Justin and I walked down and pulled him farther up on the sand. After the rain, the river was fresh and beautiful, but she wasn't going to get my boat.

Willy stood up and began waving at a man and his son in a boat coming up the Illinois side of the river. Mike told us they needed to find a part for the jonboat; the engine had cut out and they couldn't get it restarted. The father and son cruised across the intervening channel and Willy went down to hitch a ride back to shore. He knew the man. "Willy knows everybody in this county," said Mike.

Mike was a construction engineer. He and his friend Frank, who would soon join us, had both worked for the State of Missouri creating nature walkways across the state. The state had provided them with a crew of convicts from their prisons to do the manual labor and together they had built walkways through forests and even up cliffs at scenic spots, dynamiting limestone, felling trees, pick-axing walkways.

"Have any trouble with the convicts?" I asked.

"No. They knew if they gave us any grief, they'd be back in the clinker."

Some time later Willy returned in a red kayak with the gas line for the jonboat. Justin jumped up to inspect the kayak, and Willy let him take it out on the river. Away he went with its double paddle, skimming at good speed up the river and shouting out that it was much faster than old Natty Bumpo. I glanced over at our aging canoe, but Natty Bumpo said nothing, maintaining his dignity.

Next morning Frank arrived. He had a greying beard and thoughtful eyes. Recently he had ruptured a disc in his back working construction. He was unemployed, living alone after his wife left him. He had little hope of finding construction work again, so he was trying organic gardening.

Mike dished out oatmeal, boiled eggs, and fried up some wonderful Italian sausages. He put on some coffee to boil and, naturally enough, the conversation began to wander. We talked of Africa, where Mike had done construction work (watching men fell jungle trees, dig long trenches beneath them, then saw them into long boards lengthwise by hand, one man standing on top of the tree, one beneath in the trench), of African politics (the terrible dictatorship of Mobutu Sese Seko), of organic farming, of the ruin large chemical companies had brought to the farming way of life and to the environment, of the loss of subsistence farming know-how, of chickens jammed into cages in long warehouses for the mass market and of the loss of chicken breeds that were adapted to farm life, of the dangers of living in a technologically interdependent society, of volcanoes and asteroids and other natural disasters that had disrupted life on this planet, of the shifting of continental plates, and of the ice age, of organic fertilizers and natural pest reduction, of the depletion of aquifers, of Buffalo ranching, of beautiful women, of back problems, of the imperfection of the medical arts, of sun spots and their possible effects on computer chips, of home-grown vegetables (Frank offered us one of his home-grown chili peppers. It was cold, crisp, juicy, and mellow), of Africans' love of dog meat, of Lewis' and Clark's relishing the taste of puppies, of local politics—the differing concerns of townsfolk and farmfolk that Willy was trying to balance, of divorces, of loneliness, of riverboats, and home towns. A normal conversation. Sipping coffee, five American men: free, frank, friendly. They were good company.

The morning was cool, misty, spitting rain. Justin and I cut up through a narrow slough in Gilbert Island that Willy had told us about. "It goes all the way through the island," he had said. The forest rose all around us, thick limbs arching high overhead, a tangle of broken brush on either side. Water striders skated away and crowds of black whirlygigs twirled away in panic as we approached. We slid over mossy trunks half submerged and eased through gravelled shallows. But a hundred yards into the slough we were stopped by fallen trees; we turned around and made our way back. A long grey watersnake swam along the surface, its protruding head held steady like a periscope. Another snake lay among rocks on the bank, a leathery coil of black and silver-grey.

That afternoon we found a rather odd sandy beach across from the little town of Louisiana, Missouri. Someone had camped there before, nailing a sign to a tree: "Crocketville Airport: Fly Hirst Planes at Own Risk. Money Refundable if You Live." Near shore, we found a four-foot figure of a round-headed man shaped from the sand—arms, torso, feet, everything—its six-inch sand penis sticking straight up. Justin reached down and modified the little man in the interests of modesty.

At dusk, an old man and his wife anchored just off shore in a pontoon boat to do a little fishing. They had a spaniel aboard dressed in a dog's life jacket.

"What's the jacket for?" I called.

"Oh, he's half blind, you know. If the precious little darling falls in the water, he might not see the boat." I looked at Justin. He grinned.

It was a damp, still night. All around us in the dark forest, tree frogs were singing their peculiar love songs—grating, clicking, croaking, percussive songs—rather like modern teen music. Warm, thick air rose from the river blurring the scattered lights of the town across the river. Beyond the hills there was a silent flickering of lightning.

The rains returned about midnight, pouring down for some four hours. The little sand man ran away in the night. *Hic transit gloria mundi.*

Lazy By Design

Sunday morning. We left our tent and packs and paddled across the river. Scattered thunderclouds still loitered over the hills; a litter of logs and branches were floating from the mouth of the tributary Salt River, and the Mississippi current shoved a wide carpet of the debris up against the shore. We paddled through it and tied Natty up beneath an ancient cottonwood, then climbed a long rickety stairway up a steep bank to a gravel road that skirted the forested hills on that side of the river.

We found our way to an old brick church. One last chance to look at Marquette's church after three centuries. One thing is certain: the Indians scattered onto reservations do not attend the churches in these towns. But then, they no longer live here either.

The priest at St. Joseph's was a man of odd description: portly, with small eyes, turned-up nose, heavy jowels, thick neck, and rounded shoulders; there was a heavy, hoggish look to him coupled with a wonderful sense of humor; he often laughed: a hissing, rasping laugh that shook his hefty body. He looked out over the small congregation and said, "I told you I was lazy. Someone down in Mexico, Missouri said to me, 'They've got you figured out, father.' 'How's that?' I asked. 'You don't *do* anything!' she said." The jowels shook, the body joggled to that rasping, whispering laugh.

"That's right!" he affirmed. "You all know that your former priest burned out, needed time off for physical and emotional recovery. He did everything for you, more than you realize. Now he's burned out. I won't burn out because I don't *do* anything." The laugh took over again.

"Actually," he continued when he had recovered himself, "that's by design. You have a parish council. You need to take responsibility for your own parish. You need to get a list of priorities and go after them. But I do think we're making progress."

He went on to say that God is lenient, but he acts from a position of strength. He had once been in charge of a student dorm at Notre Dame University. Soon after taking over responsibilities, he had discovered that some of the students were smoking marijuana. "I could have sent them all home immediately," he said. "But instead I sent in this redneck student to tell them they were embarrassing the new rector. Eleven out of twelve apologized the next day.

"One day they had an outrageous pillow fight with the other wing of the dorm. I sent word that as long as the lobby was in the same shape as before, everything would be okay. After a while I walked in and there were feathers and vacuums everywhere." That hoarse, shaking laugh again.

"Lenient, but from a position of strength. You see?

"You want eternal life, or do you want to go to hell? Then start treating your neighbors better and use the confessional regularly."

I enjoyed the man. A straight talker. Huck Finn hated the mealy-mouthed platitudes of the preachers. I do too. There's nothing makes me more ill in church than the constant, crooning affirmation that Almighty God is really a very nice old codger who requires little from us but a corresponding level of niceness.

The Eucharist was the same as always: a flow of words and gestures: the same words, the same gestures, the same antiphonal responses flowing back and forth like a river, the same wine and water poured together, the same wafer raised, the same mystery made present: recurrent current of the of the unending.

It was a warm and heavy afternoon and we decided to cut loose and drift down the river. But we had no intention of working hard. We returned to camp, packed up, and took to the river.

I leaned back, opened our book, told Justin to keep an eye out for barges, and began to read of how Huck and Jim met the Duke of Bilgewater and the King, of their outrageous performances of the Royal Nonesuch where the king comes prancing out on stage on all fours, naked, and painted up as "splendid as a rainbow," of how the duke contrived to disguise black Jim to prevent his arrest as an escaped slave by dressing him up in a Shakespearean costume with a white horse-hair wig, painting his face blue, "like a man that's been drownded nine days," and then nailing a sign up on the raft: "Sick Arab—but harmless when not out of his head."

We laughed our way down the river for nine miles, only lifting our paddles when we needed to miss a snag or avoid a barge. I believe in leisure, though God knows I've found precious little of it in my own life. Josef Pieper was surely right to call leisure the basis of culture. This runs smack against the raging workaholic current of modern life, but leisure, says Pieper, is "a form of silence, of that silence which is the prerequisite of the apprehension of reality: only the silent hear."

We camped on Pharr's Island and built a fire. The two of us sat close, looking out across the river at cows grazing between hay bales on green, sunlit hills. We listened to the great river swirling by our sandy, forested island. In time, evening strolled out of the forest to join us and threw gold in the fire.

Scaled Symbols

We were now about a hundred miles above St. Louis. I was no longer in a hurry. It was a quiet section of river, no towns visible, just miles and miles of steady current and long, tree-sheltered islands.

Once we entered a zone of rancid odor; a dead, three-foot-long catfish, bloated thick as a log floated by. It stunk outrageously, having become what it once enjoyed eating.

Egrets stood like white flags along broad mudflats. Herons lifted off of fallen logs and flapped away shrieking. Along the sloughs, bank lines hung from tree limbs. We saw one whipping about in the water, so we paddled over and Justin pulled it up. A carp flaked green and gold and orange flipped madly about and Justin dropped line and fish back into the water.

About eight in the evening, we arrived at Lock and Dam 25. As we waited to pass through, the clouds that had accompanied us all day turned several shades of red, then deepened to purple, and moved away like a sea tide leaving a sandy dusting of stars. By the time we passed through the lock, sky and river were black, glittering with stars above and shoreside lights below. The lockmaster told us we could camp around behind the lock, but when I sent Justin ashore with a flashlight, he found only mud and rock and weed and no place to stake a tent. We decided to run on with the night. But night is the natural enemy of working man; darkness brings anxiety.

The current was quick. We crossed to the left side and were carried swiftly along the black, forested bluffs, staring ashore for a patch of sand and peering ahead for unseen snags. Reading *Huckleberry Finn*, it seems an easy thing to float downriver at night. When they got their raft out in the middle, Huck says,

> "We left her alone, and let her float wherever the current wanted her to; then we lit the pipes, and dangled our legs in the water and talked about all kinds of things. Sometimes we'd have that whole river all to ourselves for the longest time. Yonder was the banks and islands, across the water; and maybe a spark—which was a candle in a cabin window—and sometimes on the water you could

see a spark or two—on a raft or scow, you know; and maybe you could hear a fiddle or a song coming over from one of them crafts. It's lovely to live on a raft. We had the sky up there all speckled with stars, and we used to lay on our backs and look up at them."

But in a canoe, in fast water, at night, it is different. Huck's sparks ashore have become, in the course of the last century, blazing yard lights that light up long, tree-covered yards, and the couple sparks on a raft or scow have multiplied exponentially into the blinding, sweeping glare of a big barge's thousand-million megawat searchlight. There is no music.

Five or six miles downriver, beyond a bend in the river, we could see a searchlight sweeping the river this way and that; we didn't know if the barge was coming our way or not.

I maneuvered near shore a half dozen times seeing something pale that might be sand, but each time it turned out to be rocks and I quickly swerved for deeper water. High bluffs dropped away into little forested valleys, then rose steeply again into the stars. Moonlit limestone outcroppings leaned from the heavy forest, sometimes falling away into sudden cliffs, then dropping back into treetops and brushwood. The anxious silence of the night was powerful, made stronger by the faint drone of a distant plane passing away beneath the stars. We skimmed the shore for a long, complicated hour. The silence increased—a negative presence, a river of nonsound swirling ever stronger and deeper.

Watching. Listening. Waiting. Working the paddles. Attentive. Ready. Longing for solid ground. This was not Liesure's silence, but the worried silence of working too late.

Black trees above the bluffs comb through the stars. The distant barge has long since vanished around the bend. It's impossible to see snags in the black water. Riding a solid log raft

might make such a journey possible, but riding the black running water in a tippy canoe . . .

"There! Along that bank!" I murmur.

Justin leans toward shore and stares.

I twist the paddle and we glide shoreward. Grey sand scattered with brush and occasional boulders slips up to greet us.
We run ashore, the prow grinding to a stop on solid sand. Justin
climbs out and pulls us up. The sand is firm. We turn and sur-
vey the black river. The dark, witchy silence of recent hours has
quite suddenly grown gentle, calm, grandmotherly.

We rose to a blue sky and strong sunlight. After breakfast, Justin wandered the sand shore looking for shells while I washed
pans in the river; a father's work is never done. He called me
over. A foot-long gar lay in the sand, its greenish scales lapping like armor toward its gilled head and the long, bony snout
lined with fine teeth. The dead fish was covered in butterflies:
brown ones with folded wings, yellow ones slowly opening and
closing, black-laced wings, orange wings and reddish wings like
stained glass. Each butterfly had attached itself to the fish with
its delicate proboscis and was sucking out the fishy salts.

We knelt down quite close and watched. Occasionally a butterfly would flicker away into the sunny air, then return. Some
would alight on sand near the dead fish and suck at the clear
juices that had penetrated the sand. Eleven butterflies on one
fish, butterflies feeding on the dead lifegiver.

Yellow-green pastured hills came down to braided rows of dark
green cornfields. Orchards thick with summer's heat alternated
with riverside homes. Motorboats competed with jet skis. If a
barge trundled by upriver, pushing against the current, we'd
slide in behind it and ride the heavy waves it boiled out in its
wake, each rolling waterhill shoving us downriver.

Ahead of us we finally saw the high bluffs that mark the mouth of the Illinois River: miles of high limestone cliffs. Joliet and his men, plus the Indian boy the Illinois sachem had given them, were running along these bluffs "frightful for their height and length," when they were startled by the sight of two huge monsters painted high on the rock face:

> They are as large as a calf, with horns on the head like a deer, a fearful look, red eyes, bearded like a tiger, the face somewhat like a man's, the body covered with scales, and the tail so long that it twice makes the turn of the body, passing over the head and down between the legs, and ending at last in a fish's tail. Green, red, and a kind of black, are the colors employed. On the whole, these two monsters are so well painted, that we could not believe any Indian to have been the designer, as good painters in France would find it hard to do as well; besides this, they are so high upon the rock that it is hard to get conveniently at them to paint them.

They were seventeenth-century men, frightened by these painted beasts. Were the figures a warning to keep enemies away? Were they a representation of evil spirits? Did they bear some relation to the river itself? The men were still discussing the significance of these two monsters when, "sailing gently down a beautiful, still, clear water," they heard the noise of rushing waters. "I have seen nothing more frightful," wrote Marquette, "a mass of large trees, entire, with branches, real floating islands, came rushing out of the mouth of the river Pekitanoui, so impetuously, that we could not, without great danger, expose ourselves to pass across." This was the mouth of the mighty Missouri River in floodstage, centuries before it was imprisoned by locks and dams.

Perhaps those two winding-tailed, scaly, fish-finned monsters were symbols of these two great rivers that join forces just beyond these cliffs. Life-destroyers they certainly were. The Indians who traveled them in long, unwieldy, dug-out canoes would naturally fear their currents and whirlpools. The experienced Frenchmen in their much-more-maneuverable birchbark canoes were themselves terrified.

Justin and I camped on a little towhead across from the high cliffs. The next day we would pass the mouth of the Missouri and approach the great city of St. Louis and the end of our journey.

The island had been much used. Burnt logs and scattered cinders lay about the sand. In the tangle of driftwood on the upriver side, someone had placed an actual porcelain toilet. It stank. Its white ceramic presence seemed a testimony to someone's inability to cope with the natural world. Huge cockroaches scuttled from under logs.

I chopped wood for our fire and stopped to watch a large, black beetle trying again and again to climb a three-inch sand dune. Its jointed legs paddled up through rolling sand grains, almost launching the beetle over the crest, but each time old Sisyphus the Beetle slid back down. I sawed a log into ten-inch lengths. Sisyphus was still paddling up the dune. I snapped small twigs of various sizes and laid the kindling into a tepee shape, plucked a handful of dry grass, gave it a twist, and slid it into the stick tepee. I struck fire and watched a wisp of smoke crackle into flame. Sisyphus was treadmilling sand. Bright flames snapped up through the tepee and began licking into the cut lengths of driftwood. A couple feet away, in the light and growing heat of the fire, as if he had no choice, Sisyphus was still rowing and sliding. I opened a can of cream-of-chicken soup, shook it into the pan, poured in a can of pork and beans and a can of whole kernel corn. Sisyphus was stroking up the rolling sand wave. I propped the grill over the fire, put on our blackened pot and glanced over at the back of the big beetle glimmering green in the firelight. The heat increased and still the legs paddled on. After a few minutes, my gourmet stew began to bubble. I put in the spoon and stirred and glanced over at the oarsman. The black bug stopped his paddling, his back split open like an egg and he hatched a pair of wings. He raised his wings and flew away.

Ah, yes, bright bug, could you at last imagine the possible?

Justin had found a knotted rope hanging from a tree limb above the water. While I was cooking up our belly munitions, he stripped off his t-shirt, climbed the bank, grabbed tight, and jumped. I saw him swing way out over the darkening water and, at that moment of weightlessness, let go and splash into the river. He came up and swam hard for shore since the current was washing him quickly toward a half-submerged cottonwood snag.

I watched him splash ashore and grab the rope. He called me to join him, but I smiled and shook my head. It was enough to watch him do what I had done as a boy. The ending of things was closing in around me. I watched him swing away again, his hands grasping the knot on the rope, his legs spread, a toe just skimming the flat, flowing surface, leaving little staccato prints across the water as if he were typing his brief story across the water—the wide, rolling page of river blue behind him, the distant tree line a green border to the blue, passing page—then that moment again at the top of the arc—weightless, caught timeless in my memory.

Endings

And then only fragments remain: a little, green sliver of a boat rocking south through late July on a broad running current of brown water. . . houses clustered high along the cliff edge, then pouring down a slope into Alton, Illinois . . . a white casino riverboat churning upriver, then turning about as if it had lost its way and drifting back to its moorings . . . no one on deck; everyone inside jerking levers, watching their cards, while all the talk is of losses . . . the last, and newest, river-wide dam and lock on the Mississippi—and the ugliest: rectangles of concrete joined and jointed . . . and then oil-company terminals clotting the shoreline . . . iron barges rusting side-by-side along rotting banks . . . tugs pushing by to left and right . . . the distant hum of a power plant . . . a smoke stack rising impossibly high into the blue sky casting a yellow pall eastward. The great industrial city was near, gateway to the west. But like other river cities, St. Louis is diminishing: a city of 850,000 has shrunk to 350,000.

A man was sitting on a sandbank in the afternoon sunlight fishing. His children ran and shouted. Behind him an arid plain.

It has been long since I saw my children. And how should I set my house in order when I return home? For the world runs round and round and round and who can order what will not stay still? My children, addicts for excitement, move to the edge of the whirling wheel where the pull is strongest, then dart away like sparks. And who will call them back to the still and quiet center of the turning world, to the "point of intersection of the timeless/ With time"?

A flying heron squawked. I saw it through willow trees flying slowly upriver. Somewhere along the side of a sandy, willow-shaded island, a blackbird sent out its cracked soprano trill. A warm breeze rustled over us as swallows—dark, fleet shadows, skimmed the waters . . .

And Joliet, Marquette, the Beaver, the Mole, the Indian lad and the others—traveling always just ahead of us, sometimes almost visible—what became of them? On they went. As in some mythic adventure, they passed through the roaring whirlpools where the Indians said a Manitou lived who devoured all who passed. At one point they found a greasy soil of three colors: purple, violet, and red, and also a heavy red sand. Marquette rubbed some on his wooden paddle, and it took the color so well, he said, "that the water did not efface if for fifteen days that I used it in rowing." They met a band of Indians armed with guns whose shouts the Frenchmen interpreted as war cries, but who were actually only calling them over for a talk. The Frenchmen had the courage to approach, and the Indians took them into their huts and fed them buffalo meat, bear's oil, and white plums.

The weather grew hotter, and they began noticing cane breaks along shore. Cottonwoods, elms, and "white-wood" (sycamores?) rose to prodigious heights. Through the heavily wooded shores, they could hear the bellowing of buffalo. Quail came down to the water, and once they killed a little red, yellow, and green parrot. The mosquitoes were awful. They wrapped their canvas sails around their bodies for protection and kept moving south.

One day they spotted a village and heard, in the distance, "Indians exciting one another to the combat by continual yells." This time the hostility was real, for these Indians were afraid of white men, afraid because the Spanish had allied themselves to the tribe's enemies farther south. The Frenchmen began to pray. The Indians, armed with bows, arrows, axes, war-clubs, and shields—but not firearms—were in a fury. They "prepared to attack us by land and water; some embarked in large wooden canoes, a part to ascend, the rest to descend the river, so as to cut off our way, and surround us completely."

Young warriors leapt into the water and swam toward the two canoes to capsize them. When the current began to carry the French canoes away, one swimming warrior threw his war-club at them, but it sailed harmlessly over the canoe. Marquette stood up in his canoe holding high the feathered peace calumet he had received from the Illinois sachem and making gestures to explain that they had not come as enemies, though his companions grasped their guns, ready to return a volley if fired upon. The Indians in the long, dugout canoes paddled near as the Frenchmen approached shore. Indians on all sides of them nocked their arrows and prepared to shoot, but just then some old men on shore, evidently seeing the calumet, shouted for the young men to stop the attack. Two of the chiefs waded out, threw their bows and quivers into the French canoes, and pulled them safely to shore.

(One can only assume that if one arrow had been released, or a nervous Frenchman had fired his gun at the thrower of the war club, we might well have never heard the story of this journey; the little party of voyageurs would almost certainly have disappeared without trace.)

At first Marquette had to communicate with signs, "for not one understood a word of the six languages I knew." But at last they found an old man who spoke a little Illinois.

After an uneasy night in this village, they followed an Indian canoe of ten men to a village downriver called Akamsea. Near the mouth of the Akamsea (or Arkansas) River, two canoes approached. The chief was standing up, singing a song, and holding a calumet. He led them to the village, and thence to the war-chiefs' scaffold beneath which they sat down on rush mats surrounded by the whole tribe. The men were naked, with short hair, and noses and ears pierced and inserted with beads. The women were dressed in skins, their hair braided in two plaits that fell behind the ears, but wore no ornaments.

Under the war chiefs' scaffold they learned that they were just days from the great sea (though in reality they were much farther from the sea than they thought), which the French rightly concluded must be the Gulf of Mexico. But they also learned that the way would be impassible since enemy tribes controlled the river to the south and were armed with European firearms. "During this converse, they kept bringing us wooden dishes of sagamity, Indian corn whole, or pieces of dog-flesh; the whole day was spent in feasting."

That evening, the chiefs held a secret council. Some wanted to kill the Frenchmen in order to plunder their goods, but the head chief refused. He called in the Frenchmen and danced the elaborate calumet dance, thus ensuring their safety.

Joliet and Marquette then conferred with each other as to what they should do: push on to the sea, or return. They concluded they should take the information they had already gained and return. They had no wish to fall into the hands of the warlike Indians to the south, nor into the hands of the Spanish, who, they felt certain, would imprison them.

After a day's rest, they began their 1700-mile return voyage, forcing their way up the Mississippi "which gave us great trouble to stem its currents," to the white cliffs of the Illinois River. They followed the beautiful Illinois River two hundred miles until they came upon a tribe of Indians at a village called Kaskaskia. There they were well-received and Marquette was asked to come back to instruct the village of Christianity. One of the chiefs of the tribe, along with some of his young men, then guided the voyageurs back to "Ilinois lake" (Lake Michigan).

The little party made their way up the long western shore of the lake and back to Green Bay, arriving there at the end of September, 1673.

Joliet, as head of the expedition, went on in order to deliver his report to the governor in distant Montreal, but within sight of that city, his canoe capsized in heavy rapids. His companion—the man whose name is lost—also lost his life, drowned. Heartbreakingly, the Indian boy also drowned. Joliet was cast up unconscious on a rock amid rapids where he was rescued by local French fishermen. He had lost his companions, his journal, his map, pelts they had traded for with the Indians, virtually his entire investment. Later, he tried to piece together an account of the great exploration and drew a map from memory, but the only journal account is apparently Marquette's.

Louis Joliet, who had made the trip partly to advance his trade in furs, gained little by his great voyage of discovery. He was put aside by more famous and well-placed men. "The discoverer of Mississippi," says historian John Gilmary Shea, "was rewarded as if in mockery with an island in the gulf of St. Lawrence." There Joliet built a fort, a home for his family, and a trading post. But eleven years later, the island was captured by the English and he and his family, while trying to escape by boat, fell into the hands of the English commander. Joliet lost his boat, and all his goods once again, and the island too, but eventually regained his freedom when the English retired from the walls of Quebec. He hired on as a hydrographer for the French government and spent more time in the west, but his dreams of wealth through trading came to nothing. And thus he passes away into history, an apparition who rarely returns.

Jacques Marquette remained in Green Bay through the next summer fighting a debilitating spell of diarrhea that often issued in "a bloody flux," but he finally regained enough strength to attempt the journey back to Kaskaskia on the Illinois River. He and two French companions set out that autumn, but, like Allouez who would follow him later, they were delayed on this journey by Lake Michigan freezing over and were forced to construct a rude log cabin where they spent a miserable winter. Recurrent dysentery wracked Marquette's thin body, but he was alive and a little better when the ice broke that spring. The three arrived in Kaskaskia a few days before Easter, and Marquette, though terribly weakened by his ordeal, preached the faith to some 500 chiefs and old men and to thousands of young men, women, and children on the eve of Good Friday, 1675. The tribe received him, says the account, with "joy and approbation," and "besought him to return as soon as possible among them, since his malady obliged him to leave them."

But it was not Marquette who would return; he died on the journey up Lake Michigan, "having become so weak and exhausted, that he could no longer help himself, nor even stir, and had to be handled and carried like a child" by his two companions, one of whom was that same "Beaver" who had accompanied him on the exploration of the Mississippi. The Beaver reported that Father Marquette in his last extremity "nevertheless maintained in this state an admirable equanimity, joy, and gentleness, consoling his beloved companions, and encouraging them," finally passing away on an obscure shore of Lake Michigan on Saturday, May 18, 1675.

Five years later, the Beaver joined the Jesuits and was sent back to Kaskaskia, the mission Marquette had so briefly begun. There among the Illinois Indians, the Beaver, now known as Brother Jacques, served for over thirty years before dying at the age of eighty. It was the old Beaver who worked to build Marquette's mission, and Marquette's celebrated journey finds a kind of fulfillment in this virtually unknown man.

And then again, the fragments: a long, straight canal diked on either side by broken rock and weeds: the nine-mile-long Chain of Rocks Canal . . . garbage trucks rattling over an iron bridge to a massive dump beyond the levee . . .the guttural roar of huge front-end loaders, the reek of city waste in the air . . . seagulls tipping and diving. . . on shore a black man shouting frantically, leaping, flapping his arms like a bird, pointing toward the city. That way lieth madness? We paddled near, but could make nothing of his desperate warnings. And then a final dam and canal lock and out we swept into a strong current rocking us, swinging us sideways, a long roiling roadway of dark water lifting and falling and swirling us strangely, sweeping us inexorably toward the city skyline. Far away we spotted the silver hoop of the St. Louis Arch.

St. Louis

There they are—standing on the upper deck of a docked riverboat, just below the St. Louis Arch. Sqump and Snoof have lettered colorful signs decorated with bright crayon flowers and have hung them over the railings: WeLcoMe, and You Made It! I see their little blonde heads peering over the white railings, staring at two tanned strangers; their hands go up and the little one begins dancing up and down; and there below the railing I see Alexander's brown little head; and there I see the light brown hair of my wife blowing in the summer sun, she is smiling and waving; and over there, a surprise, the grey hair of my mother who has come to meet us too (my father is stuck at home in his wheelchair, too ill to travel.)

We wave our paddles and shoot swiftly by the old riverboat on the current, rudder in behind it, and scrape ashore onto cobblestones that run down into the mud-brown water. Justin steps out, leaning on his paddle like a cane, and hugs his mother with one strong arm. I clamber over our backpacks and step out to find her arms too.

Part Five

PANDEMONIUM AGAIN

Is this the Region, this the Soil, the Clime,
Said then the lost Arch-Angel, this the seat
That we must change for Heav'n, this mournful gloom
For that celestial light?

—*Paradise Lost*

Highway Home

With scratched and beaten Natty Bumpo strapped to the roof of the old truck; my wife at last beside me; Justin tucked safe into a seat behind me; all three daughters: Johanna, Andrea, and Julia, plus little Alexander stuffed in back between packs and tent; spaghetti and bread stuffed in our bellies; we were running west for Kansas on a crowded interstate highway at night. Taillights were rushing past us on all sides of the multilane highway. There was the hiss and roar of semitrucks through our open windows (our air conditioner was broken), the sound of tires tearing up the night, the wind buffeting our faces; everywhere traffic of all descriptions was speeding past us and away up the road.

"Dad, why are you driving so SLOW?" asks my youngest daughter Snoof. I glance at the speedometer: 40 miles per hour.

"Feels fast to me."

It's a mad world. But what of it? My long-enduring love beside me, my son safe, my daughters and littlest son with me again, let the shatterbrained world rush on by.

Later

Always in a hurry, Justin steps into his little red convertible and turns the key. He's supposed to run his mother's paper route tonight; she's in Columbia, Missouri, taking care of his grandmother in her trailerhouse. As usual, he's running late. He hurries out of Lawrence, Kansas, and hits the highway doing eighty. A vast storm front is moving in from the south and west and a few large drops begin hitting his windshield. There's lightning darting all over the sky ahead of him, backlighting thunderheads building high into the stars. It's a bad night to run a paper route.

Ten miles west, he drives into a running wall of rain. He slows to 70, but the old fast demon has long been his companion, urging him on. He charges on through heavy windsnapping sheets of rain. His front tires are worn, but this doesn't worry him. On an icy day just last winter, on this same stretch of highway, he swerved to miss a deer, slid sideways on the ice, and bounced off the concrete partition that divides the highway—but this doesn't worry him either. He's fast approaching a semi-truck ahead. In his fast-paced living, he has smashed a friend's car, backed into a pickup, missed a turn and hit a telephone pole, cracked his car frame running over a parking block—all in separate accidents—but none of this worries him.

He eases left and surges past the slowing tractor-trailer. The wind buffets his little red car as he pulls past the high truck cab, its great wheels spinning like turbines, a fine white spray hissing from beneath the wheels like steam. He can scarcely see the black highway in the chaos of rain and lightning and spinning wheels. Directly ahead is another long eighteen-wheeler, its red taillights shrouded in whipped spray. He eases off to 60 as the amber running lights of the great machine burn past him. The little car—his little glass-fronted, canvas-tented escape pod—

sways and shakes in the wind. He crests a hill and speeds down the far side leaving the two tractor-trailers behind. In a blind valley falling away to his right, a distant farmhouse jumps white into its place among dark trees and grey outbuildings, quivers, then vanishes. Thunder hits the air above him and then he hits the water pools and begins to slide right. He jerks left and stomps the brake. His tires catch pavement and whip him full force head-on into the concrete partition. The little car smashes the three-foot concrete wall and the momentum flips it onto its passenger door, he is slammed flat against that door with the car shooting down the highway in a spray of sparks and a hail of glass, his left hand clamped to the steering wheel; his shoes and shirt ripped from his body. The car hits the partition again, slam-rolling up onto the concrete ridge and catapulting down the highway, then hammering down on its wheels and sliding to a stop. Still flattened against the passenger door, his eyes open and he sees back down the highway the oncoming headlights of the two semi-trucks side-by-side. He pushes his body from the passenger door and squeezes out the shattered driver's window and falls onto the pavement. He crouches in the rain, his hands moving over his body checking for breaks and wounds. But there is no time. He straightens up, blinded by the swerving headlights of the oncoming trucks.

As the rain sweeps across Columbia, Missouri, his mother is praying. She lies in bed in the darkness, the little fan whirring near her head, the trees outside whipping and shaking in the violent winds, the lightning cracking. She prays through the darkness for the son she knows is in trouble. The noise of rain fills the room where she cannot sleep.

The trucks are roaring and gasping and squealing like wounded animals as they brake and swerve. But the charging machines cannot stop; the great engines built for speed and power cannot break their momentum for a boy stumbling across a con-

crete highway through a blaze of headlights . . . they both blast through and up the road, just avoiding the wrecked car.

The rain is falling all around. Across the roadside grasses and over the shoulder of a nearby hill quiet and dark, falling for miles around and down the valleys, washing the black hills and sweeping along the winding rivers, on and on cloud and thunder ride the darkness over the sleeping farms, echoing over the boxed and insulated suburbs where late-nighters stare vacantly into winking screens, slashing over the sleepless street lights, and pelting the steaming highrises where janitors dustmop the quiet halls and empty the waste cans, and drumming over a faceless apartment block where an old woman who cannot sleep turns her back on the flickering blue light of the television to watch the rain coursing down the plate glass of her darkened apartment, and on over the flat-roofed factories where the graveyard shift attends to the clank and hum of its machines and no one hears the rhythm of the rain on the flat roof, and on over the newspaper offices where night editors work their stories, out along the threading highways and back-gravel roads ditch-filled with running water where the occasional headlights still pass on, and over the wet forests and stone-knuckled ridges and down the pasture hills where black cattle flash awake and vanish into night, and across the dilapidated, rain-sacked little towns, and on down the rainy rivers and on and on through the thundering night.

He staggers backwards and sits down in the grass. He hears the radio in the crumpled car across the highway still thumping out the rhythms, still bopping the same tunes as if the Angel of Death had not so recently passed over. To his right he sees the red lights of both semis pulling to a stop a couple-hundred yards up the highway, one behind the other. He looks left and sees another semi slowing and pulling over as it nears, its headlights glaring at the crumpled car. The diesel engine slows to a *steady growl and the big rig squeaks to a stop. A man climbs out into the rain and begins setting red flares to warn oncoming vehicles. The flares, one-at-a-time, begin sparkling and spitting and bleeding red down the black highway. The man doesn't see Justin.*

Across the center partition on the other side of the highway, a little car has stopped. A woman is clambering over the concrete partition calling out, "Oh my God! Is anybody in there?" She peers into the smashed car pulling her wet hair back behind her ears. "Where are you? Oh my God! Oh my God! Where are you? Where are you?" Her clothes are soaked in the ongoing rain. She looks back down the highway, searching for a body. Lightning flashes. "Where are you? Where are you? Where are you?" Then she catches sight of something out of the corner of her eye. She glances across the road to where a boy is standing up, half-naked in the rain. She runs across the asphalt and shouts, "Come here! Come here! Let me take a look at you!" Her name is Jamie Strickland and she is a nurse.

She takes him by the arm and walks him slowly back up the highway in the rain toward the stopped semi. "Can we use your cab to check this boy out?" she calls.

"Sure. Climb on up. I'll be there in a minute!"

In the overhead light of the truck cab, she examines and prods. He is shivering with cold and is covered with cuts, but there seem to be no broken bones. She asks the necessary questions.

Soon the truck driver returns and climbs in out of the rain and slams the door. He reaches back and offers Justin a t-shirt, but it's too small for Justin and he is bleeding from cuts all over his head and back and arms. His mother, who prayed all that long night, will be pulling dime-sized pieces of glass out of his arms and back for two weeks.

He remains a mystery to me. As he was then through those long weeks on lake and river, so he is now, a phantom moving in and out and into my life, sometimes materializing bright with life beside me, often fading away along his own thoughts and his own ways. But how can that mystery be revealed to me when not yet known to himself? He is yet a boy, half-created, a riddle whose last lines have yet to be written. If he has not yet defined and fully understood himself, I should not be surprised that he remains an enigma to his mother and me. And how could I expect two months on the water to overcome the continuing distractions of our overly busy lives? Two quiet months of hard canoeing, of campfires and conversations, of sleeping under the silent stars cannot replace 16 years of a speed-addicted, media-juiced culture. But it was something. Something real, and still, and quietly enduring. There, for a time, the stories were ours, the adventure was our own, and the once-upon-a-time fairytale was once our time. However long he lives, whatever decisions he makes, however he chooses to define and lead his life, those two months are ours for good.

For the waves are still running with the wind, and the ground sometimes takes on the motion of the waves, and the currents are still running to an unknown sea, and sometimes I feel the twist of a sudden swirl or am caught floating backwards in a quiet eddy, and feeling this, I will glance back and see our reflections there.

About the Author

Steven Faulkner teaches Creative Writing at Longwood University, a beautiful school in the forested hills of southern Virginia. He has published essays in *DoubleTake, Wisconsin Trails magazine, Southern Humanities Review, Dos Passos Review,* and other journals. One essay was anthologized in *Beacon's Best of 1999.*

He was for many years a truck driver, roofer, grave vault maker, newspaper and doughnut delivery driver, and for fourteen years, a carpenter. He returned to college, working nights to support his wife and seven children, and acquired the necessary degrees from the University of Kansas. He has been married to his wife Joy for 34 years. His oldest son, David, designed the maps for this book, and his second son, Seth, designed the cover. Both are art directors and graphic designers in Kansas City. This is Steven Faulkner's first book.